The Science of Consciousness

Psychological, Neuropsychological and Clinical Reviews

Edited by Max Velmans

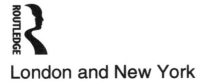

London and New York

First published 1996
by Routledge
11 New Fetter Lane, London EC4P 4EE

Simultaneously published in the USA and Canada
by Routledge
29 West 35th Street, New York, NY 10001

Routledge is an International Thomson Publishing company

Typeset in Times by LaserScript, Mitcham, Surrey
Printed and bound in Great Britain by
Mackays of Chatham PLC, Chatham, Kent

British Library Cataloguing in Publication Data
A catalogue record for this book is available from the British Library

Library of Congress Cataloguing in Publication Data
A catalogue record for this book has been requested

ISBN 0–415–11081–5 (hbk)
ISBN 0–415–11082–3 (pbk)

Contents

Illustrations

Contributors

Professor Bernard J. Baars and Professor Katharine McGovern, The Wright Institute, 2728 Durant Avenue, Berkeley, California 94707, USA

Professor John M. Gardiner, Department of Psychology, The City University, Northampton Square, London EC1V OHB, England

Professor John F. Kihlstrom, Department of Psychology, Yale University, Box 2082051, New Haven, CT 06520, USA

Professor Benjamin Libet, Department of Physiology, School of Medicine, University of California, San Francisco, California 94143–0444, USA

Professor Anees A. Sheikh, Dr Robert G. Kunzendorf and Katharina S. Sheikh, Department of Psychology, Marquette University, Milwaukee, WI 53233, USA

Dr Max Velmans, Department of Psychology, Goldsmiths College, University of London, New Cross, London SE14 6NW, England

Professor Patrick D. Wall, Sherrington School of Physiology, United Medical and Dental Schools, University of London, St Thomas's Campus, Lambeth Palace Road, London SE1 7EH, England

Dr Andrew W. Young, MRC Applied Psychology Unit, 15 Chaucer Road, Cambridge CB2 2EF, England

Preface

Of all the problems facing science, none are more challenging (and fascinating) than those posed by consciousness. These problems are of interest to many disciplines, but especially to psychology, neuropsychology and to clinicians who need to take account of the mind/body relation in their practice. In recent years, the ferment of activity in these and related areas is creating a new science of consciousness which attempts to integrate the findings of traditional 'third-person perspective' science with the 'first-person' evidence of human experience.

This book begins with an overview, and places the emerging science of consciousness within its historical context. We examine the ways in which consciousness is being investigated within cognitive psychology, focusing particularly on the question of what the function of consciousness might be, and on the relation of conscious processing to nonconscious processing in perception, learning, memory and 'information dissemination' within the human brain. We turn to the evidence from neuropsychology, examining the neural conditions for consciousness, the scope and limits of current technology used to investigate these conditions, the dissociations of consciousness which may follow brain damage, and their implications. We then consider mind/body interactions in clinical and experimental settings, including the extensive evidence for the somatic effects of imagery, biofeedback, hypnosis, meditation, placebo effects and the changes in theoretical understanding suggested by such effects. The book ends with fundamental theoretical questions such as 'What and where are conscious experiences?' and 'How can the study of conscious experiences be a science?' In the emerging science of consciousness there is a need for empirical investigations to proceed hand in hand with a reconsideration of such basic questions.

The invited authors are active researchers who have each been pioneers of some aspect of this new science. Each chapter presents an original synthesis and a review of the state-of-the-art. Many of the chapters also suggest ways in which theories of consciousness might develop and directions for future research. Unusually for works of this kind, the chapters are simply written. The authors were challenged to present their subject in ways that would interest not only their colleagues, but also a new generation of students and researchers. It has been a privilege to edit a text with chapters as clear and engaging as these.

Max Velmans, July 1995

Chapter 1

An introduction to the science of consciousness

Max Velmans

The problems surrounding consciousness and mind are often thought to be among the most complex facing philosophy and science. Yet the first psychological laboratory, founded by Wilhelm Wundt in Leipzig in 1879, was set up to study consciousness using the method of 'experimental introspection'. In Wundt's laboratory, controlled, measurable stimuli were used to bring about given conscious states. Rather like chemical compounds, these states were thought to have a complex structure and the aim of introspection was to analyse this structure into its fundamental, component elements. However, disagreements about the composition of given experiences proved to be very difficult to settle and in the early years of the twentieth century both consciousness and 'experimental introspectionism' were outlawed from psychology by decree. The founder of behaviourism, John Watson, declared that 'The time seems to have come when psychology must discard all reference to consciousness . . . its sole task is the prediction and control of behavior and introspection can form no part of its method' (1913: 163).

Within the last ten years, all this has changed. From 1984 to 1994 there were around 1,500 experimental and theoretical papers dealing with consciousness (listed in PsycLit on CD-ROM), including publications in major scientific journals such as *The Journal of Experimental Psychology* and the *Behavioral and Brain Sciences*. From 1989 to 1994 PsycLit also lists around 400 relevant chapters and books. *Consciousness and Cognition*, a journal entirely devoted to consciousness research within cognitive science, was founded in 1992. *The Journal of Consciousness Studies*, which follows a more interdisciplinary approach, was founded in 1994.

In part, this change is consequent on the growing recognition that a psychology that does not deal with consciousness is incomplete – psychology is the study of behaviour *and* experience. Scientific interest has been fostered by the development of more sophisticated methods for studying experience and for relating experience to brain and body changes in experimental and clinical settings. Renewed interest in consciousness also follows the recognition that consciousness and the 'mind/body problem' present not one problem, but many. Some of the problems are conceptual and continue to vex philosophy and science; but many of the problems are already amenable to empirical research.

Broadly speaking, the problems posed by consciousness focus around four central questions:

Q1. What is consciousness?
Q2. Is consciousness causally efficacious?
Q3. What is the function of consciousness?
Q4. What is the relationship of consciousness to the brain?

DEFINITIONS

What consciousness is taken to *be* (Question 1) is partly a matter of arbitrary definition – and some confusion in the literature has resulted from differences in definition. In the present text we follow the common usage in which the term 'consciousness' is synonymous with 'awareness' or 'conscious awareness' (sometimes 'phenomenal awareness'). The 'contents of consciousness' encompass all that we are conscious of, aware of, or experience. These include not only experiences that we commonly associate with ourselves, such as thoughts, feelings, images, dreams, body experiences and so on, but also the experienced three-dimensional world (the phenomenal world) beyond the body surface.

In some writings 'consciousness' is synonymous with 'mind'. However, given the extensive evidence for nonconscious mental processing (Dixon, 1981; Kihlstrom, 1987; Velmans, 1991a) this definition of consciousness is too broad. In the present text 'mind' refers to psychological states and processes which may or may not be 'conscious'.

In other writings 'consciousness' is synonymous with 'self-consciousness'. As one can be conscious of many things other than oneself (other people, the external world, etc.), this definition is too narrow. Here, self-consciousness is taken to be a special form of *reflexive* consciousness in which the object of consciousness is the self or some aspect of the self.

The term 'consciousness' is also commonly used to refer to a state of wakefulness. Being awake or asleep or in some other state such as coma clearly influences what one can be conscious of, but it is not the same as consciousness in the sense of 'awareness'. When sleeping, for example, one can still have visual and auditory experiences in the form of dreams. Conversely, when awake there are many things at any given moment that one does *not* experience. So in a variety of contexts it is necessary to distinguish 'consciousness' in the sense of 'awareness' from wakefulness and other states of arousal, such as dream sleep, deep sleep, coma and so on.

The above, broad definitions and distinctions are widely accepted in the contemporary scientific literature (see, for example, Farthing, 1992), although it is unfortunate that some writers continue to use the term 'consciousness' in idiosyncratic ways. Agreeing on definitions is important. Once a given reference for the term 'consciousness' is fixed, the investigation of its nature can begin, and this may in time transmute the meaning (or sense) of the term. As John Dewey notes, to grasp the meaning of a thing, an event or situation is to see it in its relations to other things; to note how it operates or functions, what consequences follow from it; what causes it, what uses it can be put to (1991 [1910]: Chapter 9). Thus, to understand what consciousness is, we need to understand what causes it, what its function(s) may be, how it relates to nonconscious processing in the brain and so on. As our scientific understanding of these matters deepens, our understanding of what consciousness *is* will also deepen. A similar transmutation of meaning (with growth of knowledge) occurs with basic terms in physics such as 'energy' and 'time'.

PHILOSOPHICAL BACKGROUND

Current scientific investigations of consciousness take place in the context of a philosophical debate about its nature which, in the Western tradition, extends back some 2,500 years to the ancient Greeks. Over this period there have been many theories about how mind and body relate, and about how consciousness and the brain relate. These theories can be broadly categorized in terms of what they take the 'substance' of consciousness to be. Traditionally, theories have been either dualist or monist. Either the universe is composed of *two* kinds of sub-stance, a mental (conscious, spiritual) substance and a physical substance ('substance dualism') – or the mental and the physical are aspects of, or reducible to, *one and the same thing*.

Varieties of dualism

Traditional theories can be further differentiated in terms of whether they think consciousness has causal efficacy (Question 2 above). Modern substance dualists usually argue that consciousness engages in a two-way causal interaction with the brain (as in the 'dualist-interactionism' of Eccles, 1980; Sherrington, 1942; Penfield, 1975; Foster, 1991). For example, according to Eccles (1980) the brain transmits perceptual input to the 'self-conscious mind', while the latter initiates muscular movement and control through the exercise of free will. A similar two-way interaction was proposed 2,500 years ago by Plato and 300 years ago by Descartes. However, not all dualists are interactionists. For example, Thomas Huxley (1898) argued that the brain causes conscious experience, but con-sciousness has no causal effects on the brain ('epiphenomenalism'), while Leibniz (1686) argued that activities in the mind and brain are perfectly aligned (correlated) but do not causally interact ('parallelism').

Varieties of monism

Contemporary monist theories come in many variants, both reductionist and nonreductionist. Twentieth-century philosophy of mind has been predominantly reductionist, attempting to show that consciousness can be understood entirely in terms of materialist science. Up to the 1960s it was commonly argued that consciousness is nothing more than a form of behaviour (the 'behaviourism' of Watson, 1913; Skinner, 1953), or a disposition to behave in certain ways (as in the 'dispositional behaviourism' of Ryle, 1949). Following the subsequent rise of cognitive science and neuropsychology, behaviourism (in its radical forms) has few contemporary adherents. Reductionists now maintain that science will eventually show consciousness to be just a state of the brain ('central-state identity theory' or 'physicalism' as in Place, 1956; Armstrong, 1968; Churchland, 1988; Searle, 1993). Alternatively, they maintain that consciousness is nothing more than a set of internal causal relationships or brain functions that may be found not just in brains but also in 'thinking' machines (as in the 'functionalism' of Dennett, 1991; Putnam, 1975; Van Gulick, 1988). There are many other variants of dualism and reductionism (see readings in Blakemore and Greenfield, 1987; Bleakley and Ludlow, 1992; Marcel and Bisiach, 1988).

Dualism versus reductionism

Broadly speaking, dualism gives full weight to the fact that the material stuff of brains seems to be different in kind from conscious experience in its many different forms. However, it splits mind and consciousness from the brain. In Descartes' classic formulation of this position (1972 [1644]), consciousness consists of *res cogitans*, a nonmaterial substance without extension in space, which 'thinks'. The material world, including the brain, consists of *res extensa* (substance that extends in space). For sciences which have been developed exclusively to investigate the material world, this poses problems. For example, it is not easy to see how one can investigate nonmaterial stuff with physical equipment. Nor is it easy to understand how a nonmaterial consciousness and a material brain might causally interact. While such problems might not be insuperable (see Foster, 1991), the attractions of reductionism are clear. If consciousness is just a state of or function of the brain as reductionists claim, such problems do not arise.

On the other hand, reductionists face the difficulty that the rich, sensuous 'qualia' of everyday experience do not *seem* to be just brain states or functions. To be ontologically identical all their properties would have to be identical – but conscious experiences and the neural stuff of brains seem to have few if any properties in common. An itch in the toe, for example, might be *caused* by or *correlate* with a state of the brain, but it seems to have irritating properties and a spatial location (in the toe) that seem very different to the properties of brain states described in physiological textbooks. Given this, it is not obvious how science *could* show these to be (ontologically) one and the same. Reductionist philosophers have proposed various 'solutions' to this problem (see, for example, Place, 1956; Churchland, 1988; Dennett, 1991; Searle, 1993). However, no generally accepted solution to the problem of 'qualia' exists.

A related problem arises from our inability to (directly) observe other people's experiences. In principle, one might be able to observe everything there is to observe about someone else's brain physiology and activity, and still not know how that person experiences the world (Nagel, 1974; Jackson, 1982, 1986). In short, 'first-person perspective facts' cannot be fully reduced to 'third-person perspective facts' (cf. Goldman, 1993; Velmans, 1991a, 1991b, 1993b; and debates between Dennett, Fenwick, Gray, Harnad, Humphrey, Libet, Lockwood, Marcel, Nagel, Searle, Shoemaker, Singer, Van Gulick, Velmans and Williams in Ciba Foundation Symposium 174, 1993). If so, reductionism is destined to fail.

A unified, nonreductionist approach

Given the problems with dualism and reductionism, it is important to consider nonreductionist forms of monism (attempts to a find a way of healing the split induced by dualism, without reducing consciousness to something other than it appears to be). An early version of this is the 'dual-aspect theory' of Spinoza (1876 [1677]) – the view that mind and matter are manifest aspects of something deeper in Nature, which appear to interact by virtue of some unfolding, grounding process within Nature itself. A twentieth-century variant of this is 'neutral monism' (James, 1970 [1904]; Mach, 1897 [1885]; Russell, 1948), which develops the view that events in the external world can be viewed as 'psychological' or 'physical', depending on how they are construed. A red spot, for example, is psychological in so far as its appearance is dependent on colour coding processes in the visual system – but it is physical in so far as it is dependent on the frequency of electromagnetic energy, the ambient light intensity and so on. However, dual-aspect theory and neutral monism have little to say about how conscious experiences relate to the brain as such (about causal interactions, neural correlates and so on). Neural correlates and their accompanying experiences are not just *construed* to be different, but are *observed or experienced* to be different (to have different properties) by external observers and subjects, respectively. This needs to be accounted for in any monist theory.

One contemporary proposal (Velmans, 1991b, 1993b) is that neural correlates and accompanying experiences encode identical information that appears to be 'formatted' in different ways because it is viewed from different, third- and first-person perspectives. Observations always require an *interaction* of an observed event with given observing apparatus, and the (interoceptive) means by which a subject accesses his or her own representational states is very different to the means available to an external observer (exteroceptors supplemented by physical equipment). Consequently, how the subject's representational states appear to the external observer and subject is very different. Rather like wave-particle descriptions in physics, first- and third-person descriptions are complementary and mutually irreducible. For completeness, psychology requires both forms of description. A deeper analysis of this and related issues is given in Velmans, 1991b and 1993b.

This brief sketch of some classical and contemporary views of consciousness suggests something of the complex background against which empirical studies of consciousness take place. The issues are fundamental, and the prevailing attitude towards them can influence the course of psychological science (during the behaviourist period the study of consciousness was eliminated from psychology by decree). Current investigations of consciousness have flourished despite such philosophical differences, as one does not need to fully understand what consciousness is *prior* to investigating it. It is enough that working definitions of consciousness are sufficiently similar to enable different investigators to direct their attention to similar phenomena. This applies also to experimental investigations of the consciousness/brain relationship. One can, for example, investigate the neural causes or correlates of a given conscious experience irrespective of whether one is a dualist, reductionist or dual-aspect theorist.

STUDIES OF CONSCIOUSNESS IN COGNITIVE PSYCHOLOGY

Memory, attention and consciousness

One of the main aims of cognitive psychology is to provide a functional description of the human mind in information processing terms. But how does conscious awareness *relate* to human information processing? Is consciousness causally active in certain forms of information processing (Question 2 above)? If so, what is its function (Question 3 above)? According to William James (1950 [1890]), the current contents of consciousness define the 'psychological present' and are contained in 'primary memory' (a form of short-term working store). The contents of 'secondary memory' (a long-term memory store) define the 'psychological past', and while they remain in secondary memory they are unconscious. James also suggested that stimuli which enter consciousness are at the *focus of attention*, having been selected from competing stimuli to enable effective interaction with the world. Stimuli at the focus of attention are also given significance and value by their contextual surround – a conscious 'fringe' or flowing consciousness 'stream'. These ideas, developed around 100 years ago, are still the focus of much psychological research.

James' linking of consciousness to primary memory, for example, was reintroduced into experimental psychology by Waugh and Norman (1965) and various attempts have been made to specify more precisely how consciousness relates to such a short-term store (e.g. Baddeley, 1993; Ericsson and Simon, 1984). It is generally thought that only information at the focus of attention enters primary memory (and consciousness), in which case it may later be consciously recognized or recalled. However, there is also much evidence for implicit memory – the ability to acquire and use long-term information in advance of or in the absence of any ability to consciously remember that information (see Gardiner in Chapter 3 below; and reviews by Reber, 1989; Schacter, 1987).

The processes which govern how stimuli are selected for focal attention and consciousness have been extensively researched since Cherry's (1953) investigations of the 'cocktail party problem'. In a cocktail party situation, the conversation one attends to enters consciousness, while the competing conversations seem to form a relatively undifferentiated background noise. However, all speech waveforms arrive concurrently at the eardrum. So how does the brain select the required message from such complex auditory stimuli? At the same time, if one's name is mentioned by someone across the room, one's attention might switch – suggesting that, to some extent, even nonattended messages are analysed.

The extent of preconscious analysis

Early experiments by Cherry (1953) and Broadbent (1958) indicated that subjects could not report the identity or meaning of stimuli on nonattended channels, although they could report some of their physical features. This suggested that preattentive analysis is restricted to physical cues, while analysis for meaning requires focal attention. Only stimuli at the focus of attention enter short-term memory, become conscious and can be subsequently remembered. However, later experiments demonstrated that the meaning of nonattended stimuli affected the processing of attended stimuli, indicating that analysis of meaning of non-attended stimuli can take place without conscious awareness or subsequent recall (Lewis, 1970; Corteen and Wood, 1972; Forster and Govier, 1978; Groeger, 1984a, 1984b). Subsequently, it was thought that the meaning and significance of input stimuli in different channels are analysed in a parallel, automatic, pre-conscious fashion, without mutual interference, up to the point where each stimulus is matched to its previous traces in long-term memory (Norman, 1969; Posner, 1978; Posner and Boies, 1971; Shiffrin and Schneider, 1977). More complex processing (for example, the identification of novel stimuli or novel stimulus combinations) was assumed to require focal attention and consciousness.

Posner and Snyder (1975), for example, developed a two-process theory in which preattentive, preconscious processing is thought of as a fast, automatic, spreading activation in the central nervous system. This activates not only memory traces of a given input stimulus but also related traces that share some of its features. For example, reading the word 'doctor' also activates or 'primes' semantically related features in the word 'nurse,' making the latter easier to recognize (Meyer et al., 1975). However, this process has no effect on unrelated traces (for example, 'doctor' does not prime 'bread'). By contrast, attentional processing occurs only after such spreading activation; it is relatively slow and serial in nature, and cannot operate without intention and awareness. This process not only activates the traces of related stimuli but also inhibits the activation of unrelated stimuli (making them harder to recognize). Evidence for this complex theory was gathered by Neely (1977). Evidence for the preconscious, parallel activation of traces which share features with an input stimulus, followed by selection of the most pertinent traces (and inhibition of nonpertinent traces), has also been found in studies of speech perception (Pynte et al., 1984; Swinney, 1979, 1982) and visual masking (a procedure where visual stimuli are prevented from reaching consciousness by the presentation of a subsequent visual stimulus or 'mask' – Marcel, 1980).

However, it is unlikely that preattentive input analysis is limited to spreading activation, and theories of preattentive and focal-attentive processing have continued to develop. La Berge (1981) and Kahneman and Treisman (1984) point out that different *forms* of attention may have to be devoted to different stages of input analysis. Attention may, for example, be devoted to physical features if one is searching for a target input stimulus, but other resources may be required to integrate the set of features at the location found by the search. In addition, the results of input analysis need to be disseminated to other processing modules.

Velmans (1991a) argues that preattentive, preconscious analysis might not be restricted to accessing the meaning of simple, familiar stimuli. Treisman (1964a, 1964b) and Lackner and Garrett (1973), for example, have found evidence for semantic and syntactic analysis of phrases and sentences in nonattended channels – although whether nonattended processing can proceed beyond the analysis of single words is still in dispute (cf. Kihlstrom in Chapter 2 below). More to the point, there is reason to doubt that input analysis is 'conscious' even for messages at the focus of attention. For example, if one silently reads the sentence 'The forest ranger did not permit us to enter the park without a permit', one experiences phonemic imagery ('inner speech') in which the stress pattern on the word 'permit' changes appropriately – from per*mit* (a verb) to *per*mit (a noun). For this to happen, the semantic and syntactic analysis required to determine the role of the word in the sentence must take place *before* its phonemic image enters consciousness. Nor are the detailed operations of input analysis in any sense 'conscious'. Velmans (1991a) concludes from this, and other evidence, that consciousness *follows* input analysis rather than *entering into it*.

The relation of consciousness to information processing

Such considerations force a re-examination of the way consciousness relates to focal-attentive processing, and similar questions can be raised about the many other forms of information processing which have been thought to require attention and consciousness for their operation; for example, stimulus selection and choice (Mandler, 1975,1985; Miller, 1987), learning and memory (Baars, 1988; James, 1950 [1890]; Underwood, 1979; Waugh and Norman, 1965), and the production of complex, flexible or novel responses (Mandler, 1975, 1985; Romanes, 1895; Shiffrin and Schneider, 1977; Underwood, 1982). It may be, for example, that consciousness relates closely not to the *detailed operation* of attentional processing, but to the *results* of such processing which need to be disseminated throughout the processing system to enable its integrated functioning, based on continuously updated, pertinent information. This possibility has been suggested by Navon (1991), Van Gulick (1991) and Velmans (1991a), and has been developed in depth by Baars (1988), and by Baars and McGovern (in Chapter 4 below).

It is also clear that one needs to define the meaning of a 'conscious process' more precisely. A process may be said to be 'conscious' in the sense that one is conscious of its operations (certain aspects of problem solving are conscious in this sense, but not, for example, the processing involved in visual perception); a process may also be said to be 'conscious' in the sense that its *output* enters consciousness (as in silent reading and the other forms of attentional processing mentioned above); a process may also be said to be 'conscious' in so far as consciousness causally affects or enters into that process. Whether any form of human information processing is 'conscious' in the last sense is a much debated issue (see Velmans, 1991a, 1991b, 1993b, and accompanying open peer reviews).[1]

The fringes of consciousness

James (1950 [1890]) stressed that the significance and value of conscious material at the focus of attention are indicated by the relatively vague feelings that surround it. Mangan (1993) argues that such feelings provide *contextual* information about conscious material at the focus of attention, in a highly condensed form. For example, the goodness-of-fit of currently focused on material with prior material stored in long-term memory may be manifest in consciousness as a simple feeling of its 'rightness' or 'wrongness'. According to Mangan, the unconscious process which produces such feelings may resemble the computation discovered by Hopfield (1982), in which the goodness-of-fit of an immense number of interacting, neuron-like nodes is condensed into a single metric or index. In their present form, connectionist networks do not require such computations in order to settle into stable states. Consequently, Mangan suggests that there may be a second network in the human brain that generates a goodness-of-fit metric (or its analogue), thereby overseeing the operations of a more basic network that settles into stable states in the normal way. Another possibility is a more sophisticated network which generates a global, state-of-the-system metric as an emergent property (Velmans, 1993c). Whether or not such ideas are borne out by experiment, it is clear that contextual processing and its accompanying conscious 'fringe' need to be incorporated into any complete model of brain function and accompanying experience.

Other studies of consciousness in psychology

The relation of consciousness to focal attention and primary memory is fundamental to its understanding in information processing terms. However, there are many other areas of psychology in which the contents of consciousness have been investigated. For example, studies of perception and psychophysics have extensively charted the way specific contents of consciousness (percepts) relate to environmental stimuli and brain processing (see, for example, Boff *et al.*, 1986). Other prominent areas of investigation include the study of consciousness in imagery (Finke and Shepard, 1986; Paivio, 1986), emotion (Ortony and

Turner, 1990; Mandler, 1975) and dreams (Foulkes, 1990; Llinás and Paré, 1991; the whole of *Consciousness and Cognition*, 3(1), 1994). There is also a continuing debate about methodological issues; for example, over how to determine when a process is conscious (Holender, 1986; Reingold and Merikle, 1993; Shanks and St. John, 1994; Kihlstrom in Chapter 2 below), about the value and limitations of introspection (Ericsson and Simon, 1984; Nisbett and Wilson, 1977; Farthing, 1992) and about the necessary conditions for a science of consciousness (Harman, 1994; Velmans 1993a).

THE NEUROPSYCHOLOGY OF CONSCIOUSNESS

Initial thoughts about the neural conditions required for consciousness

Following the investigations of the brain stem by Moruzzi and Magoun (1949), it is now generally accepted that the Reticular Activating System plays a major role in the regulation of different states of arousal (waking, sleeping and so on). Finding the necessary and sufficient neural conditions for conscious *awareness*, however, remains a formidable task (see Chapter 5 (Libet) and 6 (Young) below). The varied *contents* of consciousness are likely to draw on information that is widely distributed throughout the brain. But what happens to this information to make it conscious? Cognitive psychological theory suggests that the neural conditions for consciousness are closely linked to processes (and structures) responsible for attention and short-term memory – and within neuropsychology this suggestion has been developed by Bogen (1995), Dimond (1980), Crick and Koch (1990), and Newman and Baars (1993) (see review by Newman, 1995).

Cognitive studies also suggest that the initial 250 milliseconds (msec) (or so) of input processing is preconscious (Neely, 1977; Posner and Snyder, 1975). This is consistent with evidence from Libet (1973) that direct microelectrode stimulation of the cortex has to proceed for at least 200msec before neural conditions develop that are adequate to support conscious experience. Libet *et al.*(1979) also found evidence that the brain compensates for this preconscious processing time by 'marking' the time of arrival of stimuli at the cortical surface with an early evoked potential, and then referring experienced time of occurrence 'backwards in time' to this early time-marker (this remarkable finding is debated in the commentaries accompanying Libet, 1985; the discussion following Libet, 1993; and Velmans, 1993b).

Clinical dissociations of consciousness from psychological functioning

Studies with brain damaged patients have revealed many different forms of *dissociation* between psychological functioning and conscious awareness (reviewed by Young in Chapter 6 below). A classic example is the case of 'blindsight'. Weiskrantz *et al.* (1974), for example, examined a patient with lesions in his right hemisphere striate cortex who had no awareness of stimuli projected to his blind (left) hemifield (see also Weiskrantz, 1986). When persuaded to guess, he could nevertheless point accurately to spots flashed in the blind area, discriminate horizontal from vertical lines, and discriminate colour, movement and, to a limited extent, simple forms. A similar dissociation of awareness from ability to discriminate has been found for touch ('blindtouch') produced by somatosensory cortex damage (Paillard *et al.*, 1983). In amnesia, produced by lesions in the medial temporal lobe (including the hippocampus), patients may learn new motor skills and have implicit acquisition of semantic information although they have no (overt) conscious recognition or recall of what they have learned (Schacter, 1987, 1989, 1992; Mayes, 1992).

Given the close theoretical linkage of consciousness to focal attention, it is significant that in some of these conditions awareness is in part dissociated from aspects of focal attention (cf. Velmans, 1991a). Weiskrantz *et al.* (1974) found, for example, that a blindsighted subject could direct his attention to a screen and discriminate between stimuli projected to his blind hemifield without accompanying visual awareness of the stimuli. There is also evidence that amnesics can attend to and respond appropriately to a sequence learning task without having any explicit awareness of the sequence being learned (Nissen and Bullemer, 1987).

Such findings are troublesome for functionalist theories of consciousness, in that they demonstrate conscious awareness to be dissociable from many of the functions with which it is commonly identified. At the same time, neural differences between functions accompanied or not accompanied by consciousness may provide clues about the neural conditions which support conscious awareness (cf. Chapters 4 (Baars and McGovern) and 5 (Libet) below). Area V1 in the visual system, for example, appears to be one important component of neural systems which support visual awareness (cf. Cowey and Stoerig, 1992; Chapter 6 (Young) below).

The divisibility of consciousness

For Plato, Descartes and modern dualists such as Popper and Eccles (1977) the unity of consciousness is indivisible. However, dissociations also appear to occur *within* the contents of consciousness. For example, patients with *prosopagnosia* (usually caused by bilateral lesions to occipital-temporal cortical regions) are able to perceive familiar faces, but do not consciously recognize them (cf. Young in Chapter 6 below). They may, however, show evidence of unconscious recognition. One technique used to demonstrate such dissociations is a variant of the 'Guilty Knowledge Test', sometimes used in criminal investigations, in which a guilty person may have an involuntary physiological response to stimuli related to the crime. For example, one prosopagnosic subject studied by Bauer (1984) was shown photographs of familiar faces, each of which was accompanied by five names (one correct name and four distracters). When the subject was asked to *choose* the correct name his performance was no better than chance (22 per cent). But his skin conductance reaction to the correct name rose to maximal levels on 61 per cent of the trials (well above chance). In short, such patients consciously experience faces and *unconsciously* recognize them. However, tacit recognition is not accompanied by the ability to put a name to the face or the usual conscious feelings of 'familiarity'.

In *anosognosia*, patients appear to be unaware of their impairments and may actively deny them. Anton (1899), for example, found patients who denied their own blindness, and others who denied their deafness. Landis *et al.*(1986) found patients with prosopagnosia who denied their recognition problems. Lack of insight into memory impairments is also common (McGlynn and Schacter, 1989). Anosognosia may be thought of as an impairment in self-monitoring (Young and de Haan, 1993), or (from a first-person perspective) as a deficit in self-awareness. Schacter (1989) accounts for dissociations of consciousness in terms of disconnections of specific processing modules from a general conscious awareness system. However, the anosognosias are generally specific to a given impairment rather than reflecting any global lack of self-awareness. This opens up the possibility that self-monitoring (and accompanying self-awareness) may not rely on just one centralized monitoring mechanism (Bisiach *et al.*, 1986; Young and de Haan, 1993), although it might simply be that self-monitoring in all domains is not always accurate.

A further, dramatic dissociation of consciousness occurs within 'split-brain' patients, whose corpus callosum has been sectioned in an operation to relieve focal epilepsy (cf. Springer and Deutsch, 1993). Severing the corpus callosum prevents direct communication between the left and right cerebral cortices, although subcortical connections remain between the two halves of the brain. Surprisingly, such patients seem outwardly normal. Typically, however, they report being aware of stimuli (such as pictures or names of objects) projected to their left hemisphere (which controls speech), but deny awareness of the identity of stimuli projected to the right hemisphere. On the other hand, if objects corresponding to the stimuli are hidden behind a screen, the right hemisphere can identify them by touch, picking them out from other objects with the left hand, which it controls (Gazzaniga, 1970). The right hemisphere also appears able to understand concrete concepts, being able to identify (with the left hand) an object that 'goes with' the stimulus it receives, for example picking out a lighter when shown a cigarette (Gazzaniga, 1970, 1985); it is also generally superior to the left hemisphere in visuo-spatial tasks, although inferior in verbal and conceptual tasks (Gazzaniga and Le Doux, 1978).

What split-brain findings imply for the unity of consciousness and the relation of consciousness to the brain has been much debated. According to Eccles (1980) the ability to introspect and verbally communicate one's experience is required for full self-consciousness. Consequently, only the left hemisphere is fully conscious. Gazzaniga (1985, 1988) develops a similar view, arguing that consciousness is associated with a specialized *interpreter system* which nearly always exists in the left hemisphere. This 'makes sense' of input from left and right hemisphere modules to produce a coherent narrative which is fed to a language module (for report), thereby producing the *illusion* of a unified consciousness.

On the other hand, Sperry (1985) maintains that in the normal brain conscious unity is not an illusion. Rather, it is an emergent property of brain functioning, that 'supervenes' (regulates, coordinates) the brain activity from which it emerges. In the bisected brain (according to Sperry) each hemisphere has an associated consciousness of its own. Not only can the right hemisphere perceive, learn, engage in intelligent action and so on, but it may also have self-consciousness and a sense of social awareness (Sperry *et al.*, 1979). Striking evidence of right hemisphere ability was, for example, found by Gazzaniga and Le Doux (1978) in one exceptional patient whose right hemisphere was able to communicate its experiences by spelling out answers to questions with Scrabble letters, using the left hand (see Springer and Deutsch, 1993 for further evidence; and discussion in Farthing, 1992).

The integration of consciousness

Given the distributed nature of information processing in the brain and the many dissociations of consciousness discussed above, it is remarkable that the contents of consciousness generally appear bound into a coherent, relatively well-integrated stream. But how does the brain solve this 'binding problem'?

One possibility is that there are specific regions of the brain where all currently relevant information comes together and becomes conscious (as proposed by Bogen, 1995; Dimond, 1980; Penfield, 1975; Posner and Rothbart, 1992; Gray, 1995). However, according to Dennett (1991) and Dennett and Kinsbourne (1992) a fixed consciousness 'location' is ruled out by the distributed nature of information processing in the brain in both location and time. Indeed, Dennett and Kinsbourne oppose the view that the brain integrates such distributed information to produce a unified conscious stream. They also oppose the widely held view that the brain constructs integrated experiences by 'filling in' missing or impoverished information (on the basis of information stored in memory, expectations and so on) *prior to* the appearance of stimuli in consciousness. Rather, the brain simply produces 'multiple drafts' of ongoing events. The most recent draft is the one that defines the current contents of consciousness – and if this is inconsistent with previous drafts it simply overwrites it and we forget the previous draft. Our subjective experience of a unified conscious stream is, on this account, an illusion produced by an 'Orwellian' rewriting of history.

However, clear evidence that the brain 'fills in' impoverished information has been found, for example in studies of artificial scotoma (areas of blindness in vision). In one experiment, Ramachandran and Gregory (1991) asked subjects to fixate the centre of a monitor displaying television 'snow'. To one side of the fixation point they created an artificial 'blind spot' – a small grey square without any 'snow'. After fixating the screen for a few seconds subjects experienced the square to be filled with snow, like the surround. If the entire screen was subsequently made uniformly grey (like the square) subjects saw the surround as grey, but *continued to see the snow in the square*, for up to ten seconds – clear evidence of 'filling in', in this case persisting long after the need for it has passed (see also McCauley, 1993; Ramachandran, 1993).

Information integration is in any case possible without a fixed *location* (Velmans, 1992). For example, one 'binding' process suggested by Von der Malsburg (1986) involves the synchronous or correlated firing of diverse neuron groups representing currently attended-to objects or events. Although this possibility remains tentative, evidence for the existence of such binding processes (involving rhythmic frequencies in the 30–80 Hertz (Hz) region) has recently been reviewed by Crick and Koch (1990), Llinás and Paré (1991) and Shastri and Ajjanagadde (1993). Shastri and Ajjanagadde (1993) also give a detailed, innovative account of how such variable bindings might propagate over time, as attended-to representations change, within neural networks.

CLINICAL APPLICATIONS

Different forms of mind/body interaction

In principle, there are four basic ways in which body/brain and mind/consciousness might enter into causal relationships in clinical situations. There might be physical causes of physical states, physical causes of mental states, mental causes of mental states and mental causes of physical states. Establishing which forms of causation are effective in practice has clear implications for understanding the aetiology and proper treatment of illness and disease.

Within conventional medicine, physical → physical causation is taken for granted. Consequently, the proper treatment for physical disorders is assumed to be some form of physical intervention. Psychiatry takes the efficacy of physical → mental causation for granted, along with the assumption that the proper treatment for psychological disorders may involve psychoactive drugs, neurosurgery and so on. Many forms of psychotherapy take mental → mental causation for granted, and assume that psychological disorders can be alleviated by means of 'talking cures', guided imagery, hypnosis and other forms of mental intervention. Psychosomatic medicine assumes that mental → physical causation can be effective ('psychogenesis'). Consequently, under some circumstances a physical disorder (for example, hysterical paralysis) may require a mental (psychotherapeutic) intervention.

How could mental states affect illness and disease?

Although large bodies of research and clinical practice exist for each of these domains, those which assume the causal efficacy of mental states (psychotherapy and psychosomatic medicine) do not fit comfortably into the reductionist, materialist paradigm which currently predominates in Western philosophy and science.

For example, according to Churchland (1988) all descriptions of or theories about human nature based on conscious experience may be thought of as prescientific forms of 'folk psychology' which are destined to be replaced by some future, advanced neurophysiology. In short, all descriptions of mind or conscious experience will turn out to be descriptions of states of the brain. If so, all claims about mental causation would turn out to be 'prescientific' claims about physical causation – and the clinical consequence might be that psychotherapy will eventually be replaced by some advanced form of physical medicine. While confidence in the eventual success of reductionism might be premature (see the discussion of reductionism above), competition between mental and physical accounts has been very apparent in some therapeutic domains, for example in psychiatry and psychosomatic medicine (reviewed by McMahon and Sheikh, 1989).

McMahon and Sheikh point out that nineteenth-century physicians recognized the existence of 'nervous' disorders (headache, chronic fatigue, dyspepsia, etc.) for which no known structural defect could be found, but they took it for granted that the body was a machine governed by mechanistic laws on which the mind could have no influence. Consequently, somatic complaints without a discernible structural basis were frequently classified as 'imaginary'. Freud's account of conversion hysteria and its treatment gradually led to a change of medical opinion. As Freud noted, 'a disturbance that can be set right by means of psychic influences can itself have been nothing else than psychical' (quoted in Ferenczi *et al.*, 1921: 11). By the 1920s, belief in psychogenesis was widespread and was thought by its proponents to herald the dawn of a new holistic medicine. The journal *Psychosomatic Medicine* was founded in 1939, and by 1942 a chapter devoted to psychosomatic medicine had appeared in Osler's standard medical textbook *Principles and Practice of Medicine*.

However, this early enthusiasm did not fulfil its promise. As McMahon and Sheikh point out, there continued to be a mismatch between clinical observation and acceptable causal explanation. Freud himself took the view that the leap from 'a mental to a somatic innervation' (which takes place in hysteria) 'can never be fully comprehensible to us' (Freud, 1968 [1909]: 17). One response to this in subsequent theories of medicine was to treat conscious states as mere correlates of brain states; only the latter were thought to be the actual (physical) causes of somatic disorders (e.g. Troland, 1932). Another response was to redefine conscious states in behavioural terms (e.g. Sheehan, 1943). Occasionally, conditions thought to be examples of mental causation were dramatically shown to result from physical causes. For example, for many years patients with acute or chronic respiratory failure had been differentiated into 'fighters' (who battled to stay alive) and 'nonfighters' (who floated away gently, without apparent distress). Subsequently it was shown that fighters had normal pressure of carbon dioxide (Pco_2) in the blood, whereas nonfighters had been given oxygen at high Pco_2 levels and were narcotized by carbon dioxide – consequently they were underventilating and died quietly, often while being given high levels of oxygen (Donald, 1972: 318–319).

While belief in psychogenesis and psychosomatic disorders within medicine persisted, from the 1970s onwards psychological factors are given less prominence in medical textbooks (McMahon and Sheikh, 1989). A similar dilution of the causal role of mind in physiological disorders occurs over this period in the standard *Diagnostic and Statistical Manual of Mental Disorders* (DSM) published by the American Psychiatric Association. For example, DSM II, published in 1968, refers specifically to a category of 'psychophysiologic disorders'; in DSM-III-R, published in 1987, this category disappears.

Clinical evidence for the causal efficacy of mental states

In spite of a theoretical trend towards materialist accounts, clinical and experimental evidence for the causal efficacy of states of consciousness and mind on states of the body has continued to accumulate. For example, both Barber (1984) and Sheikh *et al.* in Chapter 7 below review a large body of evidence that hypnosis, the use of imagery, biofeedback and meditation may be therapeutic in a variety of medical conditions. Particularly striking (and puzzling) is the evidence that under certain conditions a range of autonomic bodily functions, including heart rate, blood pressure, vasomotor activity, pupil dilation, electrodermal activity and immune system functioning, can be influenced by imagery, hypnosis and so on – suggesting that under some circumstances the boundaries between voluntary and involuntary bodily functions may need to be redrawn.

The most widely accepted evidence for the effect of states of mind on medical outcome is undoubtedly the 'placebo effect' – well known to every medical practitioner and researcher. Simply receiving treatment and having confidence in the therapy or therapist has *itself* been found to be therapeutic in many clinical situations (cf. Skrabanek and McCormick, 1989; Wall, 1993, and Chapter 8 below). As with other instances of apparent mind/body interaction, there are conflicting interpretations of the causal processes involved. For example, Skrabanek and McCormick (1989) claim that placebos can affect *illness* (how people feel) but not *disease* (organic disorders). That is, they accept the possibility of mental → mental causation but not of mental → physical causation. However, Wall (1993, and Chapter 8 below) cites evidence that placebo treatments may produce organic changes. Hashish *et al.* (1988), for example, found that use of an impressive ultrasound machine reduced not only pain, but also jaw tightness and swelling after the extraction of wisdom teeth *whether or not the machine was set to produce ultrasound.* Wall also reviews evidence that placebos can remove the sensation of pain accompanying well-defined organic disorders, and not just the feelings of discomfort, anxiety and so on which may accompany it.

As McMahon and Sheikh (1989) note, the absence of an acceptable *theory* of mind/body interaction within philosophy and science has had a detrimental effect on the acceptance of mental causation in many areas of clinical theory and practice. Conversely, the extensive *evidence* for mental causation within some clinical settings forms part of the database which any adequate theory of mind/consciousness–body/brain relationships needs to explain.

CONCLUSIONS

In psychology's behaviourist period it was generally accepted that the study of consciousness was beyond the reach of science. The questions posed by consciousness are undoubtedly diverse, ranging from theoretical questions about its fundamental nature to empirical questions about how specific aspects of consciousness relate to specific processes in the brain. The issues addressed often cross the boundaries between philosophy, psychology, neuropsychology and clinical practice. Some of the ancient problems remain unresolved. But as psychology returns once more to its roots, it is clear that many aspects of consciousness have become the subject of a rich and rapidly developing science.

NOTE

1   Unlike other authors in the present text, in Chapter 4 below Baars and McGovern assume consciousness to be ontologically identical to the information processing with which it is most closely associated (i.e. with information dissemination). Consequently, they assume that consciousness performs the many functions attributable to information dissemination within the brain. However, it is important to note that *ontological identity* is not entailed by a close *association*, and for many authors the problem of how consciousness relates to the processes with which it is closely associated remains a serious one (see Gray, 1995; Libet in Chapter 5 below; Velmans, 1991a, 1991b, 1995, and Chapter 9 below).

REFERENCES

Anton, G. (1899) 'Über die selbstwahrnemung der herderkrankungen des gehirns durch den kranken bei rindenblindheit und rindentaubheit', *Archiv für Psychiatrie und Nervenkrankenheiten* 32: 86–127.

Armstrong, D.M. (1968) *A Materialist Theory of Mind*, London: Routledge.

Baars, B.J. (1988) *A Cognitive Theory of Consciousness*, Cambridge: Cambridge University Press.

Baddeley, A. (1993) 'Working memory and conscious awareness', in A.F. Collins, S.E. Gathercole, M.A. Conway and P.E. Morris (eds) *Theories of Memory*, Hillsdale, NJ: Lawrence Erlbaum Associates.

Barber, T.X. (1984) 'Changing "unchangeable" bodily processes by (hypnotic) suggestions: a new look at hypnosis, cognitions, imagining, and the mind–body problem', in A.A. Sheikh (ed.) *Imagination and Healing*, Farmingdale, NY: Bayworld.

Bauer, R.M. (1984) 'Autonomic recognition of names and faces in prosopagnosia: a neuro-psychological application of the guilty knowledge test', *Neuropsychologia* 22: 457–469.

Bisiach, E., Vallar, G., Perani, D., Papagno, C. and Berti, A. (1986) 'Unawareness of disease following lesions of the right hemisphere: anosognosia for hemiplegia and anosognosia for hemianopia', *Neuropsychologia* 24: 471–482.

Blakemore, C. and Greenfield, S. (eds) (1987) *Mindwaves*, Oxford: Blackwell.

Bleakley, B. and Ludlow, P. (eds) (1992) *The Philosophy of Mind*, A Bradford Book, Cambridge, MA: MIT Press.

Boff, K.R., Kauffman, L. and Thomas, J.P. (eds) (1986) *The Handbook of Perception and Human Performance*, Chichester: Wiley.

Bogen, J.E. (1995) 'On the neurophysiology of consciousness: I. An overview', *Consciousness and Cognition* 4(1): 52–62.

Broadbent, D.E. (1958) *Perception and Communication*, Oxford: Pergamon.

Cherry, C. (1953) 'Some experiments on the reception of speech with one and with two ears', *Journal of the Acoustical Society of America* 25: 975–979.

Churchland, P.S. (1988) 'Reductionism and the neurobiological basis of consciousness', in A.J. Marcel and E. Bisiach (eds) *Consciousness in Contemporary Science*, Oxford: Clarendon.

Ciba Foundation Symposium 174 (1993) *Theoretical and Experimental Studies of Consciousness*, Chichester: Wiley.

Corteen, R.S. and Wood, B. (1972) 'Autonomic responses to shock- associated words in an unattended channel', *Journal of Experimental Psychology* 94: 308–313.

Cowey, A. and Stoerig, P. (1992) 'Reflections on blindsight', in A.D. Milner and M.D. Rugg (eds) *The Neuropsychology of Consciousness*, London: Academic Press.

Crick, F. and Koch, C. (1990) 'Toward a neurobiological theory of consciousness', *The Neurosciences* 2: 263–275.

Dennett, D.C. (1991) *Consciousness explained*, London: Allen Lane.

Dennett, D.C and Kinsbourne, M. (1992) 'Time and the observer: the where and when of consciousness in the brain', *Behavioral and Brain Sciences* 15: 183–200.

Descartes, R. (1972 [1644]) *Treatise on Man*, trans. T.S. Hall, Cambridge, MA: Harvard University Press.

Dewey, J. (1991 [1910]) *How We Think*, Buffalo, NY: Prometheus.

Dimond, S.J. (1980) *Neuropsychology: a textbook of systems and psychological functions of the human brain*, London: Butterworths.

Dixon, N.F. (1981) *Preconscious Processing*, Chichester: Wiley.

Donald, K.W. (1972) discussion following M. Lader, 'Psychological research and psychosomatic medicine', in *Physiology, Emotion and Psychosomatic Illness*, Ciba Foundation Symposium no. 8, pp. 318–319, Amsterdam: North Holland.

Eccles, J.C. (1980) *The Human Psyche*, New York: Springer.

Ericsson, K.A. and Simon, H. (1984) *Protocol Analysis: verbal reports as data*, Cambridge, MA: MIT Press.

Farthing, J.W. (1992) *The Psychology of Consciousness*, Englewood Cliffs, NJ: Prentice-Hall.

Ferenczi, S., Abraham, K., Simmel, E. and Jones, E. (1921) *Psychoanalysis and the War Neurosis*, London: International Psycho-Analytic Press.

Finke, R.A. and Shepard, R.N. (1986) 'Visual functions of mental imagery', in K.R. Boff, L. Kauffman and J.P. Thomas (eds) *Handbook of Perception and Human Performance*, vol. 2: *Cognitive Processes and Performance*, New York: Wiley.

Forster, K.I. and Govier, E. (1978) 'Discrimination without awareness?' *Quarterly Journal of Experimental Psychology* 30: 289–295.

Foster, J. (1991) *The Immaterial Self: a defence of the Cartesian dualist concept of mind*, London: Routledge.

Foulkes, D. (1990) 'Dreaming and consciousness', *European Journal of Cognitive Psychology* 2: 39–55.

Freud, S. (1968 [1909]) 'Notes upon a case of obsessional neurosis', in S. Freud *Three Case Histories*, New York: Collier Books.

Gazzaniga, M.S. (1970) *The Bisected Brain*, New York: Appleton-Century-Crofts.

—— (1985) *The Social Brain: discovering the networks of the mind*, New York: Basic Books.

—— (1988) 'Brain modularity: toward a philosophy of conscious experience', in A.J.Marcel and E.Bisiach (eds) *Consciousness in Contemporary Science*, Oxford: Oxford University Press.

Gazzaniga, M.S. and Le Doux, J.E. (1978) *The Integrated mind*, New York: Plenum.

Goldman, A.J. (1993) 'Consciousness, folk psychology, and cognitive science', *Consciousness and Cognition* 2: 364–382.

Gray, J.A. (1995) 'The contents of consciousness: a neuropsychological conjecture', *Behavioral and Brain Sciences* (in press).

Groeger, J.A. (1984a) 'Preconscious influences on language production', PhD thesis, Queen's University of Belfast.

——— (1984b) 'Evidence of unconscious semantic processing from a forced error situation', *British Journal of Psychology* 75: 305–314.

Harman, W. (1994) 'The scientific exploration of consciousness: towards an adequate epistemology', *Journal of Consciousness Studies* 1(1): 140–148.

Hashish, I., Finman, C. and Harvey, W. (1988) 'Reduction of postoperative pain and swelling by ultrasound: a placebo effect', *Pain* 83: 303–311.

Holender, D. (1986) 'Semantic activation without conscious identification in dichotic listening, parafoveal vision, and visual masking', *Behavioral and Brain Sciences* 9: 1–66.

Hopfield, J. (1982) 'Neural networks and physical systems with emergent collective computational abilities', *Proceedings of the National Academy of Sciences, USA* 79: 2554–2558.

Huxley, T.H. (1898) *Collected Essays*, vol.1, London: Macmillan.

Jackson, F. (1982) 'Epiphenomenal qualia', *Philosophical Quarterly* 32: 127–136.

——— (1986) 'What Mary didn't know', *Journal of Philosophy* 83: 291–295.

James, W. (1950 [1890]) *The Principles of Psychology*, New York: Dover.

——— (1970 [1904]) 'Does "consciousness" exist?', in G.N.A. Vesey (ed.) *Body and Mind: readings in philosophy*, London: Allen & Unwin.

Kahneman, D. and Treisman, A. (1984) 'Changing views of attention and automaticity', in R. Parasuraman and D.R. Davies (eds) *Varieties of Attention*, London: Academic Press.

Kihlstrom, J.F. (1987) 'The cognitive unconscious', *Science* 237: 1445–1452.

La Berge, D. (1981) 'Automatic information processing: a review', in J. Long and A. Baddeley (eds) *Attention and Performance IX*, Hillsdale, NJ: Erlbaum.

Lackner, J. and Garrett, M.F. (1973) 'Resolving ambiguity: effects of biasing context in the unattended ear', *Cognition* L: 359–372.

Landis, T., Cummings, J.L., Christen, L., Bogen, J.E. and Imhof, H-G. (1986) 'Are unilateral right posterior cerebral lesions sufficient to cause prosopagnosia? Clinical and radiological findings in six additional patients', *Cortex* 22: 243–252.

Leibniz, G.W. (1686) *Discourse of Metaphysics, Correspondence with Arnauld, and Monadology*, trans. M. Ginsberg, London: Allen & Unwin, 1923.

Lewis, J.L. (1970) 'Semantic processing of unattended messages using dichotic listening', *Journal of Experimental Psychology* 85: 220–227.

Libet, B. (1973) 'Electrical stimulation and the threshold of conscious experience', in A. Iggo (ed.) *Handbook of Sensory Physiology*, vol. 2: *Somatosensory System*, New York: Springer-Verlag.

——— (1985) 'Unconscious cerebral initiative and the role of conscious will in voluntary action', *Behavioral and Brain Sciences* 8: 529–566.

——— (1993) 'The neural time factor in conscious and unconscious events', in *Experimental and Theoretical Studies of Consciousness*, Ciba Foundation Symposium 174, Chichester: Wiley.

Libet, B., Wright Jr., E.W., Feinstein, B. and Pearl, D.K. (1979) 'Subjective referral of the timing for a conscious experience: a functional role for the somatosensory specific projection system in man', *Brain* 102: 193–224.

Llinás, R.R. and Paré, D. (1991) 'Of dreaming and wakefulness', *Neuroscience* 44: 521–535.

Mach, E. (1897 [1885]) *Contributions to the Analysis of Sensations*, trans. C.M. Williams, Chicago: Open Court Publishing.

Mandler, G. (1975) *Mind and Emotion*, Chichester: Wiley.

——— (1985) *Cognitive Psychology: an essay in cognitive science*, Hillsdale, NJ: Erlbaum.

Mangan, B. (1993) 'Taking phenomenology seriously: the "fringe"' and its implications for cognitive research', *Consciousness and Cognition* 2(2): 89–108.

Marcel, A.J. (1980) 'Conscious and preconscious recognition of polysemous words: locating the selective effects of prior verbal context', in R.S. Nickerson (ed.) *Attention and Performance VIII*, Hillsdale, NJ: Erlbaum.

Marcel, A.J. and Bisiach, E. (eds) (1988) *Consciousness in Contemporary Science*, Oxford: Clarendon Press.

Mayes, A.R. (1992) 'Automatic processes in amnesia: how are they mediated?' in A.D. Milner and M.D. Rugg (eds) *The Neuropsychology of Consciousness*, London: Academic Press.

McCauley, R.N. (1993) 'Why the blind can't lead the blind: Dennett on the blind spot, blindsight, and sensory qualia', *Consciousness and Cognition* 2(2): 155–164.

McGlynn, S. and Schacter, D.L. (1989) 'Unawareness of deficits in neuropsychological syndromes', *Journal of Experimental and Clinical Neuropsychology* 11: 143–205.

McMahon, C.E. and Sheikh, A. (1989) 'Psychosomatic illness: a new look', in A. Sheikh and K. Sheikh (eds) *Eastern and Western Approaches to Healing*, Chichester: Wiley.

Meyer, D.E., Schvaneveldt, R.W. and Ruddy, M.G. (1975) 'Loci of contextual effects on visual word recognition', in P.M.A. Rabbitt and S. Dornic (eds) *Attention and Performance V*, London: Academic Press.

Miller, G.A. (1987) *Psychology: the science of mental life*, Harmondsworth, Penguin.

Moruzzi, G. and Magoun, H.W. (1949) 'Brain stem reticular formation and activation of the EEG', *Electroencephalography and Clinical Neurophysiology* 1: 455–573.

Nagel, T. (1974) 'What it is it like to be a bat?' *Philosophical Review* 83: 435–451.

Navon, D. (1991) 'The function of consciousness or of information?' *Behavioral and Brain Sciences* 14(4): 690–691.

Neely, J.H. (1977) 'Semantic priming and retrieval from lexical memory: roles of inhibitionless spreading activation and limited capacity attention', *Journal of Experimental Psychology: General* 106: 226–254.

Newman, J. (1995) 'Review: thalamic contributions to attention and consciousness', *Consciousness and Cognition* 4(2): 172–193.

Newman, J. and Baars, B.J. (1993) 'A neural attentional model for access to conciousness: a global workplace perspective', *Concepts in Neuroscience* 4(2): 255–290.

Nisbett, R.E. and Wilson, T.D. (1977) 'Telling more than we can know: verbal reports on mental processes', *Psychological Review* 75: 522–536.

Nissen, M.J. and Bullemer, P. (1987) 'Attentional requirements of learning: evidence from performance measures,' *Cognitive Psychology* 19: 1–32.

Norman, D. (1969) *Memory and Attention: an introduction to human information processing*, Chichester: Wiley.

Ortony, A. and Turner, T.J. (1990) 'What's basic about basic emotions?' *Psychological Review* 97: 315–331.

Osler, W. (1942) *Principles and Practices of Medicine Designed for the Use of Practitioners and Students of Medicine*, 14th edn., New York: Appleton Century.

Paillard, J., Michel, F. and Stelmach, C.E. (1983) 'Localization without content: a tactile analogue of "blindsight"', *Archives of Neurology* 40: 548–551.

Paivio, A. (1986) *Mental Representations: a dual coding approach*, Oxford: Oxford University Press.

Penfield, W. (1975) *The Mystery of the Mind: a critical study of consciousness and the human brain*, Princeton, NJ: Princeton University Press.

Place, U. (1956) 'Is consciousness a brain process?', *British Journal of Psychology* 47: 44–50.

Popper, K.R. and Eccles, J.C. (1977) *The Self and Its Brain*, New York: Springer.

Posner, K.R. (1978) *Chronometric Explorations of Mind*, Hillsdale, NJ: Erlbaum.

Posner, M.I. and Boies, S.W. (1971) 'Components of attention', *Psychological Review* 78: 391–408.

Posner, M.I. and Rothbart, M.K. (1992) 'Attentional mechanisms and conscious experience', in A.D. Milner and M.D. Rugg (eds) *The Neuropsychology of Consciousness*, London: Academic Press.

Posner, M.I. and Snyder, C.R.R. (1975) 'Facilitation and inhibition in the processing of signals', in P.M.A. Rabbitt and S. Dornick (eds) *Attention and Performance V*, London: Academic Press.

Putnam, H. (1975) *Philosophical Papers*, vol. 2: *Mind, Language and Reality*, Cambridge: Cambridge University Press.

Pynte, J., Do, P. and Scampa, P. (1984) 'Lexical decisions during the reading of sentences containing polysemous words', in S. Kornblum and J. Requin (eds) *Preparatory States and Processes*, Hillsdale, NJ: Erlbaum.

Ramachandran, V.S. (1993) 'Filling in gaps in logic: some comments on Dennett', *Consciousness and Cognition* 2(2): 165–168.

Ramachandran, V.S. and Gregory, R.L. (1991) 'Perceptual filling in of artificially induced scotomas in human vision', *Nature* 350: 699–702.

Reber, A.S. (1989) 'Implicit learning and tacit knowledge', *Journal of Experimental Psychology: General* 118: 219–235.

Reingold, E.M. and Merikle, P.M. (1993) 'Theory and measurement in the study of unconscious processes', in M. Davies and G.W. Humphries (eds) *Consciousness*, Oxford: Blackwell.

Romanes, G.J. (1895) *Mind and Motion and Monism*, London: Longmans, Green & Co.

Russell, B. (1948) *Human Knowledge: its scope and its limits*, London: Allen & Unwin.

Ryle, G. (1949) *The Concept of Mind*, London: Hutchinson.

Schacter, D.L. (1987) 'Implicit memory: history and current status', *Journal of Experimental Psychology: Learning, Memory and Cognition* 13: 501–518.

—— (1989) 'On the relation between memory and consciousness: dissociable interactions and conscious experience', in H.L. Roediger and F.I.M. Craik (eds) *Varieties of Memory and Consciousness*, Hillsdale, NJ: Erlbaum.

—— (1992) 'Consciousness and awareness in memory and amnesia: critical issues', in A.D. Milner and M.D. Rugg (eds) *The Neuropsychology of Consciousness*, London: Academic Press.

Searle, J. (1993) 'The problem of consciousness', in *Experimental and Theoretical Studies of Consciousness*, Ciba Foundation Symposium no.174, Chichester: Wiley.

Shanks, D.R and St. John, M.F. (1994) 'Characteristics of dissociable human learning systems', *Behavioral and Brain Sciences* 17(3): 367–447.

Shastri, L. and Ajjanagadde, V. (1993) 'From simple associations to systematic reasoning: a connectionist representation of rules, variables and dynamic bindings using temporal synchrony', *Behavioral and Brain Sciences* 16(3): 417–494.

Sheehan, D. (1943) 'Physiological principles underlying psychosomatic disorders', *Journal of Nervous Diseases* 98: 414–416.

Sherrington, C.S. (1942) *Man on his Nature*, Cambridge: Cambridge University Press.

Shiffrin, R.M. and Schneider, W. (1977) 'Controlled and automatic human information processing: II. Perceptual learning, automatic attending, and a general theory', *Psychological Review* 84: 127–190.

Skinner, B.F. (1953) *Science and Human Behavior*, New York: Macmillan.

Skrabanek, P. and McCormick, J. (1989) *Follies and Fallacies in Medicine*, Glasgow: Tarragon.

Sperry, R.W. (1985) *Science and Moral Priority: merging mind, brain and human values*, New York: Praeger.

Sperry, R.W., Zaidel, E. and Zaidel, D. (1979) 'Self-recognition and social awareness in the disconnected minor hemisphere', *Neuropsychologia* 17: 153–166.

Spinoza, B. (1876 [1677]) *The Ethics*, reprinted in *The Ethics of Benedict Spinoza*, New York: Van Nostrand.

Springer, S.P. and Deutsch, G. (1993) *Left Brain, Right Brain*, New York: Freeman.

Swinney, D.A. (1979) 'Lexical access during sentence comprehension: (re)consideration of context effects', *Journal of Verbal Learning and Verbal Behaviour* 18: 645–659.

—— (1982) 'The structure and time-course of information interaction during speech comprehension: lexical segmentation, access, and interpretation', in J. Mehler, E.C.T. Walker and M. Garrett (eds) *Perspectives on Mental Representation*, Hillsdale, NJ: Erlbaum.

Treisman, A.M. (1964a) 'The effect of irrelevant material on the efficiency of selective listening', *American Journal of Psychology* 77: 533–546.

—— (1964b) 'Verbal cues, language and meaning in attention', *American Journal of Psychology* 77: 206–214.

Troland, L.T. (1932) *The Principles of Psychophysiology*, vols. 1–3, New York: Van Nostrand.

Underwood, G. (1979) 'Memory systems and conscious processes', in G. Underwood and R. Stevens (eds) *Aspects of consciousness: psychological issues*, London: Academic Press.

—— (1982) 'Attention and awareness in cognitive and motor skills', in G. Underwood (ed.) *Aspects of Consciousness: awareness and self awareness*, London: Academic Press.

Van Gulick, R. (1988) 'Consciousness, intrinsic intentionality, and self-understanding machines', in A.J. Marcel and E. Bisiach (eds) *Consciousness in Contemporary Science*, Oxford: Clarendon.

—— (1991) 'Consciousness may still have a processing role to play', *Behavioral and Brain Sciences* 14(4): 699–700.

Velmans, M. (1991a) 'Is human information processing conscious?' *Behavioral and Brain Sciences* 14(4): 651–669.

—— (1991b) 'Consciousness from a first-person perspective', *Behavioral and Brain Sciences* 14(4): 702–726.

—— (1992) 'Is consciousness integrated?', *Behavioral and Brain Sciences* 15(2): 229–230.

—— (1993a) 'A reflexive science of consciousness', in *Experimental and Theoretical Studies of Consciousness*, Ciba Foundation Symposium no. 174, Chichester: Wiley.

—— (1993b) 'Consciousness, causality, and complementarity', *Behavioral and Brain Sciences* 16(2): 404–416.

—— (1993c) 'A view of consciousness from the fringe', *Consciousness and Cognition* 2: 137–141.

—— (1995) 'The limits of neurophysiological models of consciousness', *Behavioral and Brain Sciences* (in press).

Von der Malsburg, C. (1986) 'Am I thinking assemblies?', in G. Palm and A. Aertsen (eds) *Brain Theory*, Berlin: Springer.

Wall, P. (1993) 'Pain and the placebo response', in *Experimental and Theoretical Studies of Consciousness*, CIBA Foundation Symposium no. 174, Chichester: Wiley.

Watson, J.B. (1913) 'Psychology as the behaviorist views it', *Psychological Review* 20: 158–177.

Waugh, N.C. and Norman, D.A. (1965) 'Primary memory', *Psychological Review* 72: 89–104.

Weiskrantz, L. (1986) *Blindsight: a case study and implications*, Milton Keynes: Open University Press.

Weiskrantz, L., Warrington, E.K., Sanders, M.D. and Marshall, J. (1974) 'Visual capacity in the hemianopic field, following a restricted occipital ablation', *Brain* 97: 709–728.

Young, A.W. and de Haan, E.H.F. (1993) 'Impairments of visual awareness', in M. Davies and G.W. Humphries (eds) *Consciousness*, Oxford: Blackwell.

Chapter 2

Perception without awareness of what is perceived, learning without awareness of what is learned

John F. Kihlstrom

Beginning in the 1980s, psychology (and cognitive science generally) has undergone a dramatic shift in its attitude towards the psychological unconscious – that is, towards the idea that mental states and processes can influence experience, thought and action outside of phenomenal awareness and voluntary control. Once rejected out of hand as too deeply embedded in psychoanalysis or other forms of pseudoscience, or at least as too vague to be scientifically useful, the notion of unconscious processing is now taken seriously by most researchers and theorists in the field. At this point, the debate has shifted from questions about the very existence of unconscious states and processes to debates about the nature and extent of unconscious processing. Credit for this state of affairs goes to four rather different lines of research (for a more extensive discussion of this recent history, see Kihlstrom, 1987, 1995).

First, cognitive psychology now embraces a distinction between automatic and controlled processing (e.g. Hasher and Zacks, 1979, 1984; Schneider and Shiffrin, 1977; Shiffrin and Schneider, 1977; for updates, see Bargh, 1989; Logan, 1989; Shiffrin, 1988). Whether they are innate or routinized by extensive practice, automatic processes are inevitably engaged by specific inputs, independent of any intentionality on the part of the subject, and they cannot be controlled or terminated before they have run their course. We have no conscious awareness of their operation, and we have little or no awareness of the information which they process. All that enters awareness is the final product of the automatic process. Thus, automaticity represents unconscious processing in the strict sense of the term: we have no introspective access to automatic procedures, or their operations; these can be known only indirectly, by inference.

Further contributions came from the emergence of cognitive neuropsychology (Rozin, 1976).[1] Studies of the amnesic syndrome associated with bilateral lesions in the hippocampus and other medial–temporal structures, for example, revealed a distinction between two expressions of memory, explicit and implicit (Moscovitch *et al.*, 1993; Schacter, 1995). Explicit memory is conscious recollection of the past; implicit memory is reflected in any influence of past events on subsequent experience, thought and action. We now know that explicit and implicit memory can be dissociated in many different ways, indicating that implicit memory is in some sense independent of explicit memory (Roediger and McDermott, 1993). In the present context, the importance of the discovery of implicit memory is that it legitimized discussions of unconscious memories – a topic which had been virtually taboo among nonclinical psychologists.

A third influence was from research on hypnosis, producing many phenomena which seem to involve a division of consciousness (Hilgard, 1977; Kihlstrom, 1984). For example, in hypnotic analgesia (Hilgard and Hilgard, 1975), highly hypnotizable subjects appear insensitive to normally painful stimuli (such as immersion of the forearm in circulating ice water); similar phenomena can be observed in hypnotic blindness and deafness. In posthypnotic amnesia, hypnotizable subjects are unable to remember the events and experiences which transpired while they were hypnotized. In posthypnotic suggestion, they respond to cues established in hypnosis, without realizing that they are doing so, or why. Experimental studies of these and other phenomena, trying to understand them using concepts and methods appropriated from modern cognitive psychology, have provided new insights into the difference between conscious and unconscious mental life.

The fourth source, and one of central interest in this chapter, is research on subliminal influence, a subtype of implicit perception (Kihlstrom et al., 1992). Modelled on the explicit–implicit distinction drawn in memory, explicit perception is conscious perception, as reflected in the subject's ability to identify the form, location or movement of an object; implicit perception is reflected in any influence of such an object on the subject's ongoing experience, thought and action, independent of conscious perception. The evidence for implicit perception is of the same sort as that for implicit memory, including various types of priming effects, except that the event in question is in the current stimulus environment, or was so in the very recent past. And it is here that our story begins.

WHEN THE SUBJECT IS CONSCIOUS BUT UNAWARE OF THE EVENT

The problem of subliminal perception, initially raised speculatively by Leibniz (1981 [1704]), was addressed experimentally by Pierce and Jastrow (1885) in what may have been the earliest psychological experiment performed (or at least published) in America. In a series of studies of weight and brightness discrimination, Pierce and Jastrow reduced the difference between standard and comparison stimuli until they[2] were at zero confidence in choosing which object was the heavier or the brighter. Yet, when forced to guess, they proved to be more accurate than chance. Apparently, some stimulus information was registering below awareness in the perceptual-cognitive system. Pierce and Jastrow concluded that their experiments disproved the existence of a sensory threshold (limen); at the very least, they showed the influence on behaviour of subliminal stimuli – that is, stimuli which apparently were below the threshold for conscious perception.

For the better part of the twentieth century, a large number of investigators (themselves mostly ignorant of Pierce and Jastrow's work) have attempted the same sort of demonstration (for general coverage, see Bornstein and Pittman, 1992). For example, in a study by Poetzel (1960 [1917]) subjects were exposed to brief tachistoscopic presentations of a complex landscape. When asked to reproduce the stimulus by drawing, the subjects omitted many details; however, Poetzel reported that many of these details appeared in the subjects' subsequent dreams. A number of other investigators (e.g. Fisher, 1960, 1988; Haber and Erdelyi, 1967) replicated and extended these results. However, a further series of studies by Erdelyi (1970, 1972; see also Ionescu and Erdelyi, 1992) suggested that these results may well have been an artefact of shifts in the response criterion adopted by subjects in the various tests.

In a line of research that constituted part of the New Look in perception (Bruner, 1992), Bruner and his colleagues uncovered evidence for a phenomenon of perceptual defence (e.g. Bruner and Postman, 1947; McGinnies, 1949; Postman *et al.*, 1948). For example, the thresholds for perceptual identification were higher for words with threatening (or at least socially undesirable) sexual and aggressive content than for non-taboo words. This raised the paradox of the 'Judas eye' – the peepholes in Prohibition-era speakeasies, through which a bouncer could determine who could be admitted, a determination that required that the person be identified. Similarly, if thresholds for identification were determined by the content of the stimulus, then the content of the stimulus had to be processed before it could be admitted to consciousness. In other words, a great deal of cognitive analysis, including the analysis of meaning, had to take place outside of conscious awareness. Thus it was not merely detection (as in Pierce and Jastrow's experiments) but semantic processing which could take place on subliminal inputs.

The Eriksen challenge

The psychology of the 1950s had little patience for such ideas, and publication of such work elicited a host of friendly and hostile critiques. For example, Solomon and Howes (1951) argued that the threshold differences between taboo and non-taboo words were related to frequency of usage, rather than taboo content *per se*. Certainly the most powerful and influential criticism of subliminal perception came from C.W. Eriksen (1956, 1958, 1960); see also Goldiamond (1958). Perhaps reflecting the influence of functional behaviourism, Eriksen was extremely critical of any definition of awareness in terms of verbal reports or confidence ratings, and he was equally critical of the methods used to determine thresholds in subliminal perception experiments (as was Goldiamond, 1958). For example, in a typical experiment in which subjects were found to make a discriminative behavioural response to stimuli in the absence of verbal report, Eriksen noted that the thresholds in question were established on the basis of the verbal reports, but not on the basis of the discriminative response. Proper demonstration of subliminal perception would require that thresholds be determined from both dependent variables, and that the latter be lower than the former. Eriksen noted that when this was done, the two thresholds were essentially equivalent. This is indeed a difficult empirical problem for demonstrations of subliminal perception. However, Eriksen went further than this, because he evidently distrusted verbal reports as indices of conscious experience, and instead preferred discriminative behaviour for this purpose. This created a paradox (Bowers, 1984; Merikle and Reingold, 1992), because above-chance discriminative responses are the means by which perception without awareness is documented in the first place. If conscious perceptual experience is to be inferred from any discriminative response, this would seem to mean that subliminal perception is ruled out by fiat.

Interest in subliminal perception would have died there, in the 1960s, and it almost did. The phenomenon was kept on life support by Dixon's (1971, 1981) efforts, as well as those of some investigators who were influenced by psychoanalytic ideas (for reviews, see Shevrin, 1988, 1992; Shevrin and Dickman, 1980; Silverman, 1976; Silverman and Weinberger, 1985; Weinberger, 1992).[3] However, this neo-neo-Freudian research did not reach much beyond a small circle of like-minded investigators. The reasons for this state of affairs are not clear, since on the surface the studies appear to have met reasonably stringent methodological standards. Certainly the historical distrust on the part of experimental psychologists towards anything smacking of psychoanalytic theory must have played a role.

The turning point came in the early 1980s, with a new round of demonstrations of subliminal perception by Marcel (1980, 1983a, 1983b) and Kunst-Wilson and Zajonc (1980). Marcel's experiments employed a semantic-priming paradigm in which the prime was masked. When the prime and the target were semantically related, priming was observed on lexical decisions concerning the targets, even though the subjects did not detect the prime itself. Kunst-Wilson and Zajonc (1980) employed an adaptation of the mere exposure paradigm with extremely brief tachistoscopic exposures of the stimuli, which in this case were nonsense polygons. Subjects showed an enhanced preference for stimuli which had been repeatedly exposed, even though they had not detected the exposures themselves. In short order, both results were replicated by other investigators: Marcel's by Fowler and her colleagues (Fowler et al., 1981) and by Balota (1983); those of Kunst-Wilson and Zajonc by Seamon and his colleagues (Seamon et al., 1983, 1984) and by many others (for a review, see Bornstein, 1989). By presenting evidence that meaning (denotative in the case of Marcel, connotative in the case of Kunst-Wilson and Zajonc) could be processed subliminally, these experiments moved beyond the pioneering study of Pierce and Jastrow (1885), which involved only the discrimination of stimulus qualities such as brightness and weight, and seemed to fulfil the promise of the New Look.

Just when we might have thought it safe to study subliminal perception again, Holender (1986) weighed in with a vigorous criticism of studies purporting to show semantic processing in the absence of conscious awareness. Some of these experiments were in the Marcel tradition, employing masks to render the stimulus subliminal, while others employed paradigms like dichotic listening or parafoveal viewing, in which a supraliminal stimulus is merely unattended; this latter category, while of considerable interest, is not relevant here because I am concerned with awareness, not attention. With respect to ostensibly subliminal stimulation, Holender's critique closely resembled Eriksen's (1960), with an emphasis on the difficulty of establishing thresholds for stimulus detection (for other critiques of the threshold-setting procedures, see Cheesman and Merikle, 1985; Merikle, 1982; Purcell *et al.*, 1983). In particular, Holender equated conscious processing with discriminative response:

> This paper has proposed an analysis of the data relevant to the issue of SA/CI [semantic activation without conscious identification]. . . . In order to demonstrate the existence of such a phenomenon, a twofold condition, referred to as criterion 1, must be met. At the time of presentation of the critical stimulus, (1) there must be indirect measurable effects of semantic activation, and (2) the identity of the stimulus must be unavailable to the subject's consciousness, that is, he must be unable to give direct evidence of identification (e.g. through verbal report or any kind of voluntary discriminative response).
>
> (1986: 23)

Or, in the words of Merikle and Cheesman:

> Holender accepts without question the widely held assumption that perceptual awareness or consciousness is best defined as better than chance-level discriminative responding. In fact, Holender states that discriminative responding provides the only essential criterion for establishing perceptual awareness or consciousness. Thus, if an observer can respond discriminatively to a stimulus, then, by definition, the observer is aware of the stimulus; and, conversely, if an observer cannot respond discriminatively to a stimulus, then, by definition, the observer is unaware of the stimulus.
>
> (1986: 42)

Thus the literature on subliminal perception was brought full circle. And because discriminative response provides the evidence for the 'indirect measurable effects' (Holender, 1986, p. 23) in the first place – how else are we to know that the stimulus has been perceived? – subliminal perception was defined out of existence. For this reason, Holender's criterion should simply have been rejected out of hand – and, as discussed below, Merikle and Cheesman (1986) did specifically reject it. However, other investigators rose to the challenge, and sought to demonstrate subliminal perception on terms defined by Eriksen (1960) and Holender (1986) – at least so far as threshold-setting procedures were concerned.

By far the most diligent of these attempts to meet the Eriksen challenge were studies performed by Greenwald *et al.* (1989). They distinguished between attentionless processing, in which a supraliminal stimulus is not attended to because attention is directed elsewhere (e.g. dichotic listening or parafoveal viewing), and detectionless processing, in which a subliminal stimulus cannot be detected because it is not available to attention in the first place. Their experimental paradigm involved semantic priming of lexical decisions – except that, rather than deciding whether a letter string was a word, subjects were asked to decide whether a word was evaluatively positive or negative in (connotative) meaning. Positive and negative targets were preceded by positive, neutral or negative primes, which in turn were rendered undetectable by the dichoptic pattern masking technique employed earlier by Marcel (1980, 1983a, 1983b), Fowler et al. (1981) and Balota (1983). In this technique, the prime and the mask are presented to different eyes, so that the masking occurs centrally rather than peripherally. In contrast to the earlier studies, which defined subliminality in terms of the subject's ability to report the presence of the prime, Greenwald et al. (1989) adopted a stricter criterion: the subject's ability to report whether the prime appeared on the left or right of the fixation point. Note that this criterion does address Eriksen's (1960) and Holender's (1986) challenge, in that the subjects were apparently unable to make a discriminative response based on the position at which the prime appeared (but see Doyle, 1990, for a critique). Across three experiments, response latencies on the evaluative decision task were speeded when the prime and the target were evaluatively congruent, and slowed when they were evaluatively incongruent – even though the subjects were unable to detect where the prime was presented.

Although the results obtained by Greenwald et al. (1989) provide convincing evidence of subliminal perception, in terms of detectionless semantic processing, other results set limits on the effect which are important for theory. In Experiment 3, which employed simultaneous (rather than backward) dichoptic pattern masking, primes presented for 80 milliseconds (msec) affected evaluative judgements, but primes presented for 40 msec did not. Apparently, the perceptual system is unable to extract evaluative meaning from primes which are given only extremely brief exposures. Moreover, subsequent research reported by Greenwald and Liu (1985; see also Greenwald, 1992) failed to obtain evidence of subliminal perception when the primes were two-word phrases rather than single words. For example, 'enemy loses', a positive phrase constructed from two negative words, primed negative, rather than positive, targets. Apparently, the conditions which render stimuli undetectable permit meaning to be extracted from single words, but they do not allow the meaning of two or more words to be combined.[4] At least for the near future, Greenwald's (1992: 775) 'two-word challenge' – 'the task of demonstrating that attentionless unconscious cognition can extract the meaning of a two-word sequence' – has replaced Eriksen's challenge as the agenda for research on subliminal perception.

Another perspective on the limits of subliminal perception is to be found in the work of Merikle (1982, 1992) and his colleagues (Cheesman and Merikle, 1984, 1985, 1986; Merikle and Cheesman, 1986; Merikle and Reingold, 1990, 1992;

Reingold and Merikle, 1993). Merikle essentially abandoned the Eriksen challenge altogether, and defined awareness in terms of confidence levels rather than discriminative response. Thus he defined the *subjective threshold* as the point at which the subject's confidence in his or her discriminations drops to zero, and the *objective threshold* as the point at which the subject's actual discrimination performance drops to chance levels. In a typical experiment (Merikle and Reingold, 1990, Experiment 1), subjects were presented with a word accompanied by forward and backward masks. For the detection task, they were presented with two unmasked words and asked whether either was the word which had been presented previously (a question which requires only a yes or no response); for the recognition task, they were presented with the same two words again and forced to choose which one had been presented. The general finding of the research is that subjects showed above-chance recognition of words which they had failed to detect. Of course, from Eriksen's (1960) and Holender's (1986) point of view, the subjective threshold, as defined in Merikle's experiments, is just a poor index of conscious awareness. However, Merikle and his colleagues have also shown qualitative differences in the processing of stimuli presented above and below the subjective threshold. Thus recognition without detection is possible for words, but not for nonwords. Such differences strongly suggest that the subjective threshold creates qualitative rather than merely quantitative effects on processing. With respect to the limits on subliminal perception, we may speculate that semantic processing is possible for items presented near the subjective threshold, but that only perceptual processing is possible for items presented near the objective threshold.

Implicit perception

Subliminal perception does not exhaust the circumstances under which subjects process stimulus information without being aware of the stimulus. Such effects crop up in the neuropsychological literature on blindsight (Weiskrantz, 1986). Patients with lesions in the striate cortex report a lack of visual experience in regions of the field corresponding to their scotoma; but when forced to make guesses, they make better-than-chance conjectures about the presence, location, form, movement, velocity, orientation and size of the objects which have been presented to them. Note that Campion and his colleagues offered a critique of the blindsight literature which reflects some of the same issues raised earlier by Eriksen (Campion *et al.*, 1983).

Similar effects are very familiar in the clinical literature on the so-called *conversion disorders* (which are better construed as types of dissociative disorder; see Kihlstrom, 1994a), and in the experimental literature on hypnosis (for a review, see Kihlstrom, 1984; Kihlstrom *et al.*, 1992). For example, Brady and Lind (1961) reported a case of functional blindness, in which the patient denied any visual awareness; none the less, his behaviour in an instrumental conditioning situation was clearly influenced by visual cues (for a more recent case, see Bryant and McConkey, 1989b). Similarly, Bryant and McConkey (1989a) have shown that the choice behaviour of highly hypnotizable subjects who have received suggestions for total blindness is influenced by visual cues, even though the subjects deny awareness of these cues; moreover, visual presentation of disambiguating cues biases the performance of hypnotically blind subjects when they are asked to spell homophones presented aurally (Bryant and McConkey, 1989c). Similarly, Spanos *et al.* (1982) found that subjects who received suggestions for unilateral hypnotic deafness nevertheless showed intrusions from the affected ear in a dichotic listening task.

In these types of studies, the stimuli in question, while processed outside awareness, are in no sense subliminal. Rather, it is something about the subject – suffering brain damage or being in a dissociative state – which produces the impairment in conscious perception. Hypnotic blindness is not the same as blindsight: hypnotic subjects show no evidence of altered brain function (at least in the sense of lesions to the striate cortex), and hypnotic blindness may be reversed when the suggestion for it is cancelled. Blindsight may be limited to gross perceptual properties, of the sort that can be mediated by a secondary visual system, while processing in hypnotic blindness seems to extend to rather complex semantic analyses. Still, as in the truly subliminal case, perception is implicit in the subject's experience, thought or action.

WHEN THE SUBJECT IS AWARE OF AN EVENT BUT NOT OF THE KNOWLEDGE ACQUIRED FROM IT

Another variant on the unconscious acquisition of knowledge is provided by studies of *implicit learning* (Reber, 1967), in which subjects appear to learn from experience without being aware of what they have learned, or even of the fact that they have learned anything at all. Although the question of learning without awareness has a long history going back to the distinction between intentional and incidental learning (Jenkins, 1933; Thorndike and Rock, 1934; for reviews, see Adams, 1957; Razran, 1961), the modern era of this research began with Reber's (1967) studies of the learning of artificial grammars (for an overview, see Reber, 1993). In a typical experiment, Reber asks his subjects to study, in anticipation of a later memory test, a list of twenty three- to eight-letter strings, such as TSXS, TSSXXVPS and PVV, which have been generated by a finite-state artificial grammar. After the strings have been memorized to a strict criterion of learning, the subjects are informed that they conform to a particular set of grammatical rules. Finally, the subjects are presented with a set of fifty new letter strings, only some of which conform to the grammar, and asked to indicate which are legal and which are not. The general finding of Reber's experiments is that subjects show above-chance levels of performance on this task (baseline = 50 per cent accuracy), despite the fact that they are generally unable to report the grammatical rules by which the legal strings were generated. Reber claims that while subjects were consciously trying to memorize the letter strings, they also unconsciously induced the grammar which generated them.

According to Reber (1993), the cognitive structure which enables subjects to induce the artificial grammar is not a language-specific cognitive module, as Chomsky (1980) and other psycholinguists might suggest, but rather comprises a general learning system which enables both humans and nonhuman animals to pick up a wide variety of regularities in their environments. As opposed to what he calls the 'consciousness stance' characteristic of most modern cognitive psychology, which asserts that consciousness has priority and that awareness and self-reflection are the central features of human cognitive function, Reber (1993: 24–25) asserts 'the primacy of the implicit' and adopts an *implicit stance* which holds that unconscious learning processes are axiomatic: we cannot get along cognitively without them, and more information is available for unconscious use than is accessible to conscious introspection. As Reber puts it (1993: 86), 'Consciousness is a late arrival on the evolutionary scene. Sophisticated unconscious perceptual and cognitive functions preceded its emergence by a considerable margin.'

Since Reber reported his initial experiments, a number of other investigators have confirmed his essential results and have developed alternative paradigms for demonstrating and analysing implicit learning (for comprehensive reviews, see Berry, 1994, 1995; Berry and Dienes, 1993; Dienes and Perner, 1995; Lewicki, 1986; Reber, 1993; Seger, 1994). Among these is the *control of complex systems* paradigm developed by Broadbent (1977; see also Berry and Broadbent, 1995), and the *sequence learning* and *matrix scanning* paradigms invented by Nissen (Nissen and Bullemer, 1987) and Lewicki (1986; see also Lewicki *et al.*, 1987), respectively. In one version of the control of complex systems paradigm, known as the sugar-production task (Berry and Broadbent, 1984), subjects take the role of factory manager and are asked to control the production of sugar, varying only the size of the workforce. In fact, the system is programmed so that production on any given trial (after the first) is a function of the number of workers employed on that trial and the amount of sugar produced on the previous trial. Subjects typically learn to control this system fairly readily, although they are generally unable to specify the formula which governs it. Sequence learning is a variant on a serial reaction time task, in which subjects must respond to a light appearing in one of four locations on a screen. Rather than varying randomly, the location of the light is actually governed by a complex sequential pattern. Subjects learn this pattern, as indicated by decreasing response latencies as trials go on, even though they are generally unable to predict where the stimulus will occur on any given trial.

Implicit learning is sometimes categorized informally as a form of subliminal perception, but this is an error because the stimuli in question are clearly supra-liminal, and the subject is in no sense unconscious of them. Reber's subjects are aware that they are memorizing letter strings, just as Berry and Broadbent's subjects know they are reading sugar-production figures and Nissen and Bullemer's are aware of the lights flashing on the screen. In fact, the term 'implicit learning' is properly applied only to instances where conscious subjects are unaware of what they have learned from supraliminal stimuli. Based on the canonical definition of implicit memory, we can say that implicit learning is manifested when a subject's experience, thought or action reflects knowledge acquired during a learning experience, in the absence of conscious awareness of this knowledge. The fact that the knowledge acquired in implicit learning consists of rules has sometimes led proponents to categorize implicit learning as procedural learning. While the distinction between declarative and procedural knowledge is valid (Anderson, 1976; Winograd, 1975), some of the knowledge acquired in these procedures can be represented in propositional format. Therefore, it seems that the distinction between declarative and procedural knowledge should be kept separate from the distinction between explicit and implicit learning.

In any event, the fact that subjects are at least conscious *of something* while they are learning has led to some scepticism about the claim that these same subjects are simultaneously *not conscious of learning*, or *not conscious of what they have learned*. Dulany (1968, 1991, 1995; Dulany *et al.*, 1984, 1985) has been a particularly vigorous critic of Reber's claims concerning artificial grammar learning, and Shanks and St. John (1994) have recently offered an analysis of learning without awareness which, in its scope and negativism, rivals the earlier work of Eriksen (1960) and Holender (1986). According to the Shanks and St. John view, most ostensible demonstrations of implicit learning fail to meet two criteria: according to the Information Criterion, 'it must be possible to establish that the information the experimenter is looking for in the awareness test is indeed the information responsible for performance changes'; according to the Sensitivity Criterion, 'we must be able to show that our test of awareness is sensitive to all of the relevant conscious knowledge' (Shanks and St. John, 1994: 373). Put another way: if the subjects are asked the wrong questions about their conscious mental states, we cannot conclude from what they say that they do not know what they are doing, or why.

The importance of the information and sensitivity criteria can be illustrated with respect to the learning of artificial grammars (e.g. Reber, 1967, 1993). To begin with, it is probably too much to expect subjects to give a full verbal account of a Markov process or finite-state grammar. So, for example, one of the grammars most frequently studied by Reber (see Reber, 1993, Figure 2.1) is captured approximately – but only approximately – as follows:

A1. The first letter of the string can be either P or T.
A2. If the first letter was P, go to C1; otherwise go to B1.
B1. If the first letter was T, the next letter must be S.
B2. If the next letter was S, it can be repeated an infinite number of times.
B3. If S was not repeated, the next letter must be X.
B4. If the next letter was X, then the next letter can be either X or S.
B5. If the next letter was S, the string ends.
B6. If the next letter was X, the next letter must be T.

B7. If the next letter was T, go to C2.
C1. If the first letter was P, the next letter must be T.
C2. If the next letter was T, it may be repeated an infinite number of times.
C3. If T was not repeated, the next letter must be V.
C4. If the next letter was V, the next letter must be P or V.
C5. If the next letter was V, the string ends.
C6. If the next letter was P, the next letter may be X or S.
D1. If the next letter is S, the string ends.
D2. If the next letter is X, the next letter must be T.
D3. If the next letter was T, go to C2.

This is an awful lot to ask a subject to verbalize.

It turns out, however, that subjects do not have to verbalize all of this grammar, or even most of it, to achieve above-chance performance on Reber's grammaticality judgement task. It is entirely possible that conscious appreciation of a few rules, like 'There can't be an S, V or X at the beginning, or a T at the end, and there can't be too many Ts in the middle', may be enough to do the trick. But subjects probably know that this isn't the full extent of the grammar, and may not recite it in response to the experimenter's postexperimental queries. In any event, an emerging body of research strongly suggests that subjects in implicit learning experiments *do* have conscious access to at least a portion of the knowledge acquired during the acquisition period, and that this knowledge is enough to mediate above-chance performance on tests of implicit learning (Dienes *et al.*, 1991; Dulany *et al.*, 1984; Mathews *et al.*, 1989; Perruchet and Pacteau, 1990, 1991). Thus tests which at least approximate to Shanks and St. John's (1994) information and sensitivity criteria indicate that explicit learning – the subject's ability to gain conscious access to what he or she knows – plays a major role in ostensibly implicit learning.

WHEN THE SUBJECT IS SIMPLY UNCONSCIOUS

Subliminal perception and implicit learning are demonstrated in subjects who are conscious, in the sense that they know who they are where they are and that they are performing some sort of task at the behest of the experimenter. They are simply unaware of some stimulus event, or of what they are learning from episodes of which they are aware. Enough controversy has swirled about claims for subliminal perception and implicit learning to fill a book; now we add to this the more controversial claim that subjects can engage in perception and learning when they are not conscious at all – for example, when they are asleep or anaesthetized. Of course, the lack of conscious awareness precludes collecting on-line evidence of perception and learning. Aside from psychophysiological measures such as event-related potentials (ERPs) (see Kutas, 1990; Plourde and Picton, 1991), the only evidence of implicit perception during these states is the subject's memory afterwards.

Sleep

Sleepers are hard to arouse, and once awakened they remember little or nothing of what transpired while they were asleep. Thus, at least superficially, sleep seems to represent an interruption of normal waking consciousness; if sleepers are not strictly unconscious, at least they do not seem to be conscious of events in the world outside their own dreams. Nevertheless, *prima facie* evidence for information processing during sleep comes from documented cases of somnambulism, in which the sleeper engages in some activity resembling that of waking life (Kales *et al.*, 1966; Jacobson and Kales, 1967). Navigating around a room or a house, turning lights and appliances on and off, manipulating doorknobs and cabinet latches, and the like, all require some ability to perceive objects in the environment and make appropriate (if perhaps rather automatic) responses to them. So does conversational sleeptalking (Arkin, 1982).

More convincing evidence of information processing during sleep would come from studies of hypnopaedia or sleep-learning. Unfortunately, sleep-learning has proved extremely difficult to document convincingly (for reviews, see Aarons, 1976; Eich, 1990; Evans, 1979; see also Ellman and Antrobus, 1991; Bootzin *et al.*, 1990). Most formal studies of sleep-learning have yielded negative results, and the few positive findings available are troubled by improper controls or inadequate psychophysiological monitoring. For years, conventional wisdom has held that sleep-learning is only possible to the extent that the subject stays awake (Simon and Emmons, 1955).

Of course, as Eich (1990) has noted, this conclusion only held when learning was assessed in terms of explicit memory, because the studies in question examined only the subjects' ability, when awake, to consciously remember material presented while they were asleep. If there is implicit perception during sleep, perhaps traces of this perceptual activity are only retrievable as implicit memories.

Until recently, this hope was kept alive by a series of dramatic experiments conducted by Evans and his associates in the late 1960s (for a review, see Evans, 1979, 1990), which appeared to show that some subjects could respond appropriately, while sleeping, to cues set up by hypnosis-like suggestions. For example, subjects might scratch their noses when they heard the word 'itch'. Although these subjects had no waking memory of the suggestions or their response to them, Evans and his colleagues reported that in many instances they continued to respond to the cues on subsequent nights, even though the suggestions were not repeated – a form of sleep-state-dependent memory. Because discriminative response to suggestions requires perception, and the carry-over of the response to subsequent nights requires memory, Evans's sleep-suggestion phenomenon constitutes evidence for the acquisition and retention of memories – albeit memories expressed implicitly – while the subject is unconscious.

Unfortunately, a detailed critique by Wood (1989; see also Kihlstrom and Eich, 1994) has revealed a number of flaws in these experiments, including the absence of baseline information and the coding of behaviour by judges who were not blind to the suggestions which the subjects received. Particularly critical was the failure to follow conventional standardized criteria for sleep-staging: sleep was defined in terms of electroencephalogram (EEG) and electrooculogram (EOG) criteria only; unfortunately, without the electromyogram (EMG), it is difficult to differentiate Stage REM from (drowsy) waking. A follow-up study by Perry *et al.* (1978) corrected many of these problems – in fact, all except the sleep-staging – and found no difference in response to critical and control cues. Thus, regardless of the issue of sleep-staging, the failure to confirm discriminative response means that the sleep-suggestion studies do not provide evidence of implicit perception.

In the light of these results, Wood and his colleagues (Wood *et al.*, 1992) conducted a formal search for evidence of implicit memory for material presented during sleep. During either Stage REM or Stage 2 (i.e. early Stage NREM) sleep, defined in terms of conventional criteria, sleeping subjects were presented with two lists of paired associates consisting of either a homophone and a disambiguating context cue (e.g. *hare/hair–tortoise*), or a category label and exemplar (e.g. *metal–gold*). After five presentations of each list, the subjects were awakened and given tests of cued recall and free association or category generation. Compared to waking subjects who received the same presentations, sleeping subjects showed no evidence of either explicit or implicit memory of the list.

In summary, the study by Wood *et al.* (1992) echoes the conclusions offered forty years ago by Simon and Emmons: when adequate precautions are taken to ensure that subjects are truly asleep while material is presented, there is no evidence of sleep-learning in terms of either explicit or implicit memory. It is possible that subjects who are partially aroused by (or during) stimulus presentations might show some implicit memory later – a phenomenon which Wood *et al.* (1992) termed 'quasi-sleep learning'. But this is not the same as learning during sleep, and cannot count as convincing evidence of perception without awareness.

General anaesthesia

Certainly the most severe test of the hypothesis that perception and learning can occur without awareness comes from studies of surgical patients (and, on occasion, nonpatient subjects) who undergo general anaesthesia (for reviews, see Andrade, in press; Caseley-Rondi *et al.*, 1994; Cork *et al.*, 1995; Ghoneim and Block, 1992; Kihlstrom, 1993b; Kihlstrom and Schacter, 1990; see also Bonke *et al.*, 1990; Sebel *et al.*, 1993). Even more than sleep, anaesthesia is defined by lack of consciousness: adequately anaesthetized patients are unresponsive to surgical events (e.g. incisions), cannot remember them after the operation is over and have no memory of experiencing pain or distress during the procedure. Still, as in the case of sleep, the suspicion has lingered that surgical events might be processed outside awareness, stored in memory and be available postoperatively. Explicit memory for surgical events is, of course, ruled out by the definition of adequate anaesthesia. However, the possibility remains that events perceived implicitly during anaesthesia might be retained as implicit memories.

This hypothesis was initially tested by Eich *et al.* (1985), who found no evidence of implicit memory using the homophone-spelling paradigm. However, Kihlstrom and his colleagues were more successful (Kihlstrom *et al.*, 1990). Patients received repeated presentations of a list of paired associates consisting of a cue and its closest associate (e.g. *ocean-water*). In the recovery room, tests of free recall, cued recall and recognition gave no evidence of explicit memory. However, a free-association test revealed a significant priming effect, evidence of implicit memory. Significant priming in free association has since been confirmed by a number of other investigators (Bethune *et al.*, 1992; Humphreys *et al.*, 1990; Schwender *et al.*, 1994), although Cork *et al.* (1992, 1993) failed to replicate this result in an experiment in which the anaesthetic agent was changed from the inhalant isoflurane to the narcotic sufentanyl.

Shanks and St. John (1994), in a recent review, were not persuaded by evidence of subliminal perception and implicit learning, but they were especially dismissive of the findings obtained from studies of anaesthetized subjects. They asserted that evidence of 'small but reliable amounts of learning' is 'matched by a comparable number of negative results' (p. 371). They went on to suggest that the positive results obtained were due to 'inadequately administered anesthetic that left some or all of the patients at least partially conscious' (p. 371). The first statement, while roughly true, is irrelevant. The second is simply false.

We have long since passed the time when box scores, totting up positive and negative results, can have any value except as informal expository devices. As Rosenthal (1978) demonstrated elegantly, it is quite possible for an effect to be present even when only a minority of studies yield significant positive results. In fact, a comprehensive review of the literature by Kihlstrom (1993b) concluded that nine out of sixteen studies (56 per cent) published since 1977 (when this literature effectively began) yielded significant effects; Merikle and Rondi (1993), counting dependent variables rather than studies, reported a ratio of thirteen out of eighteen (72 per cent); Cork *et al.* (1995), also counting dependent variables, obtained a ratio of twenty out of forty-seven (43 per cent).[5] Moreover, the effects obtained are not necessarily weak – especially when one considers that the subjects were unconscious during the presentation phase! In the experiment by Kihlstrom *et al.* (1990), the overall magnitude of the priming effect was 10 per cent over baseline; among those subjects for whom the implicit test was not contaminated by the earlier explicit test, the priming effect was 18 per cent, with eleven out of thirteen patients in this group showing priming.

It is true that Cork *et al.* (1992) expressed uncertainty about the extent of implicit memory after anaesthesia, but they were not voicing doubts about the effect obtained by Kihlstrom *et al.* (1990). Rather, they were asking a more analytical question about the conditions under which such effects could be obtained – a question that can only be answered by more, and more systematic, research than is available to date. For example, holding the implicit memory task constant, some anaesthetic agents (e.g. isoflurane) might spare implicit memory, while others (e.g. sufentanyl) might not. Such a finding might tell us something interesting about the biological substrates of memory and consciousness (for a sustained argument along these lines, see Polster, 1993). Alternatively, holding the anaesthetic agent constant, some implicit memory tasks (e.g. repetition priming) might be spared, while others (e.g. conceptual priming) might not. In this respect, it is important to note that the unsuccessful experiment by Eich *et al.* (1985) focused on semantic priming; while the procedure employed by Kihlstrom *et al.* (1990) superficially resembles semantic priming, in fact it was a case of repetition priming, because both cue and target were presented during the study phase. This pattern of results, if confirmed in subsequent research, would seem to indicate that implicit perception under anaesthesia is analytically limited to perceptual rather than semantic processing (for a related argument about the limitations of subliminal perception, see Greenwald, 1992).

Of course, the best way to discount the positive findings on anaesthesia is to claim that the subjects are partially awake. With respect to the studies performed in our laboratory, Shanks and St. John (1994) are simply wrong to suggest that our subjects were inadequately anaesthetized. In our initial study (Kihlstrom *et al.*, 1990), we ran thirty patients, none of whom reported any memory for the tape or specific words; in our follow-up study (Cork *et al.*, 1992, 1993) we excluded three out of twenty-eight subjects on these grounds. *None* of the remaining subjects had any explicit memory of the wordlist, as is clearly indicated by the fact that there was neither any evidence of free recall, nor any differences in cued recall or recognition between critical and neutral targets. Those of us who investigate implicit perception in general anaesthesia take great care to ensure that our subjects are adequately anaesthetized by all standard criteria. Otherwise, what would be the point in doing the studies? The whole purpose of the anaesthesia research, from a theoretical point of view, is to determine the far limits of information processing outside of awareness. In most studies of implicit perception and learning, the subjects are conscious, even if they are not aware of what they are perceiving or learning. But in anaesthesia, the subjects aren't even conscious. If we can find evidence of implicit perception under these conditions, this should tell us something interesting about the processing demands of certain kinds of mental functions.

Why the difference in outcome between anaesthesia and sleep? Shanks and St. John (1994) note the seeming incongruity in claiming that implicit perception is possible during general anaesthesia, but not during sleep. However, these authors fail to recognize potentially important differences in the implicit memory tasks employed by Kihlstrom *et al.* (1990) and Wood *et al.* (1992). As noted earlier, Kihlstrom *et al.*'s paradigm involved repetition priming, while Wood *et al.*'s involved semantic priming. Perhaps Wood *et al.* would have obtained positive results with a repetition priming task; based on the currently available literature, it seems almost certain that Kihlstrom *et al.* (1990) would have obtained negative results with a test of semantic priming. In the final analysis, the situation noted by Shanks and St. John (1994) is only a paradox if one assumes that sleep actually 'renders a person less unconscious than general anesthesia' (Shanks and St. John, 1994: 371). This assumption is unlikely to be tested until someone produces a unidimensional, quantitative index of degree of consciousness. For the present, however, it is important to understand that sleep and general anaesthesia have almost nothing in common physiologically, and these qualitative differences make any comparison between the states extremely difficult.

THE LIMITS OF PRECONSCIOUS PROCESSING – OR, YOUR UNCONSCIOUS IS STUPIDER THAN YOU ARE

The question of whether nonconscious mental processes are as analytically powerful as, or even more powerful than, conscious processes is a very old one in psychology. Von Hartmann (1931 [1868]) argued for the Romantic notion that 'the Unconscious can really outdo all the performances of conscious reason' (vol. 2, pp. 39–40). More recently, a survey of research on unconscious processes published in a leading newspaper informed readers that 'Your Unconscious Mind May Be Smarter Than You' (*New York Times*, 23 June 1992). Evidence for this latter proposition came chiefly in the form of studies of implicit learning, in which complex, abstract, rule-based knowledge is apparently acquired outside of awareness. Unfortunately, at least in so far as artificial grammars are concerned, the evidence favouring unconscious procedural learning is not as compelling as evidence that the subjects' performance is mediated by consciously accessible declarative knowledge structures (Dienes *et al.*, 1991; Dulany *et al.*, 1984, 1985; Mathews *et al.*, 1989; Perruchet and Pacteau, 1990, 1991). Similar considerations appear to apply to other paradigms in which implicit learning has been claimed, such as the control of complex systems, sequence learning and matrix scanning. The subjects in implicit learning experiences may not be attending to what they are learning, and they may not have noticed that they have learned what they have learned, but this is not the same thing as truly unconscious learning. Nor, even if implicit learning should some day prove to be truly unconscious after all, is there any reason to think that it is superior to conscious, explicit learning. When it comes to learning, it is probably better to be conscious than unconscious.

Similar considerations apply to subliminal perception and general anaesthesia. These topics will probably be forever bedevilled by questions about whether subjects might not have been, even just for a moment, conscious of what was being presented to them. But the best research in this area has gone to great lengths to rule out this possibility, and enough experiments have yielded positive results for the phenomena in question to be taken seriously. Subliminal stimuli can be processed perceptually, and so can supraliminal stimuli presented during general anaesthesia. However, there appear to be strict limitations on the extent of this processing. With respect to subliminal stimulation, the general rule seems to be that the further the stimulus moves from the subjective threshold, the less likely it is to be subject to semantic analysis. And even for stimuli presented very close to the subjective threshold, semantic processing may be limited to very elementary operations, under the limits specified in Greenwald's (1992) two-word challenge. Similarly, it does appear that surgical patients (and nonpatient subjects) can process environmental events while they are under an adequate plane of general anaesthesia, and for this perception to leave a lasting trace in implicit (but not explicit) memory. However, it seems likely that this processing is limited to perceptual, rather than semantic, operations. It is unlikely that subjects process the meaning of what they have 'heard'. If intraoperative suggestions for improved postoperative recovery are effective (and this is by no means certain; see Cork *et al.*, 1995), this is most likely attributable to their prosodic character (e.g. the use of a quiet, soothing voice) rather than any particular semantic content. When it comes to perceiving and remembering, too, it is probably better to be conscious than unconscious.

In their dealings with the psychological unconscious, psychologists have had to navigate between the Scylla of Von Hartmann, with his Romantic notion of an omnipotent and omniscient unconscious, and the Charybdis of sceptics, including Eriksen, Holender, and now Shanks and St. John, who wish to limit the unconscious to the unattended and unprocessed. As with most binary choices, there is a third way: a way which is open to the idea that unconscious percepts, memories and thoughts can influence conscious mental life, but which is also prepared to concede that the extent of this influence may well be limited. In the final analysis, it is probably the case that the limits on unconscious processing are set by the means by which the stimuli are rendered consciously inaccessible. In the case of preconscious processing, where the percept or its memory trace has been degraded by masking or by long retention intervals, or the processing capacity of the subject has been limited by divided attention, nonsemantic orienting tasks, sleep (or sleepiness), or general anaesthesia, we would naturally expect the percept or memory to be limited to information about perceptual structure, or simple semantic features at best. Unconscious perception – perception without awareness of what is perceived – can occur, but it is almost certainly limited to what can be accomplished with elementary, automatic processes. To get more than that out of perception, attention, and thus conscious awareness, are probably necessary.

ACKNOWLEDGEMENTS

The point of view represented in this chapter is based on research supported by Grant no. MH-35856 from the National Institute of Mental Health. Thanks to Mahzarin Banaji, Talia Ben-Zeev, Randall Cork, Robert Crowder, Marilyn Dabady, Isabel Gauthier, William Hayward, Katherine Shobe, Elizabeth Phelps, Robert Sternberg, Michael Tarr, Heidi Wenk and Pepper Williams for their comments.

NOTES

1　Some prefer the term 'cognitive neuroscience', but I prefer to stick with the traditional label, with its emphasis on the functioning of the whole human organism, rather than the molecular and cellular analyses which preoccupy so much of neuroscience; I also like to make clear that the mental states and processes of interest to psychologists include emotional and motivational as well as cognitive ones.
2　Actually, Jastrow, who was at that time Pierce's graduate student, seems to have done most of the judging.
3　Whatever its liabilities as a scientific theory and therapeutic method, psychoanalysis has always served the important function of keeping interesting topics in psychology alive until the field is ready to address them (Kihlstrom, 1988, 1994b).
4　The only published exception to this of which I am aware is work by Silverman (1976) and others on subliminal symbiotic stimulation, in which subliminal presentation of the phrase 'Mommy and I are one' appears to have a wide variety of effects on experience, thought and action (for a review, see Weinberger, 1992). The discrepancy between Silverman's ability to show the effects of such a prime, which obviously requires considerable processing to understand, and Greenwald's inability to find priming for two-word stimuli, remains to be resolved.
5　Both figures exclude studies of postsurgical therapeutic suggestions, which are not directly relevant to the issue at hand. This is because such suggestions require both processing of the suggestion itself (which is what the debate about implicit perception and memory is all about) and positive response to the suggestion (which might not occur even if the suggestion had been heard by a subject who was wide awake).

REFERENCES

Aarons, L. (1976) 'Sleep-assisted instruction', *Psychological Bulletin* 83: 1–40.

Adams, J.K. (1957) 'Laboratory studies of behavior without awareness', *Psychological Bulletin* 54: 383–405.

Anderson, J.R. (1976) *Language, Memory, and Thought*, Hillsdale, NJ: Erlbaum.

Andrade, J. (in press) 'Learning during anaesthesia', *British Journal of Psychology*.

Arkin, A.M. (1982) *Sleeptalking: psychology and psychophysiology*, Hillsdale, NJ: Erlbaum.

Balota, D. (1983) 'Automatic semantic activation and episodic memory', *Journal of Verbal Learning and Verbal Behavior* 22: 88–104.

Bargh, J.A. (1989) 'Conditional automaticity: varieties of automatic influence in social perception and cognition', in J.S. Uleman and J.A. Bargh (eds) *Unintended Thought*, New York: Guilford.

Berry, D.C. (1994) 'Implicit and explicit learning, 25 years on: a tutorial', in C. Umilta and M. Moscovitch (eds) *Attention and Performance 15: conscious and nonconscious information processing*, Cambridge, MA: MIT Press.

—— (1995) 'How implicit is implicit learning?', in G. Underwood (ed.) *Implicit Cognition*, Oxford: Oxford University Press.

Berry, D.C. and Broadbent, D.E. (1984) 'On the relationship between task performance and associated verbalizable knowledge', *Quarterly Journal of Experimental Psychology* 36A: 209–231.

—— (1995) 'Implicit learning in the control of complex systems', in P. Frensch and J. Funke (eds) *Complex Problem Solving: the European perspective*, Hillsdale, NJ: Erlbaum.

Berry, D.C. and Dienes, Z. (1993) *Implicit Learning: theoretical and empirical issues*, Hove: Erlbaum.

Bethune, D.W., Ghosh, S., Bray, B., Kerr, L., Walker, I.A., Doolan, L.A., Harwood, R.J.

and Sharples, L.D. (1992) 'Learning during general anaesthesia: implicit recall after methohexitone or propofol infusion', *British Journal of Anaesthesia* 69: 197–199.

Bonke, B., Fitch, W. and Millar, K. (eds) (1990) *Memory and Awareness in Anaesthesia*, Amsterdam: Swets & Zeitlinger.

Bootzin, R.R., Kihlstrom, J.F. and Schacter, D.L. (eds) (1990) *Sleep and Cognition*, Washington, DC: American Psychological Association.

Bornstein, R.B. (1989) 'Exposure and affect: overview and meta-analysis of research', *Psychological Bulletin* 106: 265–289.

Bornstein, R.B. and Pittman, T.S. (eds) (1992) *Perception without Awareness: cognitive, clinical, and social perspectives*, New York: Guilford.

Bowers, K.S. (1984) 'On being unconsciously influenced and informed', in K.S. Bowers and D. Meichenbaum (eds) *The Unconscious Reconsidered*, New York: Wiley-Interscience.

Brady, J.P. and Lind, D.L. (1961) 'Experimental analysis of hysterical blindness', *Archives of General Psychiatry* 4: 331–339.

Broadbent, D.E. (1977) 'Levels, hierarchies, and the locus of control', *Quarterly Journal of Experimental Psychology* 29: 181–201.

Bruner, J. (1992) 'Another look at new look 1', *American Psychologist* 47: 780–783.

Bruner, J.S. and Postman, L. (1947) 'Emotional selectivity in perception and reaction', *Journal of Personality* 16: 69–77.

Bryant, R.A. and McConkey, K.M. (1989a) 'Hypnotic blindness: a behavioral and experiential analysis', *Journal of Abnormal Psychology* 98: 71–77.

—— (1989b) 'Visual conversion disorder: a case analysis of the influence of visual information', *Journal of Abnormal Psychology* 98: 326–329.

—— (1989c) 'Hypnotic blindness, awareness, and attribution', *Journal of Abnormal Psychology* 98: 443–447.

Campion, J., Latto, R. and Smith, Y. (1983) 'Is blindsight an effect of scattered light, spared cortex, and near-threshold vision?, *Behavioral and Brain Sciences* 6: 423–486.

Caseley-Rondi, G., Merikle, P.M. and Bowers, K.S. (1994) 'Unconscious cognition in the context of general anesthesia', *Consciousness and Cognition* 3: 166–195.

Cheesman, J. and Merikle, P.M. (1984) 'Priming with and without awareness', *Perception and Psychophysics* 36: 387–395.

—— (1985) 'Word recognition and consciousness', in D. Besner, T.G. Waller and G.E. Mackinnon (eds) *Reading Research: advances in theory and practice*, vol. 5, New York: Academic Press.

—— (1986) 'Distinguishing conscious from unconscious perceptual processes', *Canadian Journal of Psychology* 40: 343–367.

Chomsky, N. (1980) 'Language and unconscious knowledge', in *N. Chomsky, Rules and Representations*, New York: Columbia University Press.

Cork, R.C., Couture, L.J. and Kihlstrom, J.F. (1995) 'Memory and recall', in J.F. Biebuyck, C. Lynch, M. Maze, L.J. Saidman, T.L. Yaksh and W.M. Zapol (eds) *Anesthesia: biologic foundations*, vol. 2: *Integrated Systems*, New York: Raven.

Cork, R.C., Kihlstrom, J.F. and Schacter, D.L. (1992) 'Absence of explicit and implicit memory with sufentanil/nitrous oxide', *Anesthesiology* 76: 892–898.

—— (1993) 'Implicit and explicit memory with isoflurane compared to sufentanil/nitrous oxide', in P.S. Sebel, B. Bonke and E. Winograd (eds) *Memory and Awareness in Anesthesia*, Englewood Cliffs, NJ: PTR Prentice Hall.

Dienes, Z. and Perner, J. (1995) 'Implicit knowledge in people and connectionist networks', in G. Underwood (ed.) *Implicit Cognition*, Oxford: Oxford University Press.

Dienes, Z., Broadbent, D.E. and Berry, D.C. (1991) 'Implicit and explicit knowledge bases in artificial grammar learning', *Journal of Experimental Psychology: Learning, Memory, and Cognition* 17: 875–887.

Dixon, N.F. (1971) *Subliminal Perception: the nature of a controversy*, London: McGraw-Hill.

—— (1981) *Preconscious Processing*, Chichester: Wiley.

Doyle, J.R. (1990) 'Detectionless processing with semantic activation? A footnote to Freenwald, Klinger, and Liu (1989)', *Memory and Cognition* 18: 428–429.

Dulany, D.E. (1968) 'Awareness, rules, and propositional control: a confrontation with S-R behavior theory', in T. Dixon and D. Horton (eds) *Verbal Behavior and General Behavior Theory*, Englewood Cliffs, NJ: Erlbaum.

—— (1991) 'Conscious representation and thought systems', in R.S. Wyer and T.K. Srull (eds) *Advances in Social Cognition*, vol. 4, Hillsdale, NJ: Erlbaum.

—— (1995) 'Consciousness in the explicit (deliberative) and implicit (evocative)', in J. Cohen and J. Schooler (eds) *Scientific Approaches to the Question of Consciousness*, Hillsdale, NJ: Erlbaum.

Dulany, D.E., Carlson, R.A. and Dewey, G.I. (1984) 'A case of syntactical learning and judgment: how conscious and how abstract?', *Journal of Experimental Psychology: General* 113: 541–555.

—— (1985) 'On consciousness in syntactic learning and judgment: a reply to Reber, Allen, and Regan', *Journal of Experimental Psychology: General* 114: 25–32.

Eich, E. (1990) 'Learning during sleep', in R. Bootzin, J.F. Kihlstrom and D.L. Schacter (eds) *Cognition and Sleep*, Washington, DC: American Psychological Association.

Eich, E., Reeves, J.L. and Katz, R.L. (1985) 'Anesthesia, amnesia, and the memory/awareness distinction', *Anesthesia and Analgesia* 64: 1143–1148.

Ellman, S.J. and Antrobus, J.S. (eds) (1991) *The Mind in Sleep: psychology and psychophysiology*, 2nd edn., New York: Wiley.

Erdelyi, M.H. (1970) 'Recovery of unavailable perceptual input', *Cognitive Psychology* 1: 99–113.

—— (1972) 'The role of fantasy in the Poetzl (emergence) phenomenon', *Journal of Personality and Social Psychology* 24: 186–190.

Eriksen, C.W. (1956) 'An experimental analysis of subception', *American Journal of Psychology* 69: 625–634.

—— (1958) 'Unconscious processes', in M.R. Jones (ed.) *Nebraska Symposium on Motivation*, Lincoln, NE: University of Nebraska Press.

—— (1960) 'Discrimination and learning without awareness: a methodological survey and evaluation', *Psychological Review* 67: 279–300.

Evans, F.J. (1979) 'Hypnosis and sleep: techniques for exploring cognitive activity during sleep', in E. Fromm and R.E. Shor (eds) *Hypnosis: research developments and perspectives*, Chicago: Aldine.

—— (1990) 'Behavioral responses during sleep', in R. Bootzin, J.F. Kihlstrom and D.L. Schacter (eds) *Cognition and Sleep*, Washington, DC: American Psychological Association.

Fisher, C. (1960) 'Subliminal and supraliminal influences on dreams', *American Journal of Psychiatry* 116: 1009–1017.

—— (1988) 'Further observations on the Poetzl phenomenon: the effects of subliminal visual stimulation on dreams, images, and hallucinations', *Psychoanalysis and Contemporary Thought* 11: 3–56.

Fowler, C.A., Wolford, G., Slade, R. and Tassinary, L. (1981) 'Lexical access with and without awareness', *Journal of Experimental Psychology: General* 110: 341–362.

Ghoneim, M.M. and Block, R.I. (1992) 'Learning and consciousness during general anesthesia', *Anesthesiology* 76: 279–305.

Goldiamond, I. (1958) 'Indicators of perception: 1. Subliminal perception, subception, unconscious perception: an analysis in terms of psychophysical indicator methodology', *Psychological Bulletin* 55: 373–411.

Greenwald, A.G. (1992) 'New Look 3: unconscious cognition reclaimed', *American Psychologist* 47: 766–790.

Greenwald, A.G. and Liu, T.J. (1985) 'Limited unconscious processing of meaning', paper presented at the annual meeting of the Psychonomic Society, Boston, MA, November.

Greenwald, A.G., Klinger, M.R. and Liu, T.J. (1989) 'Unconscious processing of dichoptically masked words', *Memory and Cognition* 17: 35–47.

Haber, R.N. and Erdelyi, M.H. (1967) 'Emergence and recovery of initially unavailable perceptual material', *Journal of Verbal Learning and Verbal Behavior* 6: 618–628.

Hasher, L. and Zacks, R.T. (1979) 'Automatic and effortful processes in memory', *Journal of Experimental Psychology: General* 108: 356–388.

Hasher, L. and Zacks, R.T. (1984) 'Automatic processing of fundamental information', *American Psychologist* 39: 1372–1388.

Hilgard, E.R. (1977) *Divided Consciousness: multiple controls in human thought and action*, New York: Wiley-Interscience.

Hilgard, E.R. and Hilgard, J.R. (1975) *Hypnosis in the Relief of Pain*, Los Altos, CA: Kaufman.

Holender, D. (1986) 'Semantic activation without conscious identification in dichotic listening, parafoveal vision, and visual masking: a survey and appraisal', *Behavioral and Brain Sciences* 9: 1–23.

Humphreys, K.J., Asbury, A.J. and Millar, K. (1990) 'Investigation of awareness by homophone priming during computer-controlled anaesthesia', in B. Bonke, W. Fitch and K. Millar (eds) *Memory and Awareness in Anaesthesia*, Amsterdam: Swets & Zeitlinger.

Ionescu, M.D. and Erdelyi, M.H. (1992) 'The direct recovery of subliminal stimuli', in R.F. Bornstein and T.S. Pittman (eds) *Perception without Awareness: Cognitive, clinical, and social perspectives*, New York: Guilford.

Jacobson, E. and Kales, A. (1967) 'Somnambulism: all night EEG and related studies', in S.S. Kety, E.V. Evarts and H.I. Williams (eds) *Sleep and Altered States of Consciousness*, Baltimore, MD: Williams & Wilkins.

Jenkins, J.G. (1933) 'Instruction as a factor in "incidental" learning', *American Journal of Psychology* 45: 471–477.

Kales, A., Paulson, M.J., Jacobson, A. and Kales, J.D. (1966) 'Somnambulism: psycho-physiological correlates: I. All-night EEG studies. II. Psychiatric interviews, psychological testing, and discussion', *Archives of General Psychiatry* 14: 586–604.

Kihlstrom, J.F. (1984) 'Conscious, subconscious, unconscious: a cognitive perspective', in K.S. Bowers and D. Meichenbaum (eds) *The Unconscious Reconsidered*, New York: Wiley.

—— (1987) 'The cognitive unconscious', *Science* 237: 1445–1452.

—— (1988) 'Personality', in E.R. Hilgard (ed.) *Fifty Years of Psychology: essays in honor of Floyd Ruch*, Glenview, IL: Scott, Foresman.

—— (1990) 'The psychological unconscious', in L. Pervin (ed.) *Handbook of Personality: theory and research*, New York: Guilford.

—— (1993a) 'The continuum of consciousness', *Consciousness and Cognition* 2: 334–354.

—— (1993b) 'Implicit memory function during anesthesia', in P.S. Sebel, B. Bonke and E. Winograd (eds) *Memory and Awareness in Anesthesia*, New York: Prentice-Hall.

—— (1994a) 'One hundred years of hysteria', in S.J. Lynn and J.W. Rhue (eds) *Dissociation: theoretical, clinical, and research perspectives*, New York: Guilford.

—— (1994b) 'Psychodynamics and social cognition: notes on the fusion of psychoanalysis and psychology', *Journal of Personality* 62: 681–696.

—— (1995) 'The rediscovery of the unconscious', in H. Morowitz and J. Singer (eds) *The Mind, the Brain, and Complex Adaptive Systems*, Santa Fe Institute Studies in the Sciences of Complexity, vol. 22. Reading, MA: Addison-Wesley.

Kihlstrom, J.F. and Eich, E. (1994) 'Altering states of consciousness', in D. Druckman and R.A. Bjork (eds) *Learning, Remembering, Believing: enhancing human performance*, Washington, DC: National Academy Press.

Kihlstrom, J.F. and Schacter, D.L. (1990) 'Anaesthesia, amnesia, and the cognitive unconscious', in B. Bonke, W. Fitch and K. Millar (eds) *Memory and Awareness in Anaesthesia*, Amsterdam: Swets & Zeitlinger.

Kihlstrom, J.F., Barnhardt, T.M., and Tataryn, D.J. (1992) 'Implicit perception', in R.F. Bornstein and T.S. Pittman (eds) *Perception without Awareness*, New York: Guilford.

Kihlstrom, J.F., Schacter, D.L., Cork, R.C., Hurt, C.A. and Behr, S.E. (1990) 'Implicit and explicit memory following surgical anesthesia', *Psychological Science* 1: 303–306.

Kunst-Wilson, W.R. and Zajonc, R.B. (1980) 'Affective discrimination of stimuli that cannot be recognized', *Science* 207: 557–558.

Kutas, M. (1990) 'Event-related brain potential (ERP) studies of cognition during sleep: is it more than a dream?', in R. Bootzin, J.F. Kihlstrom and D.L. Schacter (eds) *Cognition and Sleep*, Washington, DC: American Psychological Association.

Leibniz, G.W. (1981 [1704]) *New Essays on Human Understanding*, Cambridge: Cambridge University Press.

Lewicki, P. (1986) *Nonconscious Social Information Processing*, Orlando, FL: Academic.

Lewicki, P., Czyzewska, M. and Hoffman, M. (1987) 'Unconscious acquisition of complex procedural knowledge', *Journal of Experimental Psychology: Learning, Memory, and Cognition* 13: 135–146.

Logan, G.D. (1989) 'Automaticity and cognitive control', in J.S. Uleman and J.A. Bargh (eds) *Unintended Thought*, New York: Guilford.

Marcel, A. (1980) 'Conscious and preconscious recognition of polysemous words: locating the selective effect of prior verbal context', in R.S. Nickerson (ed.) *Attention and Performance 8*, Hillsdale, NJ: Erlbaum.

—— (1983a) 'Conscious and unconscious perception: experiments on visual masking and word recognition', *Cognitive Psychology* 15: 197–237.

—— (1983b) 'Conscious and unconscious perception: an approach to the relations between phenomenal experience and perceptual processes, *Cognitive Psychology* 15: 238–300.

Mathews, R.C., Buss, R.R., Stanley, W.B., Blanchard-Fields, F., Cho, J.R. and Druhan, B. (1989) 'Role of implicit and explicit processes in learning from examples: a synergistic effect', *Journal of Experimental Psychology: Learning, Memory, and Cognition* 15: 1083–1100.

McGinnies, E. (1949) 'Emotionality and perceptual defense', *Psychological Review* 56: 244–251.

Merikle, P.M. (1982) 'Unconscious perception revisited', *Perception and Psychophysics* 31: 298–301.

—— (1992) 'Perception without awareness: critical issues', *American Psychologist* 47: 792–795.

Merikle, P.M. and Cheesman, J. (1986) 'Consciousness is a "subjective" state', *Behavioral and Brain Sciences* 9: 42–43.

Merikle, P.M. and Reingold, E.M. (1990) 'Recognition and lexical decision without detection: unconscious perception?', *Journal of Experimental Psychology: Human Perception and Performance* 16: 574–583.

—— (1992) 'Measuring unconscious processes', in R.F. Bornstein and T.S. Pittman (eds) *Perception without Awareness: cognitive, clinical, and social perspectives*, New York: Guilford.

Merikle, P.M. and Rondi, G. (1993) 'Memory for events during anesthesia has not been demonstrated: a psychologist's viewpoint', in P.S. Sebel, B. Bonke and E. Winograd (eds) *Memory and Awareness in Anesthesia*, New York: Prentice-Hall.

Moscovitch, M., Vriezen, E. and Goshen-Gottstein, Y. (1993) 'Implicit tests of memory in patients with focal lesions or degenerative brain disorders', in F. Boller and J. Grafman (eds) *Handbook of Neuropsychology*, vol. 8, Amsterdam: Elsevier.

Nissen, M.J. and Bullemer, P. (1987) 'Attentional requirements of learning: evidence from performance measures', *Cognitive Psychology* 19: 1–32.

Perruchet, P. and Pacteau, C. (1990) 'Synthetic grammar learning: implicit rule abstraction or explicit fragmentary knowledge?', *Journal of Experimental Psychology: General* 119: 264–275.

—— (1991) 'The implicit acquisition of abstract knowledge about artificial grammar: some methodological and conceptual issues', *Journal of Experimental Psychology: General* 120: 112–116.

Perry, C.W., Evans, F.J., O'Connell, D.N., Orne, E.C. and Orne, M.T. (1978) 'Behavioral response to verbal stimuli administered and tested during REM sleep: a further investigation', *Waking and Sleeping* 2: 317–329.

Pierce, C.S. and Jastrow, J. (1885) 'On small differences in sensation', *Memoirs of the National Academy of Sciences* 3: 75–83.

Plourde, G. and Picton, T.W. (1991) 'Long-latency auditory evoked potentials during general anesthesia: N1 and P3', *Anesthesia and Analgesia* 72: 342–350.

Poetzel, O. (1960 [1917]) 'The relationship between experimentally induced dream images and indirect vision', *Psychological Issues* 2(3, part 7): 41–120.

Polster, M.R. (1993) 'Drug-induced amnesia: implications for cognitive neuropsychological investigations of memory', *Psychological Bulletin* 114: 477–493.

Postman, L., Bruner, J. and McGinnies, E. (1948) 'Perception under stress', *Psychological Review* 55: 314–323.

Purcell, D.G., Stewart, A.L. and Stanovich, K.K. (1983) 'Another look at semantic priming without awareness', *Perception and Psychophysics* 34: 65–71.

Razran G. (1961) 'Recent Soviet phyletic comparisons of classical and of operant conditioning: experimental designs', *Journal of Comparative and Physiological Psychology* 54: 357–367.

Reber, A.R. (1967) 'Implicit learning of artificial grammars', *Journal of Verbal Learning and Verbal Behavior* 6: 317–327.

—— (1993) *Implicit Learning and Tacit Knowledge: an essay on the cognitive unconscious*, New York: Oxford University Press.

Reingold, E.M. and Merikle, P.M. (1993) 'Theory and measurement in the study of unconscious processes', in M. Davies and G.W. Humphreys (eds) *Consciousness: psychological and philosophical essays*, Oxford: Blackwell.

Roediger, H.L. and McDermott, K.B. (1993) 'Implicit memory in normal human subjects', in F. Boller and J. Graffman (eds) *Handbook of Neuropsychology*, vol. 8, Amsterdam: Elsevier.

Rosenthal, R. (1978) 'Interpersonal expectancy effects: the first 345 studies', *Behavioral and Brain Sciences* 3: 377–415.

Rozin, P. (1976) 'The evolution of intelligence and access to the cognitive unconscious', in E. Stellar and J.M. Sprague (eds) *Progress in Psychobiology and Physiological Psychology*, vol. 6, New York: Academic Press.

Schacter, D.L. (1995) 'Implicit memory: a new frontier for cognitive neuroscience', in M.A. Gazzaniga (ed.) *The cognitive neurosciences*, Cambridge, MA: MIT Press.

Schneider, W. and Shiffrin, R.M. (1977) 'Controlled and automatic human information processing: I. Detection, search, and attention', *Psychological Review* 84: 1–66.

Schwender, D., Madler, C., Klasing, S., Peter, K. and Pöppel, E. (1994) 'Anaesthetic control of 40-hz brain activity and implicit memory', *Consciousness and Cognition* 3: 129–147.

Seamon, J.G., Brody, N. and Kauff, D.M. (1983) 'Affective discrimination of stimuli that are not recognized: effects of shadowing, masking, and cerebral laterality', *Journal of Experimental Psychology: Learning, Memory, and Cognition* 3: 544–555.

Seamon, J.G., Marsh, R.L. and Brody, N. (1984) 'Critical importance of exposure duration for affective discrimination of stimuli that are not recognized', *Journal of Experimental Psychology: Learning, Memory, and Cognition* 10: 465–469.

Sebel, P.S., Bonke, B. and Winograd, E. (eds) (1993) *Memory and Awareness in Anesthesia*, Englewood Cliffs, NJ: PTR Prentice Hall.

Seger, C.A. (1994) 'Implicit learning', *Psychological Bulletin* 115: 163–196.

Shanks, D.R. and St. John, M.F. (1994) 'Characteristics of dissociable human learning systems', *Behavioral and Brain Sciences* 17: 367–447.

Shevrin, H. (1988) 'Unconscious conflict: a convergent psychodynamic and electrophysiological approach', in M. Horowitz (ed.) *Psychodynamics and Cognition*, Chicago: University of Chicago Press.

—— (1992) 'Subliminal perception, memory, and consciousness: cognitive and dynamic perspectives', in R.F. Bornstein and T.S. Pittman (eds) *Perception without Awareness: cognitive, social, and clinical perspectives*, New York: Guilford.

Shevrin, H. and Dickman, S. (1980) 'The psychological unconscious: a necessary assumption for all psychological theory?', *American Psychologist* 35: 421–434.

Shiffrin, R.M. (1988) 'Attention', in R.C. Atkinson, R.J. Herrnstein, G. Lindzey and R.D. Luce (eds) *Stevens' Handbook of Experimental Psychology*, 2nd edn., vol. 2, New York: Wiley-Interscience.

Shiffrin, R.M. and Schneider, W.F. (1977) 'Controlled and automatic human information processing: II. Perceptual learning, automatic attending, and a general theory', *Psychological Review* 84: 127–190.

Silverman, L.H. (1976) 'Psychoanalytic theory: reports of my death are greatly exaggerated', *American Psychologist* 31: 621–637.

Silverman, L.H. and Weinberger, J. (1985) 'Mommy and I are one: implications for psychotherapy', *American Psychologist* 40: 1296–1308.

Simon C.W. and Emmons, W.H. (1955) 'Learning during sleep?', *Psychological Bulletin* 52: 328–342.

Solomon, R.L. and Howes, D.H. (1951) 'Word frequency, word value, and visual duration thresholds', *Psychological Review* 58: 256–270.

Spanos, N.P., Jones, B. and Malfara, A. (1982) 'Hypnotic deafness: now you hear it – now you still hear it', *Journal of Abnormal Psychology* 90: 75–77.

Thorndike, E.L. and Rock, I. (1934) 'Learning without awareness of what is being learned or intention to learn it', *Journal of Experimental Psychology* 17: 1–19.

Von Hartmann, E. (1931 [1868]) *Philosophy of the Unconscious: speculative results according to the inductive method of physical science*, London: Routledge & Kegan Paul.

Weinberger, J. (1992) 'Validating and demystifying subliminal psychodynamic activation', in R.F. Bornstein and T.S. Pittman (eds) *Perception without Awareness: cognitive, clinical, and social perspectives*, New York: Guildford.

Weiskrantz, L. (1986) *Blindsight: a case study and implications*, Oxford: Oxford University Press.

Winograd, T. (1975) 'Frame representations and the procedural-declarative controversy', in D. Bobrow and A. Collins (eds) *Representation and Understanding: studies in cognitive science*, New York: Academic Press.

Wood, J.M. (1989) 'Implicit and explicit memory for verbal stimuli presented during sleep', unpublished doctoral dissertation, University of Arizona.

Wood, J.M., Bootzin, R.R., Kihlstrom, J.F. and Schacter, D.L. (1992) 'Implicit and explicit memory for verbal information presented during sleep', *Psychological Science* 3: 236–239.

Chapter 3

On consciousness in relation to memory and learning

John M. Gardiner

The problem of consciousness in relation to memory and learning concerns the extent to which people are aware of what they have memorized or learned. It also concerns the extent to which what has been memorized or learned affects people's awareness at a later time.

There are many possible ways in which consciousness can be studied in relation to memory and learning. This chapter focuses on recent research on what has been termed *implicit memory* (Graf and Schacter, 1985) and *implicit learning* (Reber, 1967). These terms have been widely used in the literature, but unfortunately they have also been widely used to mean quite different things. They have been used to mean (1) a kind of task that does not require awareness of what has been memorized or learned, (2) a state of consciousness defined by the absence of such awareness, and (3) a form of memory or learning, in the sense of a kind of memory or learning system, representation or process (Richardson-Klavehn and Bjork, 1988). Implicit memory and learning have been contrasted with *explicit memory* and *explicit learning*. These terms have been correspondingly used to mean (1) a kind of task that does require awareness of what has been memorized or learned, (2) a state of consciousness defined by the presence of such awareness, and (3) a form of memory or learning.

Because of this confusion, Richardson-Klavehn and Bjork (1988) recommended substituting the terms *indirect* and *direct* to name the two kinds of memory task, and, more recently, Richardson-Klavehn *et al.* (in press) recommend substituting the terms *incidental* and *intentional*. The choice of appropriate terms is important, but the problem lies not so much in the choice of terms as in their misuse. In accordance with a rule of *inconvertibility* of terms (Gardiner and Java, 1993), the same terms should not be used for different concepts. There is still a tendency in some theories to confuse concepts to do with consciousness and concepts to do with hypothetical information processing constructs, such as memory processes or forms of knowledge representation. For example, conscious recollection and familiarity are sometimes used to refer to memory processes as well as states of awareness (e.g. Jacoby, 1991).

In this chapter, the terms implicit and explicit (or, occasionally, direct and indirect) refer strictly to tasks and do not have any other meaning. The terms memory and learning, when used alone, refer to evidence that people's performance of some task, or what they become aware of in performing some task, has been influenced by some specific events or experiences from the past. The terms consciousness and awareness are used, interchangeably, to refer to people's subjective mental experiences.

This chapter is more about memory than learning, partly because there has been much more research on memory than on learning, but partly, too, because that is where my own research interests lie. There are a number of other recent reviews of both topics, including articles by Roediger and McDermott (1993); Schacter (1992); Shanks and St. John (1994); edited books by Berry and Dienes (1993); Graf and Masson (1993); Underwood (in press); and a monograph by Reber (1993). The present review is organized in five sections: tasks, findings, theories, trends, and conclusions.

TASKS

The distinction between explicit or direct tasks, and implicit or indirect tasks, continues to dominate research on memory. In explicit or direct tasks the subjects are instructed to try to consciously recollect the occurrence of specific items earlier in an experiment. These are the tasks that have traditionally been thought of as memory tests. They include free recall, cued recall and recognition tests. In implicit or indirect tasks, either the influence of the prior occurrence of test items is measured in ways that do not ostensibly refer to their prior occurrence, or else the subjects are told to ignore this prior occurrence when carrying out the task.

Implicit or indirect tasks fall into several categories. There are perceptual tasks, in which the subjects are presented with perceptually degraded versions of stimuli which they have to try to identify or complete. One such task is perceptual identification or naming (e.g. Jacoby and Dallas, 1981). In this task, subjects are presented with test items, such as words, at about threshold level, and their task is to identify or name these items. Word-stem and word-fragment completion tasks are other popular tasks of this sort (e.g. Graf and Mandler, 1984; Tulving *et al.*, 1982). Memory is inferred when subjects are shown to be more likely to identify or complete words when the words occurred earlier in the experiment than they are when the words did not. Other perceptual tasks of this kind include the identification of perceptually degraded pictures or drawings of objects (e.g. Srinivas, 1993).

There are also conceptual tasks, such as answering general knowledge questions (e.g. Blaxton, 1989), generating instances of a particular semantic category (e.g. Hamman, 1990), or free associating to particular words (e.g. Shimamura and Squire, 1984). Memory is inferred if subjects are shown to be more likely to answer the general knowledge questions, generate words as category instances, or produce them as free associates, if the words occurred earlier in the experiment than if the words did not.

Other implicit or indirect tasks involve various different kinds of judgements or decisions. For example, subjects might be asked to make preference judgements as to which items they like better or find more pleasant (e.g. Kunst-Wilson and Zajonc, 1980). Memory is inferred if subjects prefer items that occurred earlier in the experiment to items that did not. There are other tasks, too, that are not included in this selective review, such as lexical decision tasks. An effect of memory in all these implicit or indirect tasks has commonly been referred to as *priming*.

Memory and learning continue to be treated as relatively separate areas of enquiry, undoubtedly to the detriment of both, although the historical reasons for this separation are not without some foundation. In memory, the emphasis is on retention, and memory research often involves single-test measures of retention following a single opportunity to study the occurrence of the test items in the experimental context. In learning, the emphasis is on acquisition rather than retention, and learning research often involves measuring what happens over a series of study and test trials. This difference in emphasis leads to a corresponding difference in addressing the problem of consciousness. In memory, the emphasis is on what subjects become aware of during the test in which retention is measured. In learning, the emphasis is on what subjects become aware of during acquisition.

Implicit learning tasks typically require the subjects to learn sequences of stimuli that entail rather subtle rules or patterns, so subtle that subjects are thought unlikely to become aware of them during the learning task. What subjects actually do become conscious of during learning is typically assessed afterwards, by asking them, or by giving them other explicit or direct tests. One of the tasks used is artificial grammar learning (Reber, 1967). In this task, the subjects are shown examples of strings of letters that do or do not conform to a particular 'grammatical' rule. They are then asked to discriminate between grammatical and nongrammatical strings. Learning is inferred when subjects show better-than-chance ability to make such discriminations.

Another kind of task is sequence learning. For example, in one such task subjects are shown a sequence of frames containing targets whose positions in the frame are sometimes related to the positions of targets earlier in the sequence (e.g. Lewicki *et al.*, 1987). Subjects have to search for the targets and their search time is measured. Learning is inferred from a decrease in search time for the more 'predictable' targets.

A third kind of task is the control of complex dynamic systems. In one such task, for example, the subjects play a kind of computer game in which there is a sugar production factory and they have to control the level of sugar production by specifying the number of workers necessary to achieve a given level of production (Berry and Broadbent, 1984). On each trial the subjects type in a number of workers and they are then told the amount of sugar that will be produced. Some quite complex rule underlies the relation between the number of workers and the level of sugar production. Learning is inferred when subjects show an increase in their ability to control production levels.

FINDINGS

The critical evidence from all these implicit tasks involves *dissociations*: dissociations between different measures of performance, or dissociations between measures of performance and of awareness. In memory, there is evidence of dissociations between performance in implicit compared with explicit memory tasks. In learning, there is evidence of dissociations between learning performance and the subsequent ability to report (or otherwise demonstrate) awareness of what has been learned. Implicit memory tasks can be performed without any awareness of the earlier occurrence of the test items in the experiment; explicit tasks demand that performance is based on such awareness. Because of this difference, it is possible to assume that the two kinds of task respectively measure memory without awareness and memory with awareness. Hence dissociations in performance can be interpreted as dissociations in consciousness. Similarly, implicit learning tasks can be performed without any awareness of the underlying rule and so it is possible to assume that what was learned was learned without awareness. These assumptions have proved too simple. This is not to deny the existence of theoretically important dissociations between implicit and explicit task performance. It is to say that the implications of such dissociations for understanding consciousness are much less straightforward, and more controversial, than originally thought.

Some of the stronger evidence for the differential involvement of consciousness in implicit and explicit tasks comes from amnesic patients. These patients seem to have little consciousness of events or experiences that occurred only a few moments ago. Consequently, their performance in explicit or direct tasks like recall or recognition is poor. But in implicit or indirect tasks, such patients have often been found to perform nearly as well as memory-unimpaired adults. For example, amnesic patients and memory-unimpaired adults show similar amounts of perceptual priming in tasks like word-stem or word-fragment completion. Indeed, it was evidence of this sort that inspired the current revival of interest in consciousness in relation to memory and learning (Warrington and Weiskrantz, 1968, 1970). There is comparable evidence that amnesic patients show similarly preserved abilities in implicit learning tasks (e.g. Knowlton *et al.*, 1992). Normal elderly adults, too, compared with young adults, perform relatively well in implicit tasks, despite their poorer performance in some explicit tasks (e.g. Light and Singh, 1987).

There is a great deal of evidence of dissociations in normal young adults' performance in implicit and explicit memory tasks. These are dissociations in which independent variables have different effects in each kind of task. For example, many variables that have been found to affect performance in recall or recognition have been found not to affect perceptual priming, or to affect it differently. Levels of processing manipulations, which have a large effect on recall or recognition, typically have little or no effect on perceptual priming (e.g. Jacoby and Dallas, 1981). That is, if subjects have to think about the meaning of words presented at study (e.g. whether the words belong to a particular semantic category), rather than about the appearance of the words (e.g. whether the words appear in upper or lower case letters), they are much more likely to recall or recognize the words later. But perceptual priming is much the same for each level of processing. Another variable, *generating* versus reading the words at study (e.g. 'Opposite of hot ——— ?' vs. 'cold'), has opposite effects on each kind of task (Jacoby, 1983). Generating leads to better recognition, or recall, than reading, but reading leads to more perceptual priming than generating. There is also evidence that perceptual priming is surprisingly long lasting (e.g. Sloman *et al.*, 1988) and that it is highly specific to the precise stimulus configuration – even trivially superficial changes in the stimulus as presented at study and at test reduce the amount of perceptual priming (e.g. Roediger and Srinivas, 1993). Gross changes in the physical format or modality between study and test, such as auditory versus visual presentation, greatly reduce or eliminate perceptual priming (e.g. Graf *et al.*, 1985).

There has been less research on conceptual priming and it has not been so easy to dissociate conceptual priming from performance in recall and recognition tests. Amnesic patients and elderly adults tend to show relatively well-preserved priming effects in conceptual tasks, as they do in perceptual tasks. But other variables that influence recall and recognition tend to have a similar effect in conceptual priming. For example, Blaxton (1989) showed that generating compared with reading words at study enhanced both free recall performance and conceptual priming in a general knowledge test. She also found that reading enhanced perceptually cued recall (e.g. 'Sounds like chopper', as a cue for recalling 'copper') as well as perceptual priming in word-fragment completion. This pattern of dissociation corresponds with a distinction between tasks that depend on conceptual processing (free recall and general knowledge) and tasks that depend on perceptual processing (perceptually cued recall and completion), rather than a distinction between the explicit tasks (free recall and cued recall) and the implicit tasks (general knowledge and completion). Such findings have led some theorists to abandon the idea that perceptual and conceptual priming effects reflect the same kind of memory.

Normal memory-unimpaired adults also show dissociations between their performance in implicit learning tasks and their ability to demonstrate awareness of what has been learned. For example, subjects are usually unable to report what the rule is in artificial grammar learning (e.g. Reber, 1967), in sequence learning (e.g. Lewicki *et al.*, 1987), or in the control of complex dynamic systems (e.g. Berry and Broadbent, 1984). This last study showed too that giving subjects detailed verbal instructions can enhance their later verbal report without improving their ability to perform the task, and that further practice can enhance subjects' ability to perform the task without improving their verbal report. Thus it appears that subjects' consciousness of what is happening in the task can be dissociated from their ability to carry out the task.

THEORIES

Strong theoretical conclusions have been drawn about the systems, processes or forms of representation that are involved in implicit memory and learning tasks. Three main memory theories can be identified. One theory is that implicit and explicit tasks implicate different *memory systems*. A simple version of this theory is that there are two systems, a procedural system and a declarative or propositional system (e.g. Squire, 1987). Only the declarative system is open to consciousness and it is this system that is engaged in explicit tasks and which is damaged in amnesic patients and in old age. The procedural system is an action system, involved in skills, including perceptual skills, and it is expressed in behaviour, not in words.

Following his earlier distinction between episodic and semantic memory, Tulving (1983, 1994, 1995) now proposes four memory systems in addition to the procedural system. A separate perceptual representation system gives rise to perceptual priming (see also Schacter, 1990; Tulving and Schacter, 1990). This system is presemantic and it does not require consciousness of memory. There is a primary memory system, which is a short-term memory system that gives rise to awareness of present or very recent events and thoughts. And there are two long-term memory systems, the semantic system and the episodic system. The semantic system is a knowledge system that retains facts known about the world and about oneself. It is associated with noetic consciousness; that is, with feelings of knowing or familiarity. It is this system that is involved in conceptual priming. The episodic system retains personally experienced autobiographical events. It gives rise to autonoetic consciousness; that is, to conscious recollection of the previous occurrence of specific events (including the occurrence of items in a study list). It is this system that is engaged in explicit tasks and that is damaged in amnesia (see, e.g., Tulving *et al.*, 1991) and in old age.

The order in which these systems have been described corresponds with the order in which they are thought to have evolved phylogenetically, and also the order in which they are thought to develop ontogenetically. The systems are dissociable but interdependent, in the sense that later systems in the sequence depend upon the operation of earlier systems in the sequence. For example, it is possible to have a functional semantic system in the absence of a functional episodic system, but it is not possible to have a functional episodic system in the absence of a functional semantic system.

Another theory is that performance in both implicit and explicit tasks reflects *transfer appropriate processing* (Roediger, 1990; Roediger *et al.*, 1989). This theory postulates a continuum of processing that can vary from being highly perceptual to being highly conceptual. What determines performance is simply the extent to which the processing engaged by the study task transfers to – or is appropriate for – the processing demanded by the task at test. Thus, the more perceptual the processing at study the more likely it is that perceptual priming will be enhanced and the less likely it is that there will be any conceptual priming

– and vice versa. Explicit memory tests can also be more perceptually driven, or more conceptually driven, and the same principles of transfer apply in these tests too, as exemplified in the study by Blaxton (1989). This processing theory provides a better account of the evidence from memory-unimpaired adults than memory systems theory, since it allows more specific predictions to be made about the kinds of dissociation that should occur. However, this processing theory does not address the problem of consciousness directly, and it provides no natural explanation of memory impairment in amnesic patients, or in old age.

A third theory proposes an *attributional* view of memory (Jacoby, 1988; Jacoby *et al.*, 1989a). Memory is viewed as an attribution subjects make, sometimes on the basis of recollective experience, but sometimes on the basis of other conscious experiences, such as fluency or ease of processing. Sometimes, too, the experience of memory may be misattributed to something else, as when memory affects consciousness in perceptual and judgemental tasks without any awareness of the memory that is involved. Lacking conscious recollection, amnesic patients commonly misattribute the effects of memory to other experiences or events that do not involve this kind of consciousness. Memory-unimpaired adults also misattribute the effects of memory. For example, subjects may become unaware that the name Adrian Marr occurred earlier when they studied a list of names of people who are not famous. The subjects may later wrongly judge Adrian Marr to be the name of a famous person on encountering this name again in a test in which the nonfamous names from the study list are mixed together with names of people who are famous and the subjects' task is to judge which are the famous names (Jacoby *et al.*, 1989b). The subjects are told that none of the names they saw in the study list were names of famous people in this 'judgement of fame' task, so that when the subjects judge a name from the study list to be famous they do so in the absence of any awareness that this name was on the study list. Such awareness would act to oppose the effect.

There is other evidence of attributional effects when recognition is no better than chance. In these circumstances, subjects are more likely to prefer items that occurred earlier in the experiment when making affective judgements about which of two stimuli (one from the study list, one not) they like better (Kunst-Wilson and Zajonc, 1980). Subjects show a similar preference when making perceptual judgements about the two stimuli (see Mandler *et al.*, 1987). And amnesic patients have been found to prefer novel melodies that they heard earlier in an experiment to novel melodies they did not hear earlier (Johnson *et al.*, 1985).

In this attributional theory, perceptual priming is thought to reflect enhanced 'perceptual fluency', a facilitation of perception that results from perceiving the critical items earlier in the experiment. It is believed that this perceptual fluency also contributes to recognition memory (Jacoby and Dallas, 1981; see also Mandler, 1980). Subjects are assumed to attribute perceptual fluency in the recognition test to feelings of familiarity in the experimental context. Recognition may occur on this basis in the absence of recollection.

In research on learning there is theoretical debate about the type of knowledge that subjects acquire, as well as about the extent to which that knowledge is acquired without awareness. The theoretical claim that subjects acquire by induction an abstract representation of the underlying rule has been challenged by the argument that much, if not all, of the evidence can be explained in terms of fragmentary knowledge derived from learning the specific instances that conform to the rule. For example, Perruchet and Pacteau (1990) showed that subjects are sensitive to pairs of letters that are acceptable in the letter strings that exemplify the rule. The argument is that this fragmentary knowledge of instances is sufficient to account for the learning that occurs. It has also been assumed that if learning occurs in this way then subjects are likely to be conscious of the fragmentary knowledge that they acquire. A further possibility is that knowledge of the rule is initially acquired without consciousness, and that this knowledge may become open to consciousness later (Reber, 1993).

TRENDS

Theoretical controversy about the kind of knowledge that subjects acquire in implicit learning tasks and the extent to which subjects are conscious of that knowledge looks set to continue (see, e.g., Shanks and St. John, 1994). Shanks and St. John (1994) argue that a distinction between the two kinds of knowledge subjects might acquire is more tractable than a distinction between 'conscious learning' and 'unconscious learning', which is fraught with methodological difficulties. One difficulty is the sensitivity of the measures of consciousness; another is their timing. It is very difficult to tell whether subjects' inability to demonstrate awareness of knowledge might be due to the insensitivity of the measures used. And, because these measures would obviously affect subjects' consciousness if they took place during acquisition, they usually take place after the learning phase is over. Even if people cannot demonstrate awareness after learning, this does not necessarily mean they were unaware at the time the learning occurred. Dienes and Perner (in press), as well as Shanks and St. John (1994), provide a more detailed discussion of these issues. Interestingly, Dienes and Perner argue for the use of more subjective criteria for defining consciousness, and they suggest that the ability to exert some conscious control over a task need not necessarily entail consciousness of the specific knowledge that permits that control. To some extent, these ideas correspond with some recent developments in memory research.

In memory research, it has become very clear that the subject's actual state of awareness is not something that can be reliably inferred by the experimenter solely on the basis of conventional measures of performance (Tulving, 1989). One cannot tell merely from the production of some response what the subject has experienced consciously. In implicit memory tasks, for example, subjects may become aware that memory for the items presented earlier in the experiment is being surreptitiously tested. The subjects may then alter their retrieval strategy and consciously try to recollect the items. To deal with this problem, Schacter *et al.* (1989) proposed a 'retrieval intentionality criterion'. According to this criterion, and following an example set by Graf and Mandler (1984), the explicit and implicit tasks must involve exactly the same test items and conditions except for the retrieval instructions subjects are given. In addition, the experiment must include some variable known to have different effects on performance in the two tasks – levels of processing has been a popular choice (see, e.g., Roediger *et al.*, 1992). Deliberate, voluntary retrieval of study list words leads to large levels-of-processing effects. If levels of processing are shown to have no significant effect on priming, then it can be concluded that priming has been little influenced by voluntary retrieval.

Subjects can also be questioned about their awareness after they have finished the test. For example, Bowers and Schacter (1990) found that subjects who reported being aware of the presence of study list words in the test showed a typical levels-of-processing effect and subjects who reported being unaware of the presence of study list words did not (see also Java, 1994; Richardson-Klavehn *et al.*, 1994a).

The retrieval intentionality criterion is useful but its usefulness is limited. It can easily be applied to perceptual priming, but because few variables have been found to dissociate conceptual priming from performance in explicit memory tasks (see, e.g., Blaxton, 1989), it is not so easy to apply to conceptual priming. A more important limitation is that the criterion strictly applies to retrieval intention, or strategy, rather than to awareness of the earlier occurrence of specific words. Recent evidence shows that it is possible to dissociate subjects' retrieval strategy, which may be voluntary or involuntary with respect to the study list words, from their consciousness of the earlier occurrence of these words (Richardson-Klavehn and Gardiner, 1995; Richardson-Klavehn *et al.*, 1994b). The point is that subjects may become conscious of the earlier occurrence of these words either while trying to retrieve them or while responding involuntarily with the first words that come to mind (cf. Ebbinghaus, 1964 [1885]).

The technique for dissociating subjects' retrieval strategy from their awareness of the earlier occurrence of particular words has been developed using word-stem cues in both explicit and implicit tasks (Richardson-Klavehn *et al.*, 1994b). The method depends on a third kind of task in addition to the usual explicit and implicit tasks. This is a further implicit task in which subjects are given involuntary retrieval instructions (that is, to retrieve the first stem-completing word that comes to mind), but told to exclude from their responses any words that occurred in the study list and replace them with words that did not. In these test conditions, awareness of memory is used to oppose the production of particular responses (cf. Jacoby *et al.*, 1989b). Subjects should only respond with words that do not give rise to any such awareness. Richardson-Klavehn *et al.* (1994b) obtained additional convergent evidence by manipulating levels of processing in accordance with the retrieval intentionality criterion, by subsequently questioning subjects about their retrieval strategies and by making subjects take a recognition test for the words they had produced in the implicit tests.

Levels of processing had a large effect in the explicit recall task and no significant effect in the usual implicit task, while in the 'opposition' implicit task, the levels-of-processing effect was reversed. That is, significant priming occurred only following shallow levels of processing; following deep levels of processing, there was actually an inhibitory effect on priming. These results, together with the results from the questionnaire and from subsequent recognition performance, indicate that subjects adopted involuntary retrieval strategies in both implicit memory tasks, and that the difference between the effects obtained in these two implicit tasks reflects the extent to which involuntarily produced words spontaneously give rise to consciousness of memory. A later study confirmed these conclusions and provided additional convergent evidence from response latency measures (see Richardson-Klavehn and Gardiner, 1995).

These dissociations between the retrieval strategy subjects consciously adopt and their awareness of which words occurred in the study list have important theoretical implications. The main implication is that it is necessary to distinguish awareness of task goals and strategies for attaining those goals from awareness of the earlier occurrence of specific words. In memory tasks, subjects are free to adopt a voluntary retrieval strategy, an involuntary retrieval strategy, or both retrieval strategies. Awareness of retrieval strategy is not the same as awareness of the earlier occurrence of specific words. Indeed, it is probably more appropriate to think of these aspects of awareness as being orthogonal. Just as some items that come to mind during involuntary retrieval may give rise to consciousness of memory, so some items that come to mind during voluntary retrieval may give rise to no awareness of memory. If the test is explicit, subjects may for that reason exclude such items from their responses. Richardson-Klavehn et al. (1994b) have reported evidence consistent with this possibility.

Another method for separating conscious and unconscious components of memory performance has been developed by Jacoby et al. (1993). This method assumes that consciousness of memory depends on voluntary retrieval, and that involuntary retrieval does not give rise to such awareness. It further assumes that voluntary retrieval reflects controlled processes and that involuntary retrieval reflects automatic processes. The method involves a *process dissociation procedure*. Applied to priming, this procedure compares performance in an inclusion task, in which subjects are instructed to respond with words retrieved both voluntarily and involuntarily ('complete the stems with words from the study list if you can, or with any words that come to mind if you cannot'), with performance in an exclusion task, in which subjects are instructed to exclude words from the study list (cf. Richardson-Klavehn et al., 1994b). It is assumed that performance in the exclusion task is based on involuntary retrieval. The controlled processing that is assumed to be involved in voluntary retrieval is estimated by taking the difference between performance in the inclusion and exclusion tasks. The automatic processing that is assumed to be involved in involuntary retrieval is then estimated algebraically according to an independence model of the relation between the two types of processing.

It is argued that this procedure can be used to assess the extent to which priming effects are 'contaminated' by voluntary retrieval. For example, the procedure indicates that cross-modal (e.g. auditorily presented study list/visually presented test list) priming is due to such contamination (see Jacoby *et al.*, in press). But the procedure can be criticized because it does not allow for the possibility that involuntary retrieval, as well as voluntary retrieval, can lead to consciousness of memory. Performance in the exclusion task may include only a subset of words retrieved involuntarily, those that do not give rise to any consciousness of memory. Hence the procedure can lead to mistaken conclusions (for more discussion, see Richardson-Klavehn *et al.*, in press).

Another recent approach to the problem of consciousness in relation to memory has been to make use of *experiential* measures that were originally suggested by Tulving (1985) in connection with his memory systems theory. These are 'remember' and 'know' responses, where a remember response means that retrieval brings about some conscious recollection of an item's occurrence earlier in the experiment and a know response means that retrieval brings about no such recollection, only feelings of familiarity, or of knowing. In Tulving's theory, remember responses reflect retrieval from the episodic system and know responses reflect retrieval from the semantic system. An alternative interpretation is that remember responses reflect the extent to which the underlying processing is conceptually driven and that know responses reflect the extent to which the underlying processing is perceptually driven (Gardiner, 1988).

So far, these experiential measures have been mainly investigated in recognition memory, where they map on to the two components of recognition discussed by Mandler (1980) and Jacoby and Dallas (1981), conscious recollection and familiarity. There is much evidence of systematic dissociations between the two states of awareness (for reviews, see Gardiner and Java, 1993; Rajaram and Roediger, in press). Levels of processing, for example, influence remember responses and not know responses (Gardiner, 1988). Some perceptual variables influence know responses and not remember responses (e.g. Gregg and Gardiner, 1994; Rajaram, 1993). And Gardiner *et al.* (1994) found that whereas additional elaborative rehearsal increased remember responses and did not affect know responses, additional maintenance rehearsal increased know responses and did not affect remember responses.

This experiential approach provides a first-person rather than a third-person account of consciousness (see, e.g., Velmans, 1991), where by 'first person' is meant the subject and by 'third person' is meant the experimenter. As such, the approach allows inferences about consciousness that experimenters draw on other grounds to be checked against subjective claims about consciousness. For example, Mandler (1980) and Jacoby and Dallas (1981) argued that the word frequency effect in recognition memory (that is, the greater likelihood of recognizing low frequency than high frequency words) is due to an increase in familiarity rather than an increase in recollection. Contrary to this interpretation, Gardiner and Java (1990) showed that this word frequency effect occurred not in know responses, but in remember responses. So third-person and first-person accounts do not agree. By contrast, first-person and third-person accounts do agree in Gardiner et al.'s (1994) finding that additional maintenance rehearsal increased know responses, not remember responses, because maintenance rehearsal had been previously assumed to affect familiarity rather than recollection (see, e.g., Mandler, 1980).

The process dissociation procedure was originally devised to separate controlled (or intentional) processes from automatic processes in recognition memory, where these processes were assumed to correspond, respectively, with conscious recollection and familiarity (Jacoby, 1991). In recognition tests, inclusion and exclusion conditions involve a list discrimination task. Subjects are presented with two lists of words that clearly differ along some dimension, such as modality of presentation. Recognition performance can then be compared when targets are defined as items from both lists (inclusion) and when targets are defined as items from one list but not from the other (exclusion). Estimates of the two types of processing are then obtained in a similar way to that used when the procedure is applied to priming. This procedure has revealed quite a few interesting dissociations between the two estimates (see, e.g., Jacoby et al., in press). The effect of dividing attention, for example, reduces the estimate of 'recollection' but does not affect the estimate of 'familiarity' (regarded here as processes), a result that has also been obtained with remember and know responses (Gardiner and Parkin, 1990; Parkin et al., in press).

The process dissociation procedure and its relation to remember versus know responses is discussed in more detail by Jacoby et al. (in press), who have criticized these responses on the grounds that they are not independent and so cannot be interpreted without a 'correction' for independence, and by Richardson-Klavehn et al. (in press), who have in turn criticized the process dissociation procedure (see also Curran and Hintzman, 1995; Graf and Komatsu, 1994). The basic insight upon which this procedure is founded was that of using task conditions in which consciousness acts in opposing ways, either to include responses or to exclude them (e.g. Jacoby et al., 1989b). It is to be hoped that this important insight will not be lost in the course of debate about the particular way in which it has been instantiated in the process dissociation procedure.

CONCLUSIONS

To sum up, three general points can be made about the direction in which research on implicit memory and learning tasks seems to be heading. First, gross distinctions between memory 'with or without awareness', or between 'conscious' and 'unconscious' learning, are giving way to finer distinctions between different states of awareness. Second, opposition methods have been developed to dissociate awareness of memory strategy from awareness of memory for particular items, and to dissociate conscious from unconscious influences of memory. Third, there is a growing realization of the need to accept experiential criteria in defining and measuring different states of awareness, and of the need to supplement third-person accounts with first-person accounts of consciousness.

REFERENCES

Berry, D.C. and Broadbent, D.E. (1984) 'On the relationship between task performance and verbalisable knowledge', *Quarterly Journal of Experimental Psychology* 36: 209–231.

Berry, D.C. and Dienes, Z. (eds) (1993) *Implicit Learning: theoretical and empirical issues*, London: Lawrence Erlbaum Associates.

Blaxton, T.A. (1989) 'Investigating dissociations among memory measures: support for a transfer-appropriate framework', *Journal of Experimental Psychology: Learning, Memory, and Cognition* 15: 657–668.

Bowers, J.S. and Schacter, D.L. (1990) 'Implicit memory and test awareness', *Journal of Experimental Psychology: Learning, Memory, and Cognition* 16: 404–416.

Curran, T. and Hintzman, D.L. (1995) 'Violations of the independence assumption in process dissociation', *Journal of Experimental Psychology: Learning, Memory, and Cognition* 21: 531–547.

Dienes, Z. and Perner, J. (in press) 'Implicit knowledge in people and in connectionist networks', in G. Underwood (ed.) *Implicit Cognition*, Oxford: Oxford University Press.

Ebbinghaus, H. (1964 [1885]) *Memory: a contribution to experimental psychology*, trans. H.A. Ruger and C.E. Bussenius, New York: Dover.

Gardiner, J.M. (1988) 'Functional aspects of recollective experience', *Memory and Cognition* 16: 309–313.

Gardiner, J.M. and Java, R.I. (1990) 'Recollective experience in word and non-word recognition', *Memory and Cognition* 18: 23–30.

—— (1993) 'Recognising and remembering', in A.F. Collins, S.E. Gathercole, M.A. Conway and P.E. Morris (eds) *Theories of Memory*, London: Lawrence Erlbaum Associates.

Gardiner, J.M. and Parkin, A.J. (1990) 'Attention and recollective experience in recognition memory', *Memory and Cognition* 18: 579–583.

Gardiner, J.M., Gawlik, B. and Richardson-Klavehn, A. (1994) 'Maintenance rehearsal affects knowing, not remembering; elaborative rehearsal affects remembering, not knowing', *Psychonomic Bulletin and Review* 1: 107–110.

Graf, P. and Komatsu, S. (1994) 'Process dissociation procedure: handle with caution', *European Journal of Cognitive Psychology* 6: 113–129.

Graf, P. and Mandler, G. (1984) 'Activation makes words more accessible, but not necessarily more retrievable', *Journal of Verbal Learning and Verbal Behavior* 23: 553–568.

Graf, P and Masson, M.E.J. (eds) (1993) *Implicit Memory: new directions in cognition, development, and neuropsychology*, Hillsdale, NJ: Lawrence Erlbaum Associates.

Graf, P. and Schacter, D.L. (1985) 'Implicit and explicit memory for new associations in normal and amnesic subjects', *Journal of Experimental Psychology: Learning, Memory, and Cognition* 11: 501–518.

Graf, P., Shimamura, A.P. and Squire, L.R. (1985) 'Priming across modalities and priming across category levels: extending the domain of preserved function in amnesia', *Journal of Experimental Psychology: Learning, Memory, and Cognition* 11: 386–396.

Gregg, V.H. and Gardiner, J.M. (1994) 'Recognition memory and awareness: a large effect of study-test modalities on "know" responses following a highly perceptual orienting task', *European Journal of Cognitive Psychology* 6: 131–147.

Hamman, S.B. (1990) 'Level-of-processing effects in conceptually driven implicit tasks', *Journal of Experimental Psychology: Learning, Memory, and Cognition* 16: 970–977.

Jacoby, L.L. (1983) 'Remembering the data: analyzing interactive processes in reading', *Journal of Verbal Learning and Verbal Behavior* 22: 485–508.

—— (1988) 'Memory observed and memory unobserved', in U. Neisser and E. Winograd (eds) *Remembering Reconsidered: ecological and traditional approaches to the study of memory*, New York: Cambridge University Press.

—— (1991) 'A process dissociation framework: separating automatic and intentional uses of memory', *Journal of Memory and Language* 30: 513–541.

Jacoby, L.L. and Dallas, M. (1981) 'On the relationship between autobiographical memory and perceptual learning', *Journal of Experimental Psychology: General* 110: 306–340.

Jacoby, L.L., Kelley, C.M. and Dywan, J. (1989a) 'Memory attributions', in H.L. Roediger and F.I.M. Craik (eds) *Varieties of Memory and Consciousness: essays in honour of Endel Tulving*, Hillsdale, NJ: Lawrence Erlbaum Associates.

Jacoby, L.L., Toth, J.P. and Yonelinas, A.P. (1993) 'Separating conscious and unconscious influences of memory: measuring recollection', *Journal of Experimental Psychology: General* 122: 139–154.

Jacoby, L.L., Woloshyn, V. and Kelley, C.M. (1989b) 'Becoming famous without being recognized: unconscious influences of memory produced by dividing attention', *Journal of Experimental Psychology: General* 118: 115–125.

Jacoby, L.L., Yonelinas, A.P. and Jennings, J. (in press) 'The relation between conscious and unconscious (automatic) influences: a declaration of independence', in J.D. Cohen and J.W. Schooler (eds) *Scientific Approaches to the Question of Consciousness*, Hillsdale, NJ: Lawrence Erlbaum Associates.

Java, R.I. (1994) 'States of awareness following word stem completion', *European Journal of Cognitive Psychology* 6: 77–92.

Johnson, M.K., Kim, J.K. and Risse, G. (1985) 'Do alcoholic Korsakoff's syndrome patients acquire affective reactions?', *Journal of Experimental Psychology: Learning, Memory, and Cognition* 11: 22–36.

Knowlton, B.J., Ramus, S.J. and Squire, L.R. (1992) 'Intact artificial grammar learning in amnesia: dissociation of abstract knowledge and memory for specific instances', *Psychological Science* 3: 172–179.

Kunst-Wilson, W.R. and Zajonc, R.B. (1980) 'Affective discrimination of stimuli that cannot be recognized', *Science* 207: 557–558.

Lewicki, P., Czyzewska, M. and Hoffman, H. (1987) 'Unconscious acquisition of complex procedural knowledge', *Journal of Experimental Psychology: Learning, Memory, and Cognition* 13: 523–530.

Light, L.L. and Singh, A. (1987) 'Implicit memory in young and older adults', *Journal of Experimental Psychology: Learning, Memory, and Cognition* 13: 531–541.

Mandler, G. (1980) 'Recognizing: the judgement of previous occurrence', *Psychological Review* 87: 252–271.

Mandler, G., Nakamura, Y. and van Zandt, B.J.S. (1987) 'Nonspecific effects of exposure on stimuli that cannot be recognized', *Journal of Experimental Psychology: Learning, Memory, and Cognition* 13: 646–648.

Parkin, A.J., Gardiner, J.M. and Rosser, R. (in press) 'Functional aspects of recollective experience in face recognition', *Consciousness and Cognition*.

Perruchet, P. and Pacteau, C. (1990) 'Synthetic grammar learning: implicit rule extraction or explicit fragmentary knowledge?', *Journal of Experimental Psychology: General* 119: 264–275.

Rajaram, S. (1993) 'Remembering and knowing: two means of access to the personal past', *Memory and Cognition* 21: 89–102.

Rajaram, S. and Roediger, H.L. (in press) 'Remembering and knowing as states of consciousness during recollection', in J.D. Cohen and J.W. Schooler (eds) *Scientific*

Approaches to the Question of Consciousness, Hillsdale, NJ: Lawrence Erlbaum Associates.

Reber, A.S. (1967) 'Implicit learning of artificial grammars', *Journal of Verbal Learning and Verbal Behavior* 6: 317–327.

—— (1993) *Implicit Learning and Tacit Knowledge: an essay on the cognitive unconscious*, Oxford: Oxford University Press.

Richardson-Klavehn, A. and Bjork, R.A. (1988) 'Measures of memory', *Annual Review of Psychology* 39: 475–543.

Richardson-Klavehn, A. and Gardiner, J.M. (1995), 'Retrieval volition and memorial awareness: an empirical analysis', *Psychological Research* 57: 166–178 (special issue on implicit and explicit memory, ed. J. Engelkamp and W. Wippich).

Richardson-Klavehn, A., Gardiner, J.M. and Java, R.I. (1994b) 'Involuntary conscious memory and the method of opposition', *Memory* 2: 1–29.

—— (in press) 'Memory: task dissociations, process dissociations, and dissociations of consciousness', in G. Underwood (ed.) *Implicit Cognition*, Oxford: Oxford University Press.

Richardson-Klavehn, A., Lee, M.G., Joubran, R. and Bjork, R.A. (1994a) 'Intention and awareness in perceptual identification priming', *Memory and Cognition* 22: 293–312.

Roediger, H.L. (1990) 'Implicit memory: retention without remembering', *American Psychologist* 45: 1043–1056.

Roediger, H.L. and McDermott, K.B. (1993) 'Implicit memory in normal human subjects', in F. Boller and J. Grafman (eds) *Handbook of Neuropsychology*, Vol. 8, Amsterdam: Elsevier.

Roediger, H.L. and Srinivas, K. (1993) 'Specificity of operations in perceptual priming', in P. Graf and M.E.J. Masson (eds) *Implicit Memory: new directions in cognition, development, and neuropsychology*, Hillsdale, NJ: Lawrence Erlbaum Associates.

Roediger, H.L., Weldon, M.S. and Challis, B.H. (1989) 'Explaining dissociations between implicit and explicit measures of retention: a processing account', in H.L. Roediger and F.I.M. Craik (eds) *Varieties of Memory and Consciousness: essays in honour of Endel Tulving*, Hillsdale, NJ: Lawrence Erlbaum Associates.

Roediger, H.L., Weldon, M.S., Stadler, M.L. and Riegler, G.L. (1992) 'Direct comparison of two implicit memory tests: word fragment and word stem completion', *Journal of Experimental Psychology: Learning, Memory, and Cognition* 18: 1251–1269.

Schacter, D.L. (1990) 'Perceptual representation systems and implicit memory: toward a resolution of the multiple memory systems debate', in A. Diamond (ed.) *Development and Neural Bases of Higher Cognition*, New York: Annual New York Academy of Sciences.

—— (1992) 'Understanding implicit memory: a cognitive neuroscience approach', *American Psychologist* 47: 559–569.

Schacter, D.L., Bowers, J. and Booker, J. (1989) 'Intention, awareness, and implicit memory: the retrieval intentionality criterion', in S. Lewandowsky, J.C. Dunn and K. Kirsner (eds) *Implicit Memory: theoretical issues*, Hillsdale, NJ: Lawrence Erlbaum Associates.

Shanks, D.R. and St. John, M.F. (1994) 'Characteristics of dissociable human learning systems', *Behavioral and Brain Sciences* 17: 367–447.

Shimamura, A.P. and Squire, L.R. (1984) 'Paired associate learning and priming effects in amnesia: a neuropsychological approach', *Journal of Experimental Psychology: General* 113: 556–570.

Sloman, S.A., Hayman, C.A.G., Ohta, N., Law, J. and Tulving, E. (1988) 'Forgetting in primed fragment completion', *Journal of Experimental Psychology: Learning, Memory, and Cognition* 14: 223–239.

Squire, L.R. (1987) *Memory and Brain*, New York: Oxford University Press.

Srinivas, K. (1993) 'Perceptual specificity in nonverbal priming', *Journal of Experimental Psychology: Learning, Memory, and Cognition* 19: 582–602.

Tulving, E. (1983) *Elements of Episodic Memory*, New York: Oxford University Press.

—— (1985) 'Memory and consciousness', *Canadian Psychologist* 26: 1–12.

—— (1989) 'Memory: performance, knowledge, and experience', *European Journal of Cognitive Psychology* 1: 3–26.

—— (1994) 'Varieties of consciousness and levels of awareness in memory', in A. Baddeley and L. Weiskrantz (eds) *Attention: selection, awareness and control. A tribute to Donald Broadbent*, Oxford: Oxford University Press.

—— (1995) 'Organization of memory: Quo vadis?', in M.S. Gazzaniga (ed.) *The Cognitive Neurosciences*, Cambridge, MA: MIT Press.

Tulving, E. and Schacter, D.L. (1990) 'Priming and human memory systems', *Science* 247: 301–305.

Tulving, E., Hayman, C.A.G. and Macdonald, C.A. (1991) 'Long-lasting perceptual priming and semantic learning in amnesia: a case experiment, *Journal of Experimental Psychology: Learning, Memory, and Cognition* 17: 595–617.

Tulving, E., Schacter, D.L. and Stark, H.A. (1982) 'Priming effects in word-fragment completion are independent of recognition memory', *Journal of Experimental Psychology: Learning, Memory, and Cognition* 8: 352–373.

Underwood, G. (ed.) (in press) *Implicit Cognition*, Oxford: Oxford University Press.

Velmans, M. (1991) 'Is human information processing conscious?', *Behavioral and Brain Sciences* 14: 651–726.

Warrington, E.K. and Weiskrantz, L. (1968) 'New method of testing long-term retention with special reference to amnesic patients', *Nature* 217: 972–974.

—— (1970) 'Amnesic syndrome: consolidation or retrieval?', *Nature* 228: 629–630.

Chapter 4

Cognitive views of consciousness
What are the facts? How can we explain them?

Bernard J. Baars and Katharine McGovern

INTRODUCTION

No alien space visitor could fail to observe that vertebrates, including humans, engage in purposeful motion for only two-thirds of the earthly day. In the remaining third, we hibernate. When consciousness returns in the morning, a massive change in electrical activity takes place all over the cortex, as the fast, small and irregular waves of waking electroencephalograph (EEG) replace the large, slow, regular hills and valleys of deep sleep. Accompanying this faster electrical activity, we humans report a rich and varied array of conscious experiences: colours and sounds, feelings and smells, images and dreams, the rich pageant of everyday reality. Because these reports of conscious experiences, purposeful action and electrical activity covary so perfectly, we routinely infer that they reflect a single underlying reality. And it is this underlying reality – consciousness – which is of central importance in human life.

Consciousness, as the philosopher John Searle has said, is that aspect of ourselves that we are least willing to sacrifice. We can lose a thumb or our eyesight, or even sustain brain damage, and still be ourselves. Without consciousness we are nothing.

At this instant you, the reader, are conscious of some aspects of the act of reading – the colour and texture of *this page*, and perhaps the inner sound of *these words*. But you are probably not aware of the touch of your chair at this instant, or a certain background taste in your mouth, or that monotonous background noise, the soft sound of music, or the complex syntactic processes needed to understand *this phrase*; nor are you now aware of your feelings about a friend, the fleeting events of several seconds ago, or the multiple meanings of ambiguous words, as in *this case*. Even though you are not currently conscious of them, there is a good deal of evidence that such unconscious events are actively processed in your brain, every moment you are awake.

When we try to understand conscious experience we aim to explain the differences between these two conditions: between the events in your nervous system that you can report, act upon, distinguish and acknowledge as your own, and a great multitude of sophisticated and intelligent processes which are unconscious and do not allow these operations.

A LITTLE HISTORY

Our concern with consciousness is not new. At the very dawn of written thought Plato compared human experience to the shadows projected on the wall of a cave by people walking and gesturing in front of a fire. The mind, he thought, was like a bound prisoner, thrown on the cave floor with his face to the wall, able to see the fire-cast shadows but ignorant of the underlying reality. While Plato's allegory of the cave is ancient, its implications are quite modern – from the vast unknown of the cave, to the striking capacity limits of conscious experience and the helplessness of the prisoner. Very similar ideas are found in the vast Asian libraries on human consciousness, and they are common in contemporary thinking as well.

WHAT EVIDENCE IS RELEVANT TO CONSCIOUSNESS *AS SUCH*?

To study anything in science we need to treat it as a variable. The concept of gravity would have been useless had Newton been unable to imagine zero gravity. Likewise, to understand consciousness we need to compare its presence and absence; consciousness without unconsciousness is meaningless. Only if we can compare conscious and unconscious events can we ask, '*What is the difference between the two*?' Only then can we deal with the issue of consciousness *as such*.

George Mandler (in Baars, 1986) has made the penetrating observation that science is obliged to treat consciousness not as an observable datum but as an inferred concept based on public evidence. As scientists dealing with public evidence and shared reasoning, we observe only the *reports* that our subjects make about their states and contents of consciousness. Of course, we are quite confident about the veracity of others' reports about their conscious experiences because we, the scientists, are also conscious. In everyday life, we confidently assume that the consciousness of others is like ours. Existential philosophers have pondered whether we are justified in making this assumption about the private experience of others. As scientists, we realize that our understandings of others' consciousness are inferences based on their reports. Our understanding of adult human consciousness is based on an inferential chain that can be extended to infant, primate and mammalian consciousness.

In a vast number of cases we can make quite reliable inferences about human experience based on such public reports. We now have almost 200 years of evidence that under well-defined conditions perceptual reports correspond with exquisite sensitivity to the physical stimulus array. In studying perception, in practice we always treat verbal reports as representations of private conscious experience. Entire domains of research, like perception and psychophysics, depend upon this methodology.

Of course, what we infer from the experiential reports of others is not just anything: the experiences people report are overwhelmingly *about* something. They are about events in the world, or even the mind itself, as in the case of memories or mental images. For people to describe, recall, think about, act upon or make decisions regarding any event, it must first become conscious.

Unconscious representations can also be inferred from public observations, though the individual under observation cannot directly report or act deliberately on these representations. The simplest example is the great multitude of memories that are currently unconscious for us. You may recall this morning's breakfast – where was that memory and what was its status before it was brought to mind? We believe it was still represented in the nervous system, though not consciously. Unconscious memories can influence other processes without ever coming to mind. If you ground extra coffee for breakfast today, you will probably not grind more tomorrow; your actions tomorrow are shaped by unconscious memories or knowledge of having coffee grounds, even without bringing today's coffee-making to mind. A strong case can be made for unconscious representation of habituated stimuli, memories before and after recall, automatic skills, implicit learning, the rules of syntax, unattended speech, presupposed knowledge, preconscious input processing and many other phenomena. Researchers still argue about the particulars of some of these cases, but it is widely agreed that, given adequate evidence, unconscious representations may be inferred (Greenwald, 1992; Baars, 1988; Marcel, 1983).

Each of us has private access to our own experience, but from a public, scientific point of view it is crucial to treat *both* conscious and unconscious representations as inferred constructs, for only then can we treat consciousness as a variable, allowing us to talk about consciousness *as such*. As in the case of Newtonian gravity, we can compare a state with its absence. This is a bit more abstract than the familiar experimental method, because we are comparing two *inferred* entities, rather than two direct observations. But the principle of treating consciousness as a variable to be studied is exactly the same.

Notice how often in the history of science the ability to treat something as a variable creates a breakthrough. When finally Newton was able to imagine motion in space without friction, contrary to twenty centuries of Aristotelian physics, he could write the law that 'an object in motion continues in motion'. But on earth there is no such thing as frictionless motion. It required a great act of imagination for natural philosophers to treat friction as a variable with a zero point. A similar leap of imagination allowed the sciences to resolve other difficult issues such as the fact that the atmosphere does not pervade the universe, the loss of earth gravity in space, the Kelvin scale with its absolute zero degrees temperature and so on. Contrastive analysis aims to do just that with respect to consciousness. It is not a new idea in science, although it occasionally needs to be reinvented because we always fall into the trap of thinking that our local reality, the reality of earth gravity, of motion that stops, and of the conscious observer, is the only reality. Contrastive analysis forces us to reach beyond the limits of our own experience.

Using contrasive analysis we can define a large set of empirical constraints on the concept of consciousness. We can compare not just single pairs of phenomena like implicit and explicit memory, but entire sets of contrastive pairs of phenomena in various domains (see Tables 4.1 and 4.2). Together the contrasts place empirically solid and demanding constraints on any theory. Very few theories can satisfy all of the constraints (see Baars, 1988).

OPERATIONAL DEFINITIONS: CONSCIOUS, UNCONSCIOUS AND FRINGE CONSCIOUS

Conscious vs. unconscious events

Conscious representations can be operationally defined as those which:

(a) are claimed by people to be conscious;
                    and which
(b) can be reported and acted upon,
(c) with verifiable accuracy,[1]
(d) under optimal reporting conditions.

'Optimal reporting conditions' implies a minimum delay between the event and the report, freedom from distraction and the like. All this fits standard practice in the study of perception, short-term memory, problem solving, imagery and many other phenomena.

There is a curious asymmetry between the assessment of conscious and unconscious processes. Obtaining verifiable experiential reports works very nicely for specifying conscious representations; but unconscious ones are much more slippery. In many cases of apparently unconscious processes, such as all the things the reader is *not* paying attention to at this moment, it could be that the 'unconscious' representations may be momentarily conscious, but so quickly or vaguely that we cannot recall it even a fraction of a second later. Or suppose people cannot report a word shown for a few milliseconds: does this mean that they are truly unconscious of it? William James understood this problem very well, and suggested in fact that there were no unconscious psychological processes at all (1983 [1890]: 162ff.). We have called this the 'zero point' problem (Baars, 1988; see Holender, 1986; Dennett, 1991).

This is one of those tricky cases in which the criterion for unconsciousness could retreat ever further and further beyond the grasp of diligent experimenters. Jacoby and Kelley (1992) suggest an attractive answer, a criterion for unconscious events which does not solve the problem exactly, but which gives a reasonable basis for consensus. Suppose, they suggest, we ask a subject to consciously *avoid* reporting a recently acquired memory when it is cued? If they still report the memory, they must have lost track of the fact that it was acquired at a specific recent occasion (source attribution); that fact must have been unconscious. The same reasoning can be extended more widely, to any material that can be acted upon by reporting it or avoiding it. If we can act upon any event voluntarily, it is plausible to think that it must have been conscious. If not, it may have been completely unconscious, or so fleetingly conscious that it is functionally unavailable. Conscious representations allow voluntary action; unconscious representations do not.

To illustrate Jacoby and Kelley's method, we can ask the reader to fill in the blanks with any appropriate word or syllable as quickly as possible, but not to mention any masculine nouns in that process:

> mother/ ....; sister/ ....; aunt/ ....; cow/ ....; stallion/ ....; Norse/ ....; George Washing/ ....; Saturday / .... day; Abraham Lin/ ....; Thomas Jeffer/ ....; Lyndon John/ ....; automo/ ....; Ingmar Berg/ ....; garbage/ ....

If, in spite of your intention not to mention any masculine terms, you said 'Norse*men*', 'Jeffer*son*', 'John*son*', 'Berg*man*', etc. these masculine associates to the cue words were plausibly unconsciously produced. If you successfully avoided the male associates, you were probably aware that they fit the exclusion rule. While Jacoby and Kelley used a specially memorized list of words rather than existing word associates, the logic is quite similar.

If William James were to come along at this point to argue that the fact that the word represented a male could still have been conscious very fleetingly, we might answer yes, possibly, but in such a way that the representation was apparently unable to affect deliberate, voluntary operations related to it. This may not be the ultimate solution; the Jacoby and Kelley criterion only guarantees that the 'unconscious' event cannot be used in what might be called 'working consciousness' – the ability to describe, operate upon, recall, report, think about or make decisions regarding the event. All these voluntary operations are quite fundamental in our normal functioning, so that it seems reasonable to call the Jacoby and Kelley criterion a mark of 'working consciousness'.

Distinguishing this from 'functionally unconsciousness' may be the best we can do for the time being.

In sum, mental events can be defined as *unconscious* for practical purposes if:

(a) Their presence can be verified (through facilitation of other observable tasks, for example);
     although
(b) they are not claimed to be conscious;
(c) and they cannot be voluntarily reported, operated upon, or avoided;
(d) even under optimal reporting conditions.

By this definition, practised skills like typing, reading, maintaining upright posture and visual analysis are largely unconscious in their details. Likewise, blindsight, implicit memory, unattended information, subliminal stimulus processing, the details of language processing, the mechanisms of priming, etc. would be unconscious. There is again a reasonable fit between this definition and existing scientific practice.

Fringe consciousness

An interesting class of phenomena are not quite conscious or unconscious, but are nevertheless very important for our normal mental functioning. William James thought that such 'fringe conscious' events were at least as useful as focally conscious experiences. Indeed, he thought that perhaps one-third of our conscious lives may be spent in subjectively active but vague states of mind. Fringe events include feelings of rightness, beauty, coherence, anomaly, well-being familiarity, attraction, repulsion and the like.

Most people are certain when they experience something beautiful. But is the experience of beauty knowable in detail, like the sight of a red toothbrush? Surely not for most people, even when they feel quite certain about the experience. The combination of high certainty, high accuracy and low experienced detail defines a 'fringe conscious' state.

Mangan (1993) has developed James' ideas about fringe consciousness in modern terms, suggesting that fringe phenomena may not be subject to the classical capacity limitations of conscious experiences. The claim is that feelings of familiarity or coherence can be simultaneously present in consciousness along with perceptual contents, for example. As we listen to a wonderful melody, we can simultaneously feel moved by it emotionally, feel that it is familiar and have a sense of rightness and fit. Since focal conscious capacity is notoriously limited to one internally consistent content at a time, Mangan sees fringe consciousness as a means of evading that limitation. The fringe may be, in Mangan's terms, a 'radical condensation' of unconscious information in consciousness. Fringe states seem to be very useful. There is evidence that they contribute to accurate decision-making, can predict resolution of tip-of-the-tongue states and estimate the availability of a memory even before it comes to mind (McGovern, 1993).

For example, Bowers et al. (1990) asked subjects to select which of two word triplets can be 'solved', i.e. which one has a common associate, a fourth word that is closely related to the first three words. Quite often subjects will feel certain that one of the triplets 'feels right' without knowing why. Consider A and B below:

A	B
playing	still
credit	pages
report	music

Triplet A has a common associate ('card') while B does not. Subjects can tell us which triad has a solution *even when they cannot provide the missing word*. They can 'respond discriminatively to coherence that they could not identify'. Bowers et al. suggest that 'this tacit perception of coherence guided subjects gradually to an explicit representation . . . in the form of a hunch or hypothesis' (1990: 72). This feeling of coherence seems to be what William James had in mind in his discussion of fringe consciousness. Further, fringe experiences are evidently informative and useful.

Table 4.1 Contrastive evidence in perception and imagery*

1 Perceived stimuli	1 Processing of stimuli of low intensity or duration and centrally masked stimuli
	2 Preperceptual processing
	3 Habituated or automatic stimulus processing
	4 Unaccessed meanings of ambiguous stimuli
	5 Contextual constraints on the interpretation of percepts
	6 Unattended streams of perceptual input (all modalities)
2 perceived word meaning	7 Parafoveal guidance of eye movements/fixations in reading
3 Visual search based on conjoined features	8 visual search based on single features
4 Images retrieved and generated (all modalities)	9 Unretrieved images in memory
5 New visual images	10 Automatized visual images
6 Automatic images that encounter some difficulty	
7 Inner speech: currently rehearsed words in working memory	11 Currently unrehearsed words in working memory
	12 Automatized inner speech?

* Images are broadly defined here as quasi-perceptual events occurring in the absence of external stimulation; imagery and perception are considered together since recent evidence suggests that they are products of the same psychological and cortical system (Kosslyn, 1994)

Research on fringe consciousness is still in its early stages. We can, however, suggest a preliminary operational definition for fringe conscious events. They are those experiences that:

(a) can be reported by all normal subjects in similar tasks,
(b) with verifiable accuracy and high confidence;
                   and
(c) which can serve as cues for voluntary action,
(d) but which are not reported to have differentiated perceptual, imaginal or conceptual features;
(e) even under optimal reporting conditions.

TREATING CONSCIOUSNESS AS A VARIABLE

As we have said before, we can only study a phenomenon scientifically if we can treat it as a variable. In the case of consciousness we can compare waking to sleep, coma and general anaesthesia; subliminal to supraliminal input, habituated vs. novel stimuli, attended vs. nonattended streams of information, recalled vs. nonrecalled memories, and the like. We have called this contrastive method 'contrastive analysis'. Table 4.1 shows a contrastive analysis for stimulus representation. This analysis allows us to compare conscious stimuli to unconscious input processing of the same information – as in pre-perceptual processes, unattended input, habituated representations and the like. In all these cases there is evidence that the unconsciously processed stimulus is accurately represented in the nervous system, so that we can compare conscious and unconscious representations of a given input.

Contrastive analysis, as we have said, is much like the experimental method: we can examine closely comparable cases that differ only in respect to consciousness, so that consciousness becomes, in effect, a variable. However, instead of dealing with only one experimental data set, we can examine entire categories of well-established phenomena, summarizing numerous experimental studies. In this way we can highlight the variables that constrain consciousness over a very wide range of cases.

Even a broad contrastive analysis brings out some important facts. Table 4.1 shows that conscious perception involves more than just an accurate *representation* of the stimulus, because there are many kinds of stimulus representation that are not conscious. Likewise in the case of visual imagery, we see that there are unconscious analogues of images, such as habituated mental images, which have faded from consciousness but nevertheless serve to guide task performance.

Pani (1982) studied the effects of practice and automaticity on mental images of abstract geometric shapes. In his task, subjects had to keep in mind one particular shape and decide whether it was similar to or different from other shapes that were presented on a screen. As they became more skilled with practice at this task, the particular shape they tried to keep in mind faded from consciousness, *even though they were better at telling how similar or different it was from the shapes on the screen*. That fact implies that their mentally imaged shape was still being unconsciously represented and served to guide their decisions. Interestingly, the faded image returned to subjects' consciousness when the matching task became difficult or unpredictable – much like a dishabituated perceptual stimulus. Pani's experiment has significant implications for normal, highly practised mental processes.

ADVANTAGES AND DISADVANTAGES OF CONSCIOUS AND UNCONSCIOUS PROCESSES

Whatever we do really well, we tend to do unconsciously, from speaking to seeing to playing the piano. This observation has led some psychologists like George Mandler (personal communication) to wonder why consciousness is needed at all. To get at this question of the role of consciousness we can conduct another contrastive analysis, focused on the capabilities of comparable conscious and unconscious processes. Table 4.2 presents a basic set of such capability contrasts. Notice that purely conscious processes are handicapped by low computational efficiency: they are rather inefficient (slow, prone to error and vulnerable to interference), serial and limited in capacity. Consider this mental multiplication: 23 x 79. For most of us this is not easy, and the more steps are conscious, the more difficult it is. Yet mental multiplication is trivial in complexity compared to the vast amount of processing that is needed to analyse the syntax of *this sentence*. Fortunately syntactic analysis is entirely unconscious. Mental arithmetic becomes more efficient with practice, allowing predictable steps to become automatic and unconscious; but that illustrates the same point, that efficiency in conscious computations like arithmetic is only achieved when the details become unconscious.

Similar observations about the inefficiency of conscious processing can be made of skilled performances such as playing the piano. A skilled pianist is certainly aware of the outcome of her performance, the melody emanating from the piano. But she is not conscious of the individual finger placements and foot pedal movements in the piece. If we ask her to perform these movements consciously, her performance is interrupted: she performs slowly, she hesitates, she loses her place, she starts again, she makes errors. If we allow the pianist to return to her usual skilled, mostly unconscious mode of performance she resumes her error-free playing and may even carry on a conversation while playing. The conclusion here is the same. Mental activities where all aspects of the manipulations are conscious have a high rate of errors, are slow and interfere with other activities, suggesting that performing efficient step-wise computation is not the primary function of consciousness.

But the computational drawbacks of consciousness are balanced by clear advantages: consciousness has a *vast range* of possible contents, it enables novel

Table 4.2 Contrasting capabilities of conscious and unconscious process

Conscious processes	Unconscious processes
1 Computationally inefficient: Many errors, relatively low speed, and mutual interference between conscious processes	1 Very efficient *in routine tasks*: Few errors, high speed, and little mutual interference
2 Great range of contents Great ability to relate different conscious contents to each other Great ability to relate conscious events to their unconscious contexts	2 Each routine process has a limited range of contents Each routine process is relatively isolated and autonomous Each routine process is relatively context-free
3 High internal consistency at any single moment, seriality over time, and limited processing capacity	3 The set of routine, unconscious processes is diverse, can sometimes operate in parallel, and together has great processing capacity

access to an astonishing number of skills and knowledge sources, and it shows *exquisite context-sensitivity.*

As an example of its vast range, consider all the possible percepts, images, memories, concepts, intentions, fringe experiences and the like of which we can be conscious. As one poetic student put it, we can be conscious of everything from the 'rumbling of our stomach to the return of a theme in a Bach cantata'.

A conscious event, like this sentence, can create access to new information in memory, combine knowledge from different sources in the brain in novel ways and trigger unconscious rule systems that will pick up errors in any level of analysis – in the meaning, syntax, word level, sound, intonation or printing of this snetnecne. To continue the example of the piano player used above, consciousness was needed to *acquire* the novel patterns of finger placement and foot pedalling, to store these action components in memory, even though consciousness became a hindrance to the later smooth performance of the known steps.

The context-sensitivity of consciousness can easily be shown to permeate whole domains, like perception, thinking or language. Take the predominance of lexical ambiguity, the fact that most words have multiple meanings. The *Oxford English Dictionary*, for example, devotes 75,000 words to the many different meanings of the little word 'set'. 'Set' can be a verb, noun or adjective. It can be a game in tennis or a collection of silverware. We can set a value on an antique, or look at a stage set. Glamorous people make a jet-set, and unlucky ones a set of fools. The sun sets, but it is certainly not set in concrete. Mathematicians use set theory, but psychologists talk about set as readiness to do or experience something.

In the sentences above, notice how quickly we can change our mental set about the word 'set'. At each use of the word you had litttle difficulty understanding the meaning intended, providing you had sufficient *contextual* information to make it fit. But notice that the detailed process of relating contextual information to the choice of meaning is rarely conscious. Thus whatever we experience consciously is shaped by unconscious processes, just like a theatre in which we see only the actors on stage, but not the director, playwright and stagehand – who make it all work. If the same actors were off stage (unconscious) their actions would not be contextualized by the entire supportive apparatus of the theatre. The context-sensitivity of conscious events extends far beyond language to perception, action control, memory, problem solving and indeed all conscious events. While single subliminally presented words like 'book' and 'torn' can influence conscious processes, when the two words are presented as the novel *phrase* 'torn book', the integrated phrase fails to have any detectable combined influence beyond the effect attributable to the words separately (see Greenwald, 1992; MacKay, 1973). Consciousness is apparently needed to create meaningful wholes from novel combinations of known stimuli. Likewise, when we make a navigational error in driving to a new locale simply because we are so used to turning right on the street going home, the less conscious we are of our driving and of the terrain, the more we are likely to make the error. The less conscious some event is (turning right), the less it is sensitive to context (our plan to reach a new destination).

Unconscious processes have their own advantages, however. Unconscious automatisms, such as the ones that control nearly all aspects of the act of comprehending speech, show an impressive speed and accuracy in routine matters, a tendency to perform parallel or concurrent processing whenever possible and, when all unconscious resources are taken together, a vast capacity. But of course there is constant interaction between conscious and unconscious processes. In listening to a friend describe last night's party, we follow the conscious flow of meaning with no awareness of the complex acoustic, phonological, morphological, lexical, semantic, syntactic, intonational and pragmatic processes happening at the same time, all of which are needed for us to become aware of the message.

Yet we can easily prove that these sophisticated unconscious processes are going on all the time. Should our friend commit any error, such as saying 'entymology' instead of 'etymology', or lapse into German word order, we would immediately detect the error no matter which of a dozen different levels of analysis was involved. Concurrent with all this fast, complex and unconscious linguistic activity, we also maintain balance and upright posture, represent predictable aspects of all incoming stimuli and shape our actions in terms of the social and pragmatic demands of the situation.

In the laboratory, the limitations of purely unconscious language processing have been highlighted in selective attention studies. If we receive two dense flows of information, like two simultaneous stories, one in each ear, or two different ball games shown on the same television set, we can follow only a single, consistent flow of the action. Under these conditions we can present information to the 'unattended channel', the ear one is not listening to, for example. In general, it has been found that semantic priming from individual words in the unattented channel can influence the experience of the conscious, attended channel. Thus the word 'money' in the unattended message can bias understanding of the consciously perceived word 'bank' towards 'financial institution' instead of 'shoreline of a river'. However, the information in the unconscious channel does not extend to the meaning of longer passages; for example, the meaning of whole sentences in the unattended ear will not bias perceived word meanings in the attended ear (see Greenwald, 1992 for a review).

What is the critical difference then between the two columns of Table 4.2? There are several, but perhaps the most significant one is that conscious events seem to create *access* to unanticipated knowledge sources. Only conscious events can lead to an endless range of voluntary actions, activate novel unconscious knowledge sources, or allow novel connections to be made between known units. It is as if a conscious representation is made available throughout the system to specialized mental capacities like memory, skill control, decision-making, syntax processing and the like, allowing it to evoke memories, be used as a cue for skilled actions or decisions, and detect syntactic flaws. At a broad, architectural level, conscious representations seem to provide flexible access to multiple knowledge sources in the nervous system, while unconscious ones are relatively isolated and inflexible. This conclusion also follows from other contrastive analyses (see Baars, 1988).

Consistent patterns of evidence now begin to emerge from the contrastive analysis. We see the interplay of a serial, integrated and very limited stream of consciousness with an unconscious system which is distributed, is composed of autonomous specialized modules and has enormous collective capacity.

CONSCIOUSNESS HAS LIMITED CAPACITY BUT PROVIDES *GLOBAL ACCESS* TO NUMEROUS MENTAL RESOURCES

Limited capacity

Many psychologists and philosophers have noted the limitations on moment to moment conscious capacity. In each conscious moment, we tend to be conscious of only a single internally consistent 'thing', e.g. an object, intention or day-dream. This content may be complex, such as a visual landscape. But we are nevertheless limited to one content. If we superimpose one scene over a different one, like a photographic double exposure, the viewer will flip back and forth in awareness of each one. If we project one picture to the left eye and another to the right, the viewer will see only one picture at a time. One of the two competing views is always in, and the other out of consciousness. This phenomenon of binocular rivalry shows that we cannot be conscious of two different scenes at the same time. Very similar phenomena exist for hearing and the other senses, and even for rivalry between different senses.

In everyday life, we have the belief that we cannot do two 'things' at one time, such as have an intense conversation *and* drive in busy traffic. On the other hand we can walk and chew gum at the same time and we can carry on a conversation while driving on an empty tollway. Why? What is the difference? Most likely the difference is in the level of conscious involvement needed for performance of the action. If one task does not require conscious involvement (except for its initiation and termination), we *can* carry on two activities at a time. At times we can keep multiple semi-automatic activities going by switching consciousness to whichever one requires conscious guidance for the moment (Pashler, 1992).

The number and duration of items *currently rehearsed* in working memory are similarly limited; classically we talk about 7 ± 2 words or numbers in short-term memory, but that number drops to 3 or 4 when rehearsal is prevented. Likewise intentional (controlled) actions can only be carried out serially, one at a time, while automatic processes can be carried out concurrently (LaBerge, 1980). In carefully studied dual-task situations, consciously controlled tasks interfere with each other, causing errors and delay. But when one or both tasks become automated through practice, the interference declines and can disappear entirely (Shiffrin *et al.*, 1981).

Global access

Consciousness seems to be the gateway through which we gain access to a vast continent of knowledge, skills and actions. The weight of evidence suggests that consciousness is a necessary condition for learning. The more novelty needs to be learned, the more conscious involvement is required. Even in the case of implicit learning, where the regularities in the learned material seem to be acquired unconsciously (more or less), we still need to be conscious of the target stimuli that display those regularities. 'Transfer of learning' from a well-known to a new situation is immensely aided by explicit, conscious connections between old and new cases: that is why clear and explicit analogies between the known and the new are so useful. The Rutherford model of the atom was productive in physics shortly before 1900 precisely because it suggested strong analogies between the solar system (which was well understood) and the atom (which was not). The analogy would not have helped had Lord Rutherford whispered it to his colleagues in a subliminal hush. On the contrary, it required a great deal of concentrated, conscious thought to be thoroughly understood and tested.

The example of automatic error detection in a sentence (see p. 72 above) also shows that consciousness of the target sentence is required even for unconscious detection of syntactic, lexical or pronunciation errors. That is why we ask school children to *pay attention* when solving puzzles like 'what's wrong with this picture?' Further, for stimulus information to influence action it needs to reach consciousness. Unattended single words may bias conscious word comprehension, but novel combinations of unconscious words appear to have no effect, and unconscious stimuli do not lead to novel, voluntary action. Indeed all the 'ego functions', such as the ability to make a decision, to act voluntarily, or to recall events from memory, appear to require conscious involvement.

The global influence of consciousness is dramatized by the remarkable phenomenon of biofeedback training. There is firm evidence that *any* single neuron or *any* population of neurons can come to be voluntarily controlled by giving conscious feedback of their neural firing rates. A small needle electrode in the base of the thumb can tap into a single motor unit – a muscle fibre controlled by one motor neuron coming from the spinal cord, and a sensory fibre going back to it. When the signal from the muscle fibre is amplified and played back as a click through a loudspeaker, the subject can learn to control his or her single motor unit – one among millions – in about ten minutes. Some subjects have learned to play drumrolls on their single motor units after about thirty minutes of practice! However, if the biofeedback signal is not conscious, learning does not occur. Subliminal feedback, distraction from the feedback signal, or feedback via a habituated stimulus – all these cases prevent control from being acquired. Since this kind of learning only works for *conscious* biofeedback signals, it suggests again that consciousness creates global access to all parts of the nervous system.

The paradox is therefore that conscious contents are quite limited in capacity, but that they can somehow create access to a vast array of knowledge sources in the brain. How can we explain this paradox?

SOME METAPHORS FOR CONSCIOUSNESS

Over the last two centuries, scientific thought about consciousness has often been cast in terms of a small set of metaphors.

The threshold metaphor

This metaphor embodies the commonly held assumption that consciousness results from the activation of some stimulus or memory above a certain threshold value. The hypothesis was stated in an early form by J. Herbart in 1824 (Herbart, 1961 [1824]). Activation theories of memory and perception are of course the bread and butter of modern cognitive psychology. They can explain priming effects, availability of memory and other forms of readiness to respond.

A few modern theories have begun to identify activation with access to consciousness. However, a simple activation metaphor fails as an adequate account of consciousness, because it cannot handle the phenomenon of redundancy effects: stimuli or behaviours that are repeated and predictable become unconscious. This includes habituation of perceptual events and mental images, skills practised to the point of automaticity and semantic satiation for repeated meaningful words. Redundancy effects occur in all sensory modalities, probably at all levels of analysis and apparently even for abstract concepts. If some minimum amount of activation were all that is needed to enter consciousness, we would be left with the paradox that repeating activation to the point of redundancy always causes conscious contents to become unconscious! Simple, unadorned activation cannot explain the likelihood of a stimulus either coming to mind or fading from mind if the stimulus happens to become predictable.

Activation alone is inadequate as a theory of consciousness. We need something more.

The tip-of-the-iceberg metaphor

Another long tradition looks at consciousness as the tip of a large psychological iceberg. This metaphor brings out the fact that conscious experience emerges from a great mass of unconscious events. Sigmund Freud is of course the name that comes to mind most easily here, but the current view is not necessarily psychodynamic. Unconscious material is not unconscious because it has been pushed out of consciousness. Rather, the great bulk of neural systems in the cortex and elsewhere are very efficient specialized processors which are normally unconscious. Modern neuropsychology confirms the vastness of the iceberg that is under the water, compared to the small limited-capacity component that is visible and conscious.

The novelty metaphor

One line of thought about consciousness holds that consciousness is focused on novelty, 'antihabit', or that which mismatches our expectations or mental set

(Mandler, 1984). There is ample evidence that people and animals seek novel and informative stimulation; consciousness seems to have a preference for 'news'. Repetitive, predictable, 'old' stimuli tend to fade from consciousness regardless of their sensory modality, degree of abstractness or physical intensity. Novelty can be defined as change in the physical environment (dishabituation), discon-firmation of expectation (surprise), or violation of skilled routines (choice-points in the otherwise routine flow of action). The novelty metaphor captures one central function of consciousness – its ability to direct resources towards adapta-tion to novel and significant events. In the language of Piaget, consciousness comes into play more when we need to accommodate to unexpected events than when we readily assimilate to predictable ones.

However, the novelty hypothesis is obviously not enough. We can be con-scious of routine matters if they are important enough personally or biologically: our repetitive need to eat, for example, without getting habituated or bored.

The integration metaphor

In the early information processing models of cognitive psychology there was sometimes an implicit assumption that consciousness was the result of 'high level processing'. Once low level sensory information was synthesized through suc-ceeding stages of constructive information processing, the output could be made available to an 'executive' which handled conscious percepts. Neisser (1967) described multiple, primitive or low level 'preattentive processes' operating in parallel which constructed the potential contents of consciousness. The output of only one preattentive process entered consciousness and the others died out. For Marcel (1983) and Mandler (1984) conscious perception results from high level perceptual integration. In addition to theories of perception, psycholinguistic theories describe complex, hierarchical use of the rules of grammar during language comprehension, with the assumption that only the output at the highest level enters consciousness.

Several psychologists suggest that conscious contents involve the highest level of integration in some hierarchical view of the nervous system. Sensory systems have increasingly integrated and abstract anatomical maps of the sensory receptor surface. Points of light and light–dark contrast at the retina are integrated at the thalamus, whence it is in turn mapped onto higher levels in the primary visual cortex, representing lines, colours, orientations and simple shapes, pro-ceeding to at least another twenty-five increasingly complex and integrated visual maps, until finally we obtain such high level constructs as three-dimensional object constancy, moving bodies, faces, kinetic (force) representations of objects and entire, integrated multisensory scenes (Desimone and Ungerleider, 1989; Churchland and Sejnowski, 1992). Consciousness can surely access such high level information.

In language understanding, we know that adults most of the time attend to the *meaning* of speech, rather than lower levels of analysis such as pure sound, phonemes, morphemes, words, grammar and the like. For instance, try to remember the sentence before this one. In all likelihood you won't remember the sound, syntax or even the specific words; only the gist, the meaning. This fact is consistent with the idea that you devote conscious capacity to the meaning level of language.

Nevertheless, you *can* choose to pay attention to the individual words or speech sounds. When people are presented with paired comparisons between two speech sounds that differ in very tiny acoustical properties, they can generally learn to tell the difference. In fact, in learning a new language and culture we have to pay attention to *all* levels, and a singer or trained speaker can learn to attend to extremely subtle aspects of speech sounds. Thus consciousness is not limited to the high levels of analysis: it easily ranges across levels.

In perception the same pattern obtains. While we are normally conscious of entire visual scenes, we can be conscious of only a single star on a dark night, even though the starlight may be as small as a single stream of photons streaming into a single retinal receptor, out of all the millions of receptor cells. Consciousness is marked by its *flexibility* in ranging up and down perceptual and language hierarchies. If we encounter a problem in communicating our meaning to a listener, we can quickly restate the same meaning in a very different form. But we can equally well change the fast and complex movements of the tongue to avoid touching a painful tooth. After several minutes of biofeedback training even the operation of single motor neurons can come under conscious control. The critical condition for biofeedback is immediate, conscious feedback from the to-be-controlled neurons. Again, it appears that we can get conscious access to quite high levels of perceptual and conceptual analysis, but consciousness does *not* seem to be limited to high levels of analysis.

At the brain level, integration issues are often viewed in terms of the 'binding problem' (Crick and Koch, 1990). That is, how is activity in neurons at diverse cortical locations 'bound together' to produce coherent, integrated and rapidly changing conscious experiences? Objects and events have many features that change rapidly, triggering quite different activity in many different brain locations and sensory modalities, and with some asynchrony. How are multiple aspects of a stimulus, such as the red of an apple, its roundness, its spatial location, its movement towards my mouth, brought together into a single, momentary, coherent conscious experience? Crick and Koch (1990) and others have suggested that binding may be paced by a neural timing signal, specifically the 40 Hertz (Hz) waveform that can be observed in many places in the brain at the same time. However, recent studies of anaesthetized subjects shows that the 40Hz waveform can exist without consciousness (Schwender *et al.*, 1994). The status of the binding problem is an ongoing topic of debate.

The executive

Another popular view is that consciousness is closely associated with executive control over action, speech and thought. Sometimes this is identified with a 'self as agent', operating in a hierarchy of control and monitoring functions (Hilgard, 1992; Baars, 1988). Kihlstrom (1993) maintains that an activated mental representation of the self, residing in working memory, is a necessary condition for conscious experience. In this view, for example, autobiographical memory must be indexed as self-related as it is encoded in the brain. Such self-indexing presumably takes place in immediate memory. Conversely, material that is not tagged as self-related cannot be recalled as one's own past experience, though it may well emerge in tests of implicit memory, learned skills and the like. In common sense terms, practising 'pinky-trills' on the piano will improve one's playing of Mozart without having to bring up the autobiographical memory of the last time we practised trills. Indeed, recalling the last time we practised anything (such as reading sentences like this) would interfere disastrously with our ability to perform the action that was practised.

These ideas are significant because they attempt to bring the self into our cognitive architecture, which in its own way is as important as trying to make sense of consciousness. However, there are some unanswered questions. For instance, if conscious experience requires a self-system (at least for registration of autobiographical information), how could we have 'self-alien' experiences, like minor dissocations in the case of accidents, when we might experience something in a removed, dreamy or self-dissociated fashion, as if the accident were happening to someone else; or alien hand syndrome in parietal neglect (where one's hand seems to belong to someone else); or the kind of self-alien experiences that are routinely used in hypnotic induction? For example, hypnotic techniques typically ask people to experience their hands as rising by themselves, as if drawn by a string. About 20 per cent of the population is highly hypnotizable and can easily be induced to have a strong self-alien experience of this kind. But surely all these examples are conscious. If these conscious but self-alien experiences exist, conscious contents must not *require* self-tags to be conscious. This might imply that such hypnotic experiences are less likely to be recalled as autobiographical memories, a perfectly testable proposition.

Shallice (1978, 1991) has presented a very different kind of executive association with consciousness, one that is exclusively involved with the control of action. In early versions, the executive supervisor of this system *was* the conscious component, but more recently Shallice has modified the theory to explain consciousness as coherent functioning of a set of controlling modules (see below).

The searchlight metaphor

One of the ancient, embedded idioms in many languages is consciousness as something that casts a light on things, so as to clarify and enlighten one's understanding ('Ah, I *see*!'). The image of casting light is discussed as far back as Plato. The searchlight metaphor is our modern way of expressing these ideas (e.g. Lindsay and Norman, 1977; Crick 1984). It is an attractive metaphor,

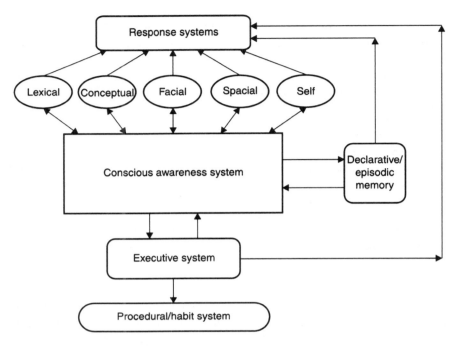

Figure 4.1 Schacter's DICE (Dissociable Interactions and Conscious Experience) model. Phenomenal awareness depends on intact connections between the conscious awareness system and the individual knowledge modules or declarative/ episodic memory. The conscious awareness system is the gateway to the executive system which is involved in initiation of voluntary action

Source: adapted from Schacter, 1990

embodying in a single image the selective function of consciousness, and the flow of conscious contents across numerous domains of memory, perception, imagery, thought and action. Crick's neurobiological version also captures what is known about the thalamocortical complex, the fact that the thalamus, nestled like an egg in the cocoon of each hemisphere, maps point-to-point into the corresponding parts of the cerebral cortex, almost like a miniature brain within the brain. The searchlight of attention can be imagined as shining out from the thalamus to the corresponding regions of the cortex.

The importance of thalamus in the neuropsychology of consciousness is highlighted by the long-known fact that lesioning the reticular and/or intra-laminar nucleus of the thalamus uniquely abolishes consciousness and produces coma. On the other hand, cortical lesions, even as large as hemispherectomies, only abolish *some* contents of consciousness, not consciousness itself (Bogen, 1995). Lesions of striate cortex, for example, produce scotoma or localized blind spots (loss of conscious contents) in the corresponding part of the visual field – but the state of consciousness in general and consciousness of other visual contents remain. Crick's thalamocortical spotlight is an elegant image, and one that may yet turn out to be true.

Both psychological and neurobiological searchlight theories are open to two unanswered questions. First, how is the *particular* focus selected? That is, what determines whether the searchlight shines on *this* content or cortical area and not some other? And second, once something is selected to be in focus, what happens to that information? What does it mean for that content to *be* conscious? Is it conveyed to a self-system, as suggested by the executive metaphor? Does it go to motor systems, to prepare them for voluntary action? Or does it go to semantic processors, which encode the meaning of the event? One can imagine a real searchlight operating in full darkness, so that one can see the light and its target but not the people who control its aim, or the audience that is looking at it. What is happening in these dark spaces? Without filling them in, the metaphor is missing some essentials. The theatre metaphor makes a stab at an answer.

The theatre in the society of mind

The theatre metaphor likens conscious experience to the brightly lit stage in a darkened auditorium. Whatever is on stage is disseminated to a large audience, as well as to the director, playwright, costume designers and stagehands behind the scenes. The focus of this metaphor is a publicity function in a vast array of specialized systems, which constitute the audience. Events on stage are privileged; they are made available to all the listeners in the auditorium.

Dennett (1991) and Dennett and Kinsbourne (1992) have criticized a particular version of the metaphor which they call the Cartesian Theater, 'a single place in the brain where "it all comes together"', much like the tiny, centrally located pineal gland in Descartes' brain. This is a bit of a red herring, however. No current model suggests that conscious contents may be found in a single, tiny point, the discrete finishing line of competing potential contents. There are many other ways to bring multiple sources of information together, for example by coordinating the dozens of perceptual maps in the nervous system. The thalamus may be in an ideal situation to do that.

Modern theatre metaphors bypass these Cartesian paradoxes. In recent versions, consciousness is not identified with any single locus. Rather, the contents of consciousness are whatever is being widely disseminated throughout the brain (Newman and Baars, 1994).

Combining the metaphors into a single, coherent theory

We can combine all five metaphors into a single integrated 'supermetaphor'. The theatre can be visualized as including useful aspects of the threshold, searchlight, iceberg, novelty and executive notions. As such a supermetaphor becomes

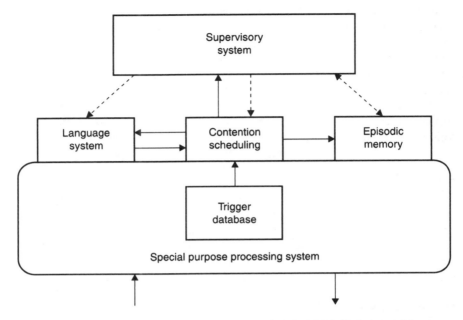

Figure 4.2 Shallice's Information Processing Model of Consciousness. The boxes represent distinct functions, not necessarily distinct anatomical locations. Arrows represent the flow of information between control systems, solid lines are obligatory communications, dashed lines are optional

Source: Shallice, 1988

enriched, it can gradually take on the features of a genuine theory. The theoretical proposals described below can be seen as steps in that direction.

MODERN THEORIES OF CONSCIOUSNESS

We are now beginning to see a small cluster of first-approximation theories that aim to account for a number of aspects of conscious experience.

Johnson-Laird: a computational view

Johnson-Laird's (1988) operating system model of consciousness emphasizes its role in controlling mental events, such as directing attention, planning and triggering action and thought, and purposeful self-reflection. Johnson-Laird proposes that the cognitive architecture performs parallel processing in a system dominated by a control hierarchy. His system involves a collection of largely independent processors (finite state automata), which cannot modify each other but which can receive messages from each other; each initiates computation when it receives appropriate input from any source. Each passes messages up through the hierarchy to the operating system, which sets goals for the subsystems. The operating system does not have access to the detailed operations of the subsystems – it receives only their output. Likewise, the operating system does not need to specify the details of the actions it transmits to the processors – they take in the overall goal, abstractly specified, and elaborate it in terms of their own capabilities.

In this model, conscious contents reside in the operating system or its working memory. Johnson-Laird believes his model can account for aspects of action control, self-reflection, intentional decision-making and other metacognitive abilities.

Schacter's Model of Dissociable Interactions and Conscious Experience (DICE)

Accumulating evidence regarding neuropsychological disconnections of processing from consciousness, particularly implicit memory and anosagnosia, led Schacter to propose his Dissociable Interactions and Conscious Experience (DICE) model. 'The basic idea motivating the DICE model . . . is that the processes that mediate conscious identification and recognition – that is, phenomenal awareness in different domains – should be sharply distinguished from modular systems that operate on linguistic, perceptual, and other kinds of information' (1990: 160–161).

Like Johnson-Laird, Schacter's DICE model assumes independent memory modules and a lack of conscious access to details of skilled/procedural knowledge. It is primarily designed to account for memory dissociations in normally functioning and damaged brains. There are two main observations of interest. First, with the exception of coma and stupor patients, failures of awareness in neuropsychological cases are usually restricted to the domain of their impairment; they do not have difficulty generally in gaining conscious access to other knowledge sources. Amnesic patients do not necessarily have trouble reading words, while alexic individuals don't necessarily have memory problems.

And, second, implicit (nonconscious) memory for unavailable knowledge has been demonstrated in many conditions. For example, name recognition is facilitated in prosopagnosic patients when the name is accompanied by a matching face – even though the patient does not consciously recognize the face. Numerous examples of implicit knowledge in neuropsychological patients who do not have deliberate, conscious access to the information are known (see Milner and Rugg, 1992). These findings suggest an architecture in which various sources of knowledge function somewhat separately, since they can be selectively lost; these knowledge sources are not accessible to consciousness, even though they continue to shape voluntary action.

In offering DICE, Schacter has given additional support to the idea of a conscious capacity in a system of separable knowledge sources, specifically to explain spared implicit knowledge in patients with brain damage. DICE does not aim to explain the limited capacity of consciousness or the problem of selecting

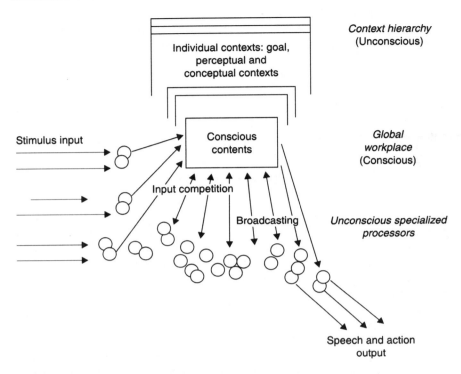

Figure 4.3 The global workspace architecture. The global workspace architecture consists of three components: the context hierarchy, the global workspace and the specialized processors

among potential inputs. In agreement with Shallice (see below) the DICE model suggests that the primary role of consciousness is to mediate voluntary action under the control of an executive. However, the details of these abilities are not spelled out, and other plausible functions are not addressed.

Shallice's supervisory system

Shallice shares an interest in the relationship of volition and consciousness with James (1983 [1890]), Baars (1988) and Mandler (1984). His earlier theory (1978) focused on conscious selection of the *dominant action system*, the set of current goals that work together to control thought and action. More recently (Shallice, 1988; Norman and Shallice, 1980), he has modified and refined the theory to accommodate a broader range of conscious functions.

Shallice describes an information processing system with five characteristics.

First, it consists of a very large set of specialized processors like Johnson-Laird's subsystems and Baars' (1988) unconscious specialized processors. There are several qualifications to this 'modularity':

a There is considerable variety in the way the subsystems can interact.
b The overall functional architecture is seen as partly innate, partly acquired, as with the ability to read.
c The 'modules' in the system include not only input processors but also specialized information stores, information management specialists and other processing modules.

Second, a large set of action and thought schemata can 'run' on the modules. These schemata are conceptualized as well-learned, highly specific programmes for routine activities, such as eating with a spoon, driving to work, etc. Competition and interference between currently activated schemata are resolved by another specialist system, *contention scheduling*, which selects among the schemata based on activation and lateral inhibition. Contention scheduling acts during routine operations.

Third, a *supervisory system* functions to modulate the operation of contention scheduling. It has access to representations of operations, of the individual's goals and of the environment. It comes into play when the operation of routinely selected schemata does not meet the system's goals; that is, when a novel or unpredicted situation is encountered or when an error has occurred.

Fourth, a *language system* is involved which can function either to activate schemata or to represent the operations of the supervisory system or specialist systems.

Fifth, more recently an *episodic memory* component containing event-specific traces has been added to the set of control processes.

Thus the supervisory system, contention scheduling, the language system and episodic memory all serve higher level or control functions in the system. As a first approximation, one of these controllers or several together might be taken as the 'conscious part' of the system. However, as Shallice points out, consciousness cannot reside in any of these control systems taken individually. No single system is either necessary or sufficient to account for conscious events. Consciousness remains even when one of these control systems is damaged or disabled. And the individual control systems can all operate autonomously and unconsciously. Instead, Shallice suggests, consciousness may arise on those occasions where there is concurrent and coherent operation of several control systems on representations of a single activity. *In this event, the contents of consciousness would correspond to the flow of information* between the control systems and the flow of information and control from the control systems to the rest of the cognitive system.

Shallice's model aims primarily to 'reflect the phenomenological distinctions between willed and ideomotor action' (1988: 319). However, the move to identify consciousness with the control of coherent action subsystems, and the emphasis

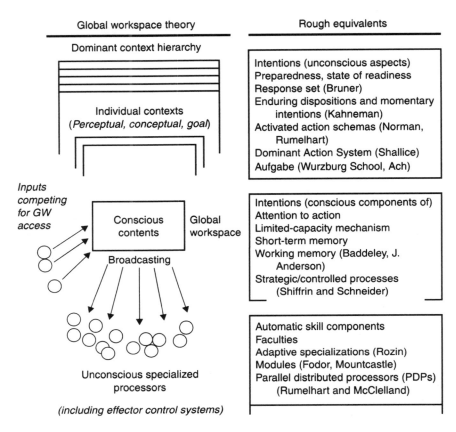

Figure 4.4 Rough equivalences between the basic concepts of GW theory and other widespread terms. Notice that global workspace (GW) theory has only three main constructs: the global workspace, unconscious specialized processors and contexts. Each one has a graphic symbol associated with it, so that the theory can be expressed in intuitively obvious diagrams

on the flow of information among the subsystems, bears a strong resemblance to the information broadcasting ideas of Baars' global workspace theory.

Baars' global workspace theory

The theatre metaphor is the best way to approach Baars' global workspace (GW) theory (Baars, 1983, 1988, in press). Consciousness is associated with a global 'broadcasting system' that disseminates information widely throughout the brain. If this is true, then conscious capacity limits may be the price paid for the ability to make single momentary messages available to the entire system for purposes of coordination and control. Since at any moment there is only one 'whole system,' a global dissemination facility must be limited to one momentary content. (There is evidence that each conscious 'moment' may be of the order of 100 milliseconds, a tenth of a second – see Blumenthal, 1977.)

Baars develops these ideas through seven increasingly detailed models of a global workspace architecture, in which many parallel unconscious experts interact via a serial, conscious and internally consistent global workspace (or its functional equivalent) (1983, 1988). Global workspace architectures or their functional equivalents have been developed by cognitive scientists since the 1970s; the notion of a 'blackboard' where messages from specialized subsystems can be 'posted' is common to the work of Baars (1988), Reddy and Newell (1974) and Hayes-Roth (1984). The global workspace framework is closely related to the well-known integrative theories of Herbert A. Simon (General Problem Solver or EPAM, Newell and Simon, 1972), Allan Newell (SOAR, 1992), and John R. Anderson (ACT*, 1983). Architectures much like this have also seen some practical applications. GW theory is currently a thoroughly developed framework, aiming to explain an exceedingly large set of evidence. It appears to have fruitful implications for a number of related topics such as spontaneous problem solving, voluntary control, and even the Jamesian 'self' as agent and observer (Baars, 1988, ch. 9).

GW theory relies on three theoretical constructs: unconscious specialized processors, a conscious global workspace and unconscious contexts.

The first construct is the *unconscious specialized processor*, the 'expert' of the psychological system. We know of hundreds of types of 'experts' in the brain. They may be single cells, such as cortical feature detectors for colour, line orientation or faces, but also entire networks and systems of neurons, such as cortical columns, functional areas like Broca's or Wernicke's, large nuclei such as locus ceruleus, etc. Like human experts, unconscious specialized processors may sometimes be quite narrow-minded. They are extremely efficient in limited task domains, able to act independently or in coalition with each other. Working as a coalition, they do not have the narrow capacity limitations of consciousness. They can receive global messages. And by 'posting' messages in the global workspace (consciousness) they can send messages to other experts and thus recruit a coalition of other experts. For routine missions they may work autonomously, without conscious involvement, or they may display their output in the global workspace, thus making their work conscious and available throughout the system. Answering a question like 'What is your mother's maiden name?' requires a mission-specific coalition of unconscious experts, which report their answer to consciousness.

The second construct is of course the *global workspace* itself. A GW is an architectural capability for system-wide integration and dissemination of information. A global workspace is much like the podium at a scientific meeting. Groups of experts at such a meeting may interact locally around conference

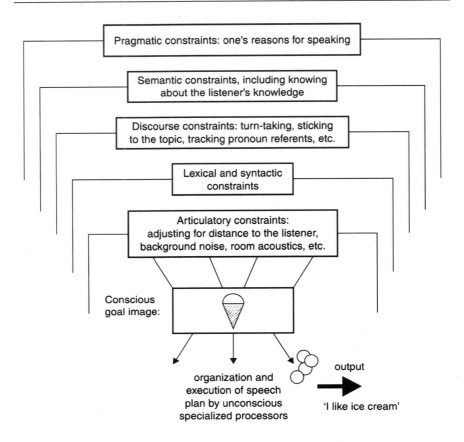

Figure 4.5 Multiple contextual constraints on utterances. Any single conscious event is influenced by multiple unconscious goal systems which together make up one kind of context hierarchy. Thus, the conscious goal image of the sentence to be spoken is constrained by all the goal contexts shown, which are normally not conscious. The conscious goal image serves to recruit and organize a set of specialized processors, which actually control the articulation of the sentence

tables, but in order to influence the meeting as a whole any expert must compete with others, perhaps supported by a coalition of experts, to reach the podium, whence global messages can be broadcast. New links between experts are made possible by global interaction via the podium, and can then spin off to become new local processors. The podium allows novel expert coalitions to form, to work on new or difficult problems, which cannot be solved by established experts and committees. Tentative solutions to problems can then be globally disseminated, scrutinized and modified.

The evidence presented in Tables 4.1 and 4.2 above falls into place by assuming that information in the global workspace corresponds to conscious contents. Since conscious experience seems to have a great perceptual bias, it is convenient to imagine that perceptual processors – visual, auditory or multimodal – can compete for access to a brain version of a GW. For example, when someone speaks to us the speech stream receives preperceptual processing through the speech specialist systems before the message in the speech stream is posted in consciousness. This message is then globally broadcast to the diverse specialist systems and can become the basis for action, for composing a verbal reply, for cueing related memories. In turn, the outcome of actions carried out by expert systems can also be monitored and returned to consciousness as action feedback.

Obviously the abstract GW architecture can be realized in a number of different ways in the brain, and we do not know at this point which brain structures provide the best candidates. While its brain correlates are unclear at this time, there are possible neural analogues, including the reticular and intralaminar nuclei of the thalamus, one or more layers of cortex, or an active loop between the sensory projection areas of the cortex and the corresponding thalamic relay nuclei. Like other aspects of GW theory, such neural candidates provide testable hypotheses (Newman and Baars, 1994).

Context, the third construct in GW theory, refers to the powers behind the scenes of the theatre of mind. Contexts are coalitions of expert processors that provide the director, playwright and stagehands behind the scenes of the theatre of mind. They can be defined functionally as *knowledge structures that constrain conscious contents without being conscious themselves*, just as the playwright determines the words and actions of the actors on stage without being visible. Conceptually, contexts are defined as pre-established expert coalitions that can evoke, shape and guide global messages without themselves entering the global workspace.

Contexts may be momentary, as in the way the meaning of the first word in a sentence shapes an interpretation of a later word like 'set', or they may be long-lasting, as with life-long expectations about love, beauty, relationships, social assumptions, professional expectations, world views and all the other things people care about. While contextual influences shape conscious experience without being conscious, contexts can be *set up* by conscious events. The word 'tennis' before 'set' shapes the interpretation of 'set', even when 'tennis' is already gone from consciousness. But, the word or perhaps concept 'tennis' was initially conscious, and needed to be conscious in order to create the unconscious context that made sense of the word 'set'.

Thus conscious events can set up unconscious contexts. The reader's ideas about consciousness from years ago may influence his or her current experience of this chapter, even if the memories of the earlier thoughts do not become conscious again. Earlier experiences typically influence current experiences as contexts, rather than being brought to mind. It is believed, for example, that a shocking or traumatic event earlier in life can set up largely unconscious expectations that may shape subsequent experiences (Baars and McGovern, 1995).

The three constructs of global workspace theory – expert processors, global workspace and contexts – are specifically defined with respect to conscious and unconscious functioning, unlike other psychological concepts, but of course they have many resemblances to well-known ideas. Figure 4.4 shows a summary of these similarities.

An example of goal contexts

The reader is doing a number of purposeful things right now, but they are not necessarily conscious, not at least unless they are interrupted. Suppose, for example, a flyspeck drifted into your visual field right now, making the next word impossible to read. Obviously you would do something to remove it, because it would be interfering with your reading, even though you probably did not hold the goal of reading in consciousness just a minute ago. Nevertheless, something goal-like was happening: why else would you remove an obstacle to reading? Moreover, your goal of reading this paragraph is probably nested under higher level goals, which you *could* bring to mind but which were not necessarily conscious either, until you were reminded of them. Further, there are likely to be high level goals – such as pursuing a decision made years ago to explore interesting psychological topics like consciousness – which are helping to guide your actions *without* being conscious. And finally, every word above can be viewed as a subgoal serving a higher-level goal, so that we are talking about a dense hierarchy of goals and subgoals, many of which were conscious, or consciously accessible at some point, some of which may be brought to mind when they are disrupted, and some of which may be entirely unconscious. This is essentially the rationale for the concept of a goal hierarchy (not in principle different from Maslow's motivational hierarchy); global workspace theory simply suggests that those goals are *contextual* when they shape action and experience. That is, the goal hierarchy helps to direct and shape a complex act like reading without itself being conscious. Figure 4.5 represents a simplified goal context hierarchy for the sentence 'I want to buy ice cream', a goal that is of course nested within longer lasting higher level goals, such as maximizing pleasure and avoiding pain.

Formally we can define *goal contexts* as future-directed, non-qualitative representations about one's own actions (Figure 4.4). Like other contexts, they shape and constrain conscious contents, including possible conscious goal images, without being conscious themselves. In everyday usage, a goal context is the same as a plan or intention. Goal contexts are similar to the notion of 'current concerns' (Singer, 1988), which is a conscious or unconscious need or value that shapes attentional selection, imagery, inner speech and action, including daydreams, sampled stream of thought and even night dreams. By definition they exert their influence on conscious experience unconsciously, unless they themselves become the objects of experience (when they are of course shaped by yet other contexts). We tend to become aware of the workings of goal contexts only when they are unexpectedly mismatched; for example, when we make errors or otherwise cannot complete our intentions.

The GW notion of goal context hierarchy differs from the goal hierarchies of Maslow and others in only one major respect: these theories have little to say about whether goals can be conscious. Note that in GW theory, consciousness is found in the global workspace and not in the high levels of the goal hierarchy. From this perspective, the remarkable thing about consciousness is not that it is always 'high level', but rather that it can range freely among levels of goals and in the goal context hierarchy.

THE MANY FUNCTIONS OF CONSCIOUSNESS

William James wrote that 'The *particulars of the distribution of consciousness*, so far as we know them, *point to its being efficacious . . .*' (1983 [1890], vol. I: 141–142). This view contrasts markedly with epiphenomenalism, which, in the words of T. H. Huxley, views conscious experience much as the 'steam whistle which accompanies the work of a locomotive [but which] is without influence upon its machinery' (quoted in James, 1983 [1890], vol. I: 130).

The evidence sketched above militates strongly against epiphenomenalism. If consciousness is a major biological adaptation, it may have not just one but a number of functions. Fundamental biological adaptations tend to accrue multiple functions. Just as the bloodstream circulates oxygen and glucose to all the body cells, takes away waste products, provides a channel for hormones, carries the white cells of the immune system, plays a role in temperature regulation and much more, we believe that consciousness has added to its fundamental functions during its evolutionary history.

The evidence suggests at least the following functions for consciousness:

1 *Definitional and context-setting function.* By relating global input to its contextual conditions, the system underlying consciousness acts to define a stimulus and remove ambiguities in its perception and understanding.
2 *Adaptation and learning function.* The more novelty the nervous system must adapt to, the more conscious involvement is required for successful problem solving and learning.
3 *Prioritizing and access control function.* Attentional mechanisms exercise selective control over what will become conscious. By consciously relating some event to higher level goals, we can raise its access priority, making it conscious more often and therefore increasing the chances of successful adaptation to it. By persuading smokers that the apparently innocuous act of lighting a cigarette is life-threatening over the long term, the medical profession has raised the smokers' conscious involvement with smoking, and created the possibility for more creative problem solving in that respect.
4 *Recruitment and control of mental and physical actions.* Conscious goals can recruit subgoals and motor systems in order to organize and carry out voluntary actions.

5 *Decision-making and executive function.* While the global workspace is not an executive system, executive access to the GW creates the opportunity for controlling any part of the nervous system, as shown by the extraordinary range of neural populations that can be controlled with conscious biofeedback. When automatic systems cannot resolve some choice-point in the flow of action, making it conscious helps to recruit knowledge sources able to help make the proper decision. In the case of indecision, we can make a goal conscious to allow widespread recruitment of conscious and unconscious resources acting for or against the goal.

6 *Error detection and editing function.* Conscious goals and plans are monitored by unconscious rule systems, which will act to interrupt execution if errors are detected. Though we often become aware of making an error in a general way, the detailed description of what makes an error an error is almost always unconscious.

7 *Reflective and self-monitoring function.* Through conscious inner speech and imagery we can reflect upon and to some extent control our conscious and unconscious functioning.

8 *Optimizing the trade-off between organization and flexibility.* Automatized, 'canned' responses are highly adaptive in predictable situations. However, in facing unpredictable conditions, the capacity of consciousness to recruit and reconfigure specialized knowledge sources is indispensable in allowing flexible responses.

In sum, consciousness appears to be the major way in which the nervous system adapts to novel, challenging and informative events in the world.

CONCLUDING REMARKS

A vast array of solid evidence is beginning to reveal the role of consciousness in the nervous system, at least in broad outline. Consciousness seems to create access to multiple, independent knowledge sources. While organization of coherent percepts and control over novel, voluntary actions may have been primary in the phylogenetic evolution of consciousness, it seems also to have acquired other functions which can be seen as contributing to adaptive action in a complex world, such as self-monitoring and self-reflection, symbolic representation of experience, control over novel actions and mental rehearsal. Consciousness provides for flexible cooperation and reconfiguration of many expert systems in the society of mind.

NOTE

1   The verifiability criterion may exclude phenomena like hallucinations and dreams, which can only be verified in a very broad way, without the precision we expect for perceptual stimuli or specific memories. While dreams and hallucinations are important, we can focus initially on cases that command the widest agreement.

REFERENCES

Ach, N. (1951 [1905]) 'Determining tendencies: awareness' (English translation by D. Rapaport), in D. Rapaport (ed.), *Organization and Pathology of Thought*, New York: Columbia University Press.

Anderson, J.R. (1983) *The Architecture of Cognition*, Cambridge, MA: Harvard University Press.

Baars, B.J. (1983) 'Conscious contents provide the nervous system with coherent, global information', in R. Davidson, G. Schwartz and D. Shapiro (eds) *Consciousness and Self-regulation*, New York: Plenum.

—— (1986) *The Cognitive Revolution in Psychology*, New York: Guilford.

—— (1988) *A Cognitive Theory of Consciousness*, New York: Cambridge University Press.

—— (in press) *Consciousness Regained: the new science of human experience*, New York: Oxford University Press.

Baars, B.J. and McGovern, K. (1995) 'Steps toward Healing: false memories and traumorgenic amnesia may coexist in vulnerable populations', *Consciousness and Cognition* 4(1): 68–74.

Baddeley, A.D. (1986) *Working Memory*, Oxford: Clarendon Press.

Blumenthal, A.L. (1977) *The Process of Cognition*, Englewood Cliffs, NJ: Prentice-Hall.

Bogen, J. (1995) 'On the neurophysiology of consciousness: I. An overview', *Consciousness and Cognition* 4(1): 52–62.

Bowers, K., Rehger, G., Balthazard, C. and Parker, K. (1990) 'Intuition in the context of discovery', *Cognitive Psychology* 22: 72–110.

Bruner, J.S. (1957) 'On perceptual readiness', *Psychological Review* 64: 123–152.

Churchland, P.S. and Sejnowski, T.J. (1992) *The Computational Brain*, A Bradford Book, Cambridge, MA: MIT Press.

Crick, F. (1984) 'Function of the thalamic reticular complex: the searchlight hypothesis', *Proceedings of the National Acadamy of Science USA* 81: 4586–4590.

Crick, F. and Koch, C. (1990) 'Towards a neurobiological theory of consciousness', *Seminars in Neuroscience* 2: 263–275.

Dennett, D. (1991) *Consciousness Explained*, Boston, MA: Little, Brown.

Dennett, D. and Kinsbourne, M. (1992) 'Time and the observer: the where and when of consciousness in the brain', *Brain and Behavioral Sciences* 15(2): 183–201.

Desimone, R. and Ungerleider, L.G. (1989) 'Neural mechanisms of visual processing in monkeys', in F. Boller and J. Grafman (eds) *Handbook of Neuropsychology*, Vol. 2, Amsterdam: Elsevier.

Fodor, J. (1983) *The Modularity of Mind: an essay on faculty psychology*, Cambridge, MA: MIT Press.

Greenwald, A. (1992) 'New Look 3, unconscious cognition reclaimed', *American Psychologist* 47(6): 766–779.

Hayes-Roth, B. (1984) 'A blackboard model of control', *Artificial Intelligence* 16: 1–84.

Herbart, J.F. (1961 [1824]) 'Psychology as a science, newly founded upon experience, metaphysics, and mathematics', reprinted in T. Shipley (ed.), *Classics in Psychology*, New York: Philosophical Library.

Hilgard, E.R. (1992) 'Divided consciousness and dissociation', *Consciousness and Cognition* 1(1): 16–31.

Holender, D. (1986) 'Semantic activation without conscious identification in dichotic listening, parafoveal vision, and visual masking: a survey and appraisal, *Behavioral and Brain Sciences* 9: 1–66.

Jacoby, L.L. and Kelley, C.M. (1992) 'A process-dissociation framework for investigating unconscious influences: Freudian slips, projective tests, subliminal perception, and signal detection theory', *Current Directions in Psychological Science* 1(6): 174–179.

James, W. (1983 [1890]) *The Principles of Psychology*, Cambridge, MA: Harvard University Press.

Johnson-Laird, P.N. (1988) 'A computational analysis of consciousness', in A. Marcel and E. Bisiach (eds) *Consciousness and Contemporary Science*, Oxford: Oxford University Press.

Kahneman, D. (1973) *Attention and Effort*, Englewood Cliffs, NJ: Prentice-Hall.

Kihlstrom, J.F. (1993) 'The psychological unconscious and the self', in G.R. Bock and J. Marsh (eds) *CIBA Symposium on Experimental and Theoretical Studies of Consciousness*, London: Wiley Interscience.

Kosslyn, S. (1994) *Image and Brain: the resolution of the imagery debate*, Cambridge: MA: Bradford.

LaBerge, D. (1980) 'Unitization and automaticity in perception', in J.H. Flowers (ed.) *Nebraska Symposium on Motivation*, Lincoln, NE: University of Nebraska Press.

Lindsay, P.H. and Norman, D.A. (1977) *Human Information Processing: an introduction to psychology*, 2nd edn., New York: Academic.

MacKay, D.G. (1973) 'Aspects of a theory of comprehension, memory, and attention', *Quarterly Journal of Experimental Psychology* 25: 22–40.

Mandler, G. (1984) *Mind and Body: psychology of emotion and stress*, New York: Norton.

Mangan, B. (1993) 'Taking phenomenology seriously: the "fringe" and its implications for cognitive research', *Consciousness and Cognition* 2(2): 89–108.

Marcel, A.J. (1983) 'Conscious and unconscious perception: an approach to the relations between phenomenal experience and perceptual processes', *Cognitive Psychology* 15: 238–300.

McGovern, K. (1993) 'Feelings in the fringe', *Consciousness and Cognition* 2(3): 119–125.

Milner, A.D. and Rugg, M.D. (eds) (1992) *The Neuropsychology of Consciousness*, London: Academic Press.

Mountcastle, V.B. (1978) 'An organizing principle for cerebral function: the unit module and the distributed system', in G.M. Edelman and V.B. Mountcastle (eds), *The Mindful Brain*, Cambridge, MA: MIT Press.

Neisser, U. (1967) *Cognitive Psychology*, New York: Appleton-Century-Crofts.

Newell, A. (1992) 'SOAR as a unified theory of cognition: issues and explanations', *Behavioral and Brain Sciences* 15(3): 464–492.

Newell, A. and Simon, H.A. (1972) *Human Problem Solving*, Englewood Cliffs, NJ: Prentice-Hall.

Newman, J. and Baars, B.J. (1994) 'A neural attentional model for access to consciousness: a global workspace perspective', *Concepts in Neuroscience* 2(3): 255–290.

Norman, D.A. (1976) *Memory and Attention*, New York: Wiley.

Norman, D.A. and Shallice, T. (1980) 'Attention to action: willed and automatic control of behaviour' (CHIP report no. 99), University of California, San Diego.

Pani, J. (1982) 'A functionalist account of mental imagery', paper presented at the Twenty-third Annual Meeting of the Psychonomic Society, Baltimore, MD.

Pashler, H. (1992) 'Attentional limitations in doing two tasks at the same time', *Current Directions in Psychological Science* 1(2): 44–48.

Reddy, R. and Newell, A. (1974) 'Knowledge and its representation in a speech understanding system', in L.W. Gregg (ed.) *Knowledge and Cognition*, Potomac, MD: Erlbaum.

Rozin, P. (1976) 'The evolution of intelligence and access to the cognitive unconscious', in J. Sprague and A. Epstein (eds), *Progress in Psychobiology and Physiological Psychology*, New York: Academic Press.

Rumelhart, D. and Norman, D. (1975) 'The active structural network', in D. Norman and D. Rumelhart (eds), *Explorations in Cognition*, San Francisco: Freeman.

Rumelhart, D.E., McClelland, J.E. and the PDP Research Group (1986) *Parallel Distributed Processing: explorations in the microstructure of cognition*, vol. 1: *Foundations*, Cambridge, MA: Bradford/MIT Press.

Schacter, D.L. (1990) 'Toward a cognitive neuropsychology of awareness: implicit knowledge and anosognosia', *Journal of Clinical and Experimental Neuropsychology* 12(1): 155–178.

Schwender, D., Madler, C., Klasing, S., Peter K. and Poppel, E. (1994) 'Anesthetic control of 40-hz brain activity and implict memory', *Consciousness and Cognition* 3(2): 129–147.

Shallice, T.R. (1978) 'The dominant action system: an information processing approach to consciousness', in K.S. Pope and J.L. Singer (eds) *The Stream of Consciousness: scientific investigations into the flow of experience*, NY: Plenum.

—— (1988) 'Information-processing models of consciousness: possibilities and problems', in A.J. Marcel and E. Bisiach (eds) *Consciousness in Contemporary Science*, Oxford: Clarendon.

—— (1991) 'The revival of consciousness in cognitive science', in W. Kessen, A. Ortony and F. Craik (eds) *Memories, Thoughts and Emotions: essays in honour of George Handlar*, Hillsdale, NJ: Erlbaum.

Shiffrin, R.M. and Schneider, W. (1977) 'Controlled and automatic human information processing: II Perceptual learning, automatic attending, and a general theory', *Psychological Review* 84: 127–190.

Shiffrin, R.M., Dumais, S.T. and Schneideer, W. (1981) 'Characteristics of automatism', in J. Long and A. Baddeley (eds) *Attention and Performance IX*, Hillsdale, NJ: Erlbaum.

Singer, J.L. (1988) 'Sampling ongoing consciousness and emotional experience: Implications for health', in M.J. Horowitz (ed.) *Psychodynamics and Cognition*, Chicago: University of Chicago Press.

Chapter 5

Neural processes in the production of conscious experience

Benjamin Libet

There is no doubt that the production or appearance of conscious experience is a function of brain processes. One need only think of the loss of awareness during an anoxia that initially depresses the forebrain selectively, as seen in a reduction of spontaneous electrophysiological ('brain wave') activity. This loss contrasts with the retention of conscious awareness when the spinal cord has been either anaesthetized or transected at a high cervical level (although, of course, somatic sensibility and motor control below the neck are lost). The questions to be addressed here are as follows: How do cerebral neurons produce conscious experience? Are there unique neuronal activities or loci that distinguish between conscious and unconscious mental events? Which brain structures are specific-ally necessary for conscious experience? Within the context of a brain with normally functioning necessary structures, is production of a conscious ex-perience finally achieved by some localized processing, or by a distributed processing in a more global fashion? I also ask whether the conscious mental phenomena that are produced by cerebral neurons can in turn influence or control some activities of those neurons. Although many if not most contemporary neuroscientists and philosophers would immediately answer no to the last question, their judgement is based on the often unstated hypothesis that the causal relationship is one-way, neural to mental only, and that feelings of free will are illusions. But this is a hypothesis that has yet to be tested and confirmed, and so the question should remain open to an experimental scientist. Our ability to carry out acts of our own will would seem to provide a kind of prima facie evidence that such a causal relationship may exist. For example, one can decide at will to flick a finger, or not to flick it, at any time one wishes to do so.

DEFINITIONAL PRINCIPLES

Before discussing possible studies that attempt to gain answers to our questions about brain and conscious experience we should clarify what is to be studied. For scientific studies, whether experimental or descriptive, we must have a workable operational definition of conscious awareness.

Introspective report of the experience

The stubborn fact is that conscious experience or awareness is directly accessible only to the subject having that experience, and not to an external observer. Consequently, only an introspective report by the subject can have primary validity as an operational measure of a subjective experience. The 'transmission' of an experience by a subject to an external observer can, of course, involve distortions and inaccuracies. Indeed there can be no absolute certainty (objectively demonstrable by externally observable events) about the validity of the report (Libet, 1987). Of course, absolute certainty does not hold even for physical observations. But in all social interactions we accept introspective reports as evidence of a subject's experience, though we may subject the report to some analyses and tests which affect our acceptance of their validity. This same general approach can be applied more rigorously in a scientific investigation. The validity of what is communicated depends upon the degree to which both individuals have had similar or related experiences. A congenitally completely blind person can never share the conscious experience of a visual image, regardless of how detailed a verbal description he or she is given by a sighted individual. The same limitation applies to all experiences in less dramatic, more subtle ways. For example, electrical stimulation of the somatosensory cortex can produce sensations related to but sufficiently different from those generated by normal sensory input, so that the subjects could only relate some roughly understandable approximation of these experiences to the experimental observer, in whom similar modes of sensory generation had never been employed (Libet *et al.*, 1964; Libet, 1973).

An important corollary of this principle is that any behavioural evidence which does not require a convincing introspective report cannot be assumed to be an indicator of conscious, subjective experience; this is so regardless of the purposeful nature of the action or of the complexity of cognitive and abstract problem-solving processes involved, since all of these can and often do proceed unconsciously, without awareness by the subject. Similarly, studies of signal detection should not be confused with those of conscious experience. The forced choice responses in signal detection studies could be made independent of introspective awareness of the signal, although they may be excellent indicators of whether some type of detection has occurred. There is, in fact, evidence that signal detection can occur with signals that are distinctly below the threshold required for any conscious awareness of the signal (see Libet *et al.*, 1991). Indeed, most sensory signals probably do not reach conscious awareness; but many of them lead to modified responses and behaviours, as in the tactile and proprioceptive signals that influence simple everyday postural and walking activities, which have therefore clearly been detected and utilized in complex brain functions.

The requirement of a reportable introspective experience also implies that it is difficult for nonhuman animals, even monkeys or chimpanzees, to supply convincingly valid responses for our purposes. Such animals may in fact have conscious experiences, but the question is – how can these be studied? Complicated cognitive and purposeful behaviours can proceed even in human beings without introspective awareness of them, and so we cannot safely assume that such behaviours in animals are expressing subjective experience. Some investigators and writers have proposed that adaptive, problem-solving behaviours in animals indicate conscious thought and experience. But even in humans, the most complex problem solving, even of mathematical problems, can and often does proceed at unconscious levels, as has been repeatedly described by many creative thinkers, artists and others.

No *a priori* rules for relating brain events to conscious mental events

Mental events and externally observable (physical) events constitute two categorically separate kinds of phenomena. They are mutually irreducible categories in the sense that one cannot, *a priori*, be described in terms of the other. There are no *a priori* rules or laws that can describe the relationship between neural, brain events and subjective, mental events. No doubt rules do exist, but they must be discovered. They can only be established by simultaneous observation of both categories of event. It also follows that even a complete knowledge of all the neural, physical events and conditions (in the unlikely case that were possible) would not, in itself, produce a description of any associated subjective experience (Libet, 1966; Nagel, 1979). This would constitute a flat rejection of a reductionist view that an adequate knowledge of neuronal functions and structures would be sufficient for defining and explaining consciousness and mental activities (e.g. Dennett and Kinsbourne, 1992).

CEREBRAL STRUCTURES OR SITES, FOR CONSCIOUS EXPERIENCE

The traditional sources of information on this issue are observed changes in conscious functions resulting from cerebral lesions due to pathological damage (tumours, etc.), accidental damage (blows or intracranial penetrations) and surgical interventions (for example, excisions of epileptic foci). These approaches have produced some interesting general findings. First, surprisingly large amounts of cerebral cortex (or forebrain generally) could be lost without losing awareness. There could of course be losses in the contents of awareness (e.g. loss of conscious vision with lesions of the primary visual cortex, etc.), but patients could remain generally aware of other events and of themselves. The well-known split-brain studies by Sperry *et al.* (1969) showed that information available to one cerebral hemisphere was not available to the other hemisphere after transection of the corpus callosum and anterior commissure. There has been some debate about whether the non-speaking right hemisphere is conscious and aware (see Gazzaniga, 1993; Sperry, 1985). A crucial test of that issue lay in the results of an entire left hemispherectomy in the adult subject (young children were known to recover most functions after a hemispherectomy). I have seen (courtesy of neurosurgeon Joseph Bogen) video-recordings of two such patients who retained only a right hemisphere after surgical or pathological loss of the left hemisphere. Although there was loss of sensory and motor function on the right side of the body, and of much though not all ability to speak, the two subjects appeared to be convincingly conscious, aware of events and appropriately responsive. They even exhibited an understandable frustration at not being able to articulate an appropriate verbal response to questions.

On the other hand, the functions of certain brain stem structures appear to be necessary to maintain the normal waking state of consciousness and awareness. The initial definitive experiment was done by the Belgian neurophysiologist Frédéric Bremer (1937), who found that transection of the brain stem at a midbrain level, in the cat, produced a permanent coma of the forebrain. More localized lesions and electrical stimulation in the brain stem led Moruzzi and Magoun (1949) to propose the reticular-activating-system (RAS), originating in the reticular formation of the pontine region of hind-brain. The RAS diffuse projection to the forebrain could produce and maintain arousal and a waking state. Further work indicated that more rostral related structures, particularly the reticular nucleus of the thalamus, might play a role in selective arousal of cortical areas and thereby in the attention mechanism. The neurosurgeon Penfield (1958) noted that pathological lesions of similar structures in man led to irreversible coma, whereas extensive losses of cerebral cortex did not. Penfield therefore proposed that the conscious process arises or even resides in the 'centrencephalic' system of the brain stem.

Necessary vs. sufficient structures and functions

The centrencephalic structures are indeed necessary for the ability to have any awareness or conscious experience, but that does not mean they are also sufficient for that ability. As we will see below, unique activities of cortical neurons must be superimposed on the state of arousal produced by the RAS, in order for awareness of an event to appear. In a more general sense many structures are necessary for conscious experience. For example, if the heart fails one loses consciousness within some seconds, but that does not mean that conscious experience is produced in the heart. Actually, it may be very difficult if not impossible to decide whether certain neuronal activities (even when uniquely required) provide the sufficient cause of awareness, or whether they are simply another necessary factor or perhaps only one of a number of potentially sufficient causes. This is so because the activity of any given structure or pattern of neurons is embedded in the enormously complex and active interconnections of the whole brain. We may have to be satisfied with attempting to discover simply whether there are unique neuronal structures or activity patterns that can lead to awareness when they are superimposed on the complex necessary activity patterns of the whole brain, without insisting on rigorous criteria for sufficiency.

On the other hand, any hypothesis or theory that purports to be a scientific one should be amenable, at least in principle, to experimental test. Potentially, the tests should be able to produce a finding that could falsify the hypothesis. Otherwise, there is no way to eliminate the many explanations that may be 'compatible with' (that is, do not contradict) the available evidence. This issue is especially important in connection with theories of brain and conscious experience. Awareness is not accessible to an external observer, and it is easy to relapse into nontestable explanations. Many published theories are in that category; for example, one could cite among these the 'multiple drafts' theory (Dennett and Kinsbourne, 1992). Experimental designs that could test these theories are not available and have not been proposed.

Metabolic indices of sites

Increases in metabolic activity of cerebral neurons have been studied by measuring rates of local uptake of significant chemical participants (e.g. of glucose or oxygen) or by measuring changes in regional cerebral blood flow (rCBF). Changes in rCBF are thought to reflect changes in nearby neuronal activity that induce regional vasodilatations, at least partly via the action of increased CO_2 production on local vessels. An early study of rCBF responses to inputs in cats was carried out by Serota and Gerard (1938), using thermocouples implanted in the brain. Noninvasive studies of rCBF in human subjects were initiated by Ingvar and Lassen (see Ingvar and Phillipson, 1977), placing multiple scintillation counters on the head to detect radiations following a brief inhalation of a suitable radioactive gas or following intravascular injection of a radioactive agent. The variety of usable agents as well as the spatial and temporal resolution of the changes with activity were improved by the development of positron-emission-tomography (PET) and, more recently, by adaptations of magnetic resonance imaging (MRI) (see brief review by Posner, 1993). These techniques make it possible to study changes in local uptake and turnover of specific metabolic and pharmacological agents, as well as local changes in blood flow.

Our question here would be – what have or can such studies show us about the way cerebral activities are involved in conscious experience? First, an increase in metabolic rate may not tell us about specific changes of neuronal activities. Inhibitory processes are probably as much a part of a cerebral action as are excitatory ones. To the extent that increases in metabolic rate are a function of increased firing of impulses, an inhibitory process would tend to decrease metabolic rate; this could make a cerebral area falsely appear to be neutral if the decrease matched any excitatory increase. Indeed, synaptic events, especially metabotropic types, may contribute to the measured overall metabolic rate without any axonal firing. For example, some slow synaptic responses have been found to be mediated via an increased synthesis of cyclic adenosine monophosphate (AMP) or cyclic guanosine monophosphate (GMP) (see Libet 1992a); these compounds are well known as second messengers in cells and their syntheses are energy consuming. Second, although the spatial resolution in PET scans has been improving impressively, the time resolution is still far short of the millisecond ranges in which many neuronal activities proceed. For example, the supplementary motor area (SMA, in the anterior mesial neocortex) was found to exhibit a selective increase in blood flow when subjects merely imagined moving their fingers; but the temporal resolution of that measured change was not sufficient to say whether SMA increased its activity before or after the mental imagery began (this question was settled later with electrophysiological techniques, as discussed below; see Libet *et al.*, 1983; Libet, 1985). Third, the studies with PET and MRI can, at best, tell us *where* in the brain some activities have changed. But they do not describe the neuronal activity patterns that may be uniquely involved and certainly not the causal relationships between brain actions and conscious experience.

ARE THERE UNIQUE NEURONAL ACTIVITIES FOR CONSCIOUS EXPERIENCE?

This is meant to be a physiological rather than an anatomical question. That is, regardless of where the relevant cerebral sites are located, can one identify unique, specific kinds of neuronal activities that elicit a conscious experience? A related question – do all neocortical activities produce a conscious response? – has been answered in the negative by direct experimental evidence (Libet, 1973; Libet *et al.*, 1967, 1991).

The best experimental tools available for studies of this question have been electrophysiological, either recording the electrical changes manifested by neural activities or electrically stimulating neuronal groups so as to elicit or modify a conscious experience. These techniques give adequate time resolution and, under suitable conditions, can give highly localized spatial resolution. One should mention recent developments in the recording of the magnetic changes produced by neural activities, and also magneto-stimulation of brain tissue. Both magneto-techniques are noninvasive, with the appropriate devices placed on or near the scalp. Magneto-recording may develop into a good competitor of electrical recordings, as the sources of magnetic changes are easier to define and interpret. Magneto-stimulation thus far appears to have limited applicability, with problems of localizability, difficulty in supplying repetitive brief pulses and accompanying acoustic noise from the apparatus.

A great deal of information has been gained about neuronal activities that correlate with certain psychological states and cognitive responses. But relatively little can be regarded as giving valid answers to our question. For example, the EEG (electroencephalographic recordings of ongoing activities) exhibits a slowing from a dominant 10/sec rhythm to 1–2/sec, when a person goes from a waking state to deep sleep. This may suggest that the 10/sec rhythm represents neuronal activity related to the waking state of consciousness, but it does not in itself point to a unique role for the 10/sec rhythm in actually producing a conscious experience. Indeed, the resting 10/sec rhythm breaks up into higher frequency, low amplitude, irregular activity when a subject is made more attentive to a sensory signal, given a thought problem and so on. This 'arousal' EEG response (thought largely to reflect a desynchronization of the individual rhythms in a large group) might be getting us a bit closer to the mechanism for awareness, but again what we have is an observed correlation rather than a directly causal relationship. On the other hand, event-related potentials (ERPs), recorded in response to a sensory signal, do provide some direct correlates of conscious experience. The early components of ERPs represent neuronal responses that are a direct function of the stimulus parameters; i.e. they vary appropriately with changes in stimulus intensity, repetition, area, etc., but these neuronal actions are not sufficient for conscious experience (Libet *et al.*, 1967). The later components (beginning at 150 milliseconds (msec) or so after the signal) may vary considerably with changes in the subject's attention, mental tasks related to the stimulus and other cognitive processes. These later neuronal responses do appear to correlate with the ability to generate a conscious sensation but attempts to identify the specifically essential components have not been successful. The well-known P300 or P3 component is a surface positive electrical deflection that peaks at about 300 msec after an unusual sensory signal. With passive reception of a series of stimuli the P3 may be entirely absent. But if the subject is asked to note mentally the instances when the expected stimulus is omitted (in a rare and randomized fashion) from a series, a very large P3 usually appears in the computer-averaged tracing of the whole series. Does that mean that the P3 represents activity that elicits awareness of the signal? However, that proposal cannot explain why subjects were aware of a passively received series of signals with no mental task, in which virtually no P3 is present in the ERPs.

The fact is that sensory signals may be received and lead even to complicated behavioural responses without the subject's awareness of the signals (e.g. Velmans, 1991a; Libet *et al.*, 1991; Taylor and McCloskey, 1990). I repeat, the distinction between detection, evaluation, conation and behavioural responses for a sensory signal on the one hand, and conscious experience or awareness of the signal on the other, must be regularly applied to any study. Any study that attempts to address the cerebral basis of conscious experience should propose a question, hypothesis and experimental design that specifically deals with awareness and not simply with any cognitive or cognitive processes, no matter how complex these processes may be. Conversely, an awareness need not be complex; it can be as simple as the 'raw feel' of a weak stimulus to the skin.

CORRELATION VS. CAUSALITY: ELECTRICAL STIMULATION

In order to demonstrate causality rather than mere correlation between neural and conscious events one would like to be able to alter or manipulate each category of events in a controlled manner, to test predictions from hypotheses about the causal relationship. Operationally, the *conscious* side of the relationship can be manipulated by the subjects themselves on instruction; for example, subjects may be asked to perform a voluntary motor act at any time of their own choosing, while the investigator monitors related neural activities, etc. (see Libet *et al.*, 1983). Controlled manipulation of the *neural* side, so as to answer questions about how neuronal activity may become sufficient to elicit a conscious experience, is a much more difficult problem with human subjects. It can be achieved to a degree by controlling the stimulus input parameters, but the cerebral neural responses to such peripheral stimulus changes are not known in sufficient detail.

Electrical stimulation of the brain

Direct electrical stimulation of cerebral tissue provides one limited avenue for such causal investigations. Electrical stimuli can be used to manipulate neural activities directly in a spatially and temporally controlled manner, thereby testing causal predictions about the effects of such controlled alterations of activity. But one should immediately spell out the *limitations of electrical stimulation.*

Intracranial electrodes are invasive

Stimulation of neural elements in the cerebral cortex can be accomplished non-invasively, electrically with a contact on the scalp, or magnetically with a coil just above the scalp. But these methods are thus far only of very limited usefulness for various technical reasons; both are not sufficiently localizable or applicable to deep neural elements. More meaningful stimulation may be achieved by subdural or intracerebral electrodes. But this requires awake human subjects in whom the intracranial insertion of electrodes and the testing requirements of the study are compatible with their therapeutic procedures as well as with the patient's condition and informed consent. The electrical stimuli in the study must be applied with parameters that are innocuous and produce no irreversible effects. In our own studies of conscious experience, reported below, the stimuli were kept to very low, near threshold values by design, and have been found to produce undesirable results in none of the hundreds of patients studied.

Electrical stimulation vs. normal activities

Electrical stimuli do not duplicate the normal arrays of spatiotemporal patterns of activities in the neurons being stimulated. Electrical stimuli act primarily by exciting axons, which are electrically far more excitable than are dendrites and cell bodies. Such axons may elicit excitatory effects, inhibitory effects or both in the same postsynaptic elements; this may or may not be conducive to developing a functional response. It should not, therefore, be surprising that the ability of electrical stimulation to elicit observable behavioural or subjective responses is severely limited to the primary sensory and motor systems (with some exceptions; e.g. Penfield, 1958). The ability to elicit sensory or motor responses by stimulating these 'excitable' areas of the brain is perhaps due to the functionally direct input or output characteristics of such areas, when compared to the remaining vast areas of 'inexcitable' or 'silent' cortex. It should be noted, however, that neuronal elements in *all* areas of the brain can respond to electrical stimuli, even when no functionally organized response is elicited (see Libet, 1973). For example, an electrophysiological response, the 'direct cortical response' (DCR), is recordable near stimuli at all cortical areas. Moreover, electrical stimuli applied to virtually any cortical area can be utilized successfully to establish conditioned behavioural responses in cats and monkeys.

Disruption of normal functions

Electrical stimuli can interfere with or even suppress the normal function of a cortical area, presumably because they may modify or disrupt normal patterns of neuronal activities. However, this feature can actually be put to experimental use. For example, the ability to suppress or disrupt normal functions has been extensively employed by Ojemann (1982) to analyse anatomical and functional aspects of language representation in the cerebral cortex.

EXPERIMENTAL APPROACHES BY LIBET *ET AL.*

I shall now outline the way in which our own experimental approaches developed when attempting to answer questions about what kinds of neuronal activities produce conscious experience, and how these may differ from those neuronal activities that produce unconscious/nonconscious mental operations. My hope is that this will provide actual examples of how the issues discussed above could be dealt with in a manner that has produced interesting and meaningful results.

Beginning in the late 1950s, my neurosurgeon colleague, the late Bertram Feinstein, made available for possible study patients in whom electrodes were inserted intracranially for therapeutic purposes (see Libet *et al.*, 1964; Libet, 1973). The patients were awake at suitable times, they could report introspective experiences and they gave their informed consent to the virtually risk-free studies (as agreed to by an independent hospital committee for the protection of human subjects).

Electrode contacts were available in the primary somatosensory system, including the postcentral cortex. These made possible electrical stimulation and electrophysiological recording at these (and additional) sites, in relation to subjective reports of a very simple awareness which could be tested for reliability. In this approach we were in accord with the suggestion by Lord Adrian (1952) that

> there is reasonable hope that we may be able to sort out the particular activities which coincide with quite simple mental processes like seeing or hearing. At all events that is the first thing a physiologist must do if he is trying to find out

what happens when we think and how the mind is influenced by what goes on in the brain.

Another principle in our experimental approach was to limit the study to cerebral changes involved in the transition from below to just above threshold level of a conscious sensory experience; this would allow us to focus on neuronal processes that may be unique to eliciting conscious experience without attempting to deal with the whole complicated substratum of cerebral activities that form a necessary background permitting the finally unique step to become effective.

Minimum time for 'neuronal adequacy'

Our initial question was of a classical physiological nature: when stimulating the sensory cortex are any of the stimulus parameters especially or uniquely significant for eliciting a threshold sensory experience? The answer might give us some idea of what neuronal activations are required at this neocortical level, bypassing the various changes normally imposed by the subcortical systems on the transmission of the message from the skin to the cortex. The most striking finding was the requirement of a surprisingly long train duration (about 500 msec) of the repetitive pulses at liminal intensity. The full relation, between the intensity (peak current) and the train duration (of the repetitive stimulus pulses) that gave a just threshold sensory experience, is seen in Figure 5.1. At the liminal intensity, all train durations were effective down to about half a second. Below half a second the required intensity began to rise rather steeply.

Do subcortical sites in the ascending somatosensory pathways also exhibit this temporal requirement? We found that stimulation in the ventrobasal thalamus and the medial lemniscus had the same requirements. However, a single pulse was sufficient in dorsal columns (spinal cord) and, as is well known, also at the skin or over a peripheral sensory nerve.

Cerebral delay with normal sensory input

Does a normal threshold sensory input (a single pulse at the skin) also require an elaboration of *cerebral* activities that persist for up to about half a second, before these activities become 'neuronally adequate' to elicit a conscious sensory experience? Answers to this question required more indirect approaches. It was already well known that a single peripheral pulse could elicit a series of cortical potentials lasting half a second and longer. What do these ERPs, recorded in the cerebral cortex in response to single pulses to the skin, tell us about the issue? We found that the early components of an ERP are neither necessary nor sufficient for the production of a sensory experience; the latter only appeared when later components were present, although we did not try to establish which component might be uniquely involved (Libet *et al.*, 1967, 1975). When late components are depressed, as by some drugs (e.g. atropine) or in general anaesthesia, conscious

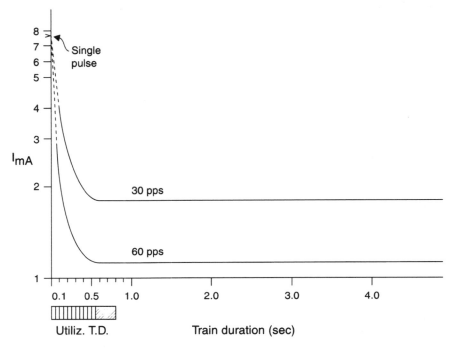

Figure 5.1 Temporal requirement for stimulation of the somatosensory (SI) cortex in human subjects. The curves are schematic representations of measurements in five different individuals, which were not sufficient in each case to produce a full curve individually. Each point on a curve indicates the combination of intensity (I) and train duration (TD) for repetitive pulses that is just adequate to elicit a threshold conscious sensory experience. Separate curves are shown for stimulation at 30 pulses per second (pps) and 60 pps. At the liminal I (below which no sensation was elicited even with long TDs), a similar minimum TD of about 600 msec ±100 msec was required for either pulse frequency. Such values for this 'utilization TD' have since been confirmed in many ambulatory subjects with electrodes chronically implanted over SI cortex and in the ventrobasal thalamus

Source: Libet, 1973: 86

sensory experiences are also depressed or lost. Another approach employed dealt with 'retroactive masking/inhibition', a phenomenon well known to psychologists. In that phenomenon, a second but stronger and spatially larger stimulus could eliminate the reportable awareness of a *preceding* relatively weak stimulus (e.g. Raab, 1963). Interstimulus intervals of up to about 100 msec (in some cases, 200 msec) were found to be effective. Such findings with two peripheral sensory stimuli are explainable by our hypothesis; the second or delayed stimulus can modify the sensory experience elicited by the first stimulus during the roughly half-second interval in which neuronal adequacy for the experience is developing. There are, of course, alternative possible explanations, as there are for any set of observations. One such was proposed by Dennett and Kinsbourne (1992), and holds that the conscious experience actually appears without appreciable delay but that the memory of it must be developed during the half second or so of subsequent cerebral activity; in such a case, the retroactive masking effect is due to an interference, by the second, delayed stimulus with the formation of the memory. I have given experimental reasons for regarding this Dennett hypothesis as improbable and much less tenable than our hypothesis (Libet, 1992b, 1993a; see also Velmans, 1993a, 1993b); one of these reasons involves our finding of a retroactive effect in which there is modulation of the experience with no loss of memory, that of retroactive enhancement (as described below).

With a first weak stimulus applied to the skin and a second suprathreshold stimulus applied to the somatosensory (SI) cortex, we were able to obtain retroactive effects with intervals of up to 500 msec or more between these two stimuli. With a large cortical electrode (10mm disc) we obtained mostly retroactive masking (Libet et al., 1973). With a small wire contact (1 mm) we obtained retroactive enhancement (Libet et al., 1992). In these tests a weak skin stimulus (S_1) was followed after five seconds by a second skin stimulus (S_2) identical to S_1. In about two-thirds of the trials the subjects reported that the subjective or felt intensity of S_2 was the same as for S_1; S_2 felt stronger in about one-sixth of the trials and weaker in about another sixth. However, when a stimulus train of pulses was applied to the SI cortex so as to begin up to 400 msec after S_2, the subjects reported S_2 as stronger than S_1 in about two-thirds of such trials. An excess of such reports (above the control level, with no SI train) was observed with intervals of 500 msec or more between S_2 and the onset of the SI train. Clearly, a delayed input could modulate the subjective content of a previous signal when applied during the half second or so of putative time for the sensory experience of that previous signal to develop. When such a modulation consists of an enhanced subjective intensity of that experience, the argument that the later stimulus disrupts the memory of the earlier stimulus becomes irrelevant.

Subjective referral backwards in time

If a substantial *neuronal* delay is required before achieving a sensory experience or awareness, is there a corresponding delay in the *subjective* timing of the experience? One cannot answer this question solely from the neural knowledge available. In fact, an experimental test of this question indicated that there is no appreciable delay for the subjective timing of a normally arriving sensory input, as illustrated in Figure 5.2 (Libet et al., 1979). In that test a train of liminal intensity pulses applied to SI cortex required about 500 msec of train duration to elicit any conscious sensation. If a threshold single pulse applied to the skin were also to require about 500 msec of cortical activity before that sensory experience could appear, then the subject should have reported that the sensation elicited by

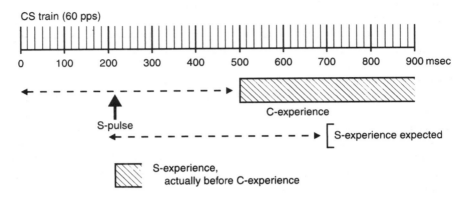

Figure 5.2 Diagram of an experiment on the subjective time order of two sensory experiences, one elicited by a stimulus train to the SI cortex (labelled CS) and the other by a threshold pulse to skin (S). CS consisted of repetitive pulses (at 60/sec) applied to the postcentral gyrus, at the lowest (liminal) peak current sufficient to elicit any reportable conscious sensory experience. The sensory experience for CS ('C-experience') would not be initiated before the end of the utilization-train duration (average about 500 msec), but then proceeds without change in its weak subjective intensity for the remainder of the applied liminal CS train (see Libet *et al.*, 1964; Libet, 1966, 1973). The S-pulse, at just above threshold strength for eliciting conscious sensory experience, is here shown delivered when the initial 200 msec of the CS train have elapsed (in other experiments, it was applied at other relative times, earlier and later). If S were followed by a roughly similar delay of 500 msec of cortical activity before 'neuronal adequacy' is achieved, initiation of S-experience might have also been expected to be delayed until 700 msec of CS had elapsed. In fact, S-experience was reported to appear subjectively before C-experience.

For the test of the subjective antedating hypothesis, the stimulus train was applied to the medial lemniscus (LM) instead of to somatosensory cortex ('CS' in the figure). The sensation elicited by the LM stimuli was reported to begin *before* that from S, in this sequence; this occurred in spite of the empirically demonstrated requirement that the stimulus train in LM must persist for 500 msec here in order to elicit any sensation (see text)

Source: Libet *et al.*, 1979: 170, by permission of *Brain*.

the cortical stimulus began before that produced by the skin pulse (when the latter was delivered 200 msec after the onset of the cortical train). In fact the subjects reported the skin pulse sensation appeared before the cortically induced one. That finding produced the paradoxical situation of, on the one hand, good evidence for up to a half-second delay required to achieve neuronal adequacy to produce the skin sensation and, on the other, the subject reporting that the skin sensation appeared with essentially no delay. After some considerable flailing about, both intellectually and experimentally, we realized that the timing reported for the subjective experience and that for neuronal adequacy need not be the same. We also realized that both timings appeared to be the same for the sensation elicited by a cortical stimulus but not for one elicited by a skin stimulus; a possible explanation for that difference (between cortical and skin stimuli) lay in the absence of a primary evoked potential in the response of the cortex to each stimulus pulse applied to the postcentral gyrus (SI cortex), in contrast to its presence with a skin pulse. All that led to the following hypothesis, in two parts (see Figure 5.3). First, some neuronal process associated with the early or primary evoked response serves as a 'time-marker'. Second, there is an automatic subjective referral of the conscious experience backwards in time to that time-marker, from the delayed time at which the neuronal state becomes adequate to produce the experience. The experience would thus appear subjectively to occur as if there were no significant delay. Fortunately, we were able to devise a crucial test of this hypothesis, one that could potentially falsify it.

The test was based on the nature of the responses to stimuli in either the ventrobasal thalamus (VB) or the medial lemniscus (LM). At both sites, effective near-threshold stimuli required the same train durations to produce a conscious sensory experience (up to about half a second) as for stimuli applied to the SI cortex. But, unlike the SI cortex, each single pulse in VB or LM should elicit the same putative timing signal (the primary evoked potential) as does the single skin pulse. Consequently, the subjective antedating hypothesis led to a startling prediction: the subjective timing of a sensory experience elicited by a stimulus train in LM (or VB) should be essentially similar to that for a skin pulse, in spite of the experimental fact that the LM stimulus does not become adequate to produce a sensation until the end of the minimum required train duration. This prediction was experimentally tested and was essentially borne out (Libet *et al.*, 1979), using patients with electrodes permanently implanted in LM to treat intractable pain (see Figure 5.3).

How does the brain distinguish unconscious from conscious mental functions?

One possibility suggested itself from our evidence that a minimum activity time is required to produce a conscious experience, whether the experience is exogenous (sensory) or endogenous (conscious intention to act voluntarily). It seemed attractive to hypothesize that neuronal activation times to produce an unconscious mental function could be less than those for a conscious one, and that the transition from an unconscious to a conscious function could be controlled simply by an adequately increased duration of the appropriate neuronal activity. I have called this hypothesis the *'time-on' theory*.

Again, it was important to carry out at least one convincing and direct experimental test of a general prediction of this theory. The availability of patients with electrodes permanently implanted in the ventrobasal thalamus made such a test possible (Libet *et al.*, 1991). As noted, stimuli in VB require up to about 500 msec of repetitive pulses to elicit a near-threshold conscious sensory experience (usually a

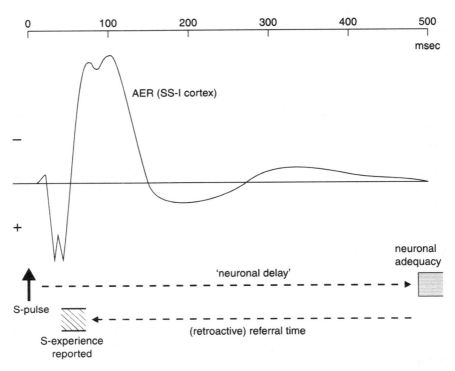

Figure 5.3 Diagram of hypothesis for subjective referral of sensory experience backwards in time. The average evoked response (AER) based on 256 averaged responses delivered at 1/sec, recorded at the somatosensory cortex (labelled SS-I here), was evoked by pulses just suprathreshold for sensation and delivered to the skin of the contralateral hand. Below the AER, the first line shows the approximate delay in achieving the stage of neuronal adequacy that appears (on the basis of other evidence) to be necessary for eliciting the sensory experience. The lower line shows the postulated retroactive referral of the subjective timing of the experience, from the time of neuronal adequacy backwards to some time associated with the primary surface-positive component of the evoked potential. The primary component of the AER is relatively highly localized to an area on the contralateral postcentral gyrus in these awake human subjects. The secondary or later components, especially those following the surface-negative component after the initial 100 to 150 ms of the AER, are more widely distributed over the cortex and more variable in form, even when recorded subdurally (see, for example, Libet *et al.*, 1975). This diagram is not meant to indicate that the state of neuronal adequacy for eliciting conscious sensation is restricted to neurons in the primary SS-I cortex of postcentral gyrus; on the other hand, the primary component or 'timing signal' for retroactive referral of the sensory experience is more closely restricted to this SS-I cortical area

Source: Libet *et al.*, 1979: 172, by permission of *Brain*

paraesthesia, like tingling or pins-and-needles felt in a specific part of the body). The train durations could be varied randomly among stimuli so as to include brief trains (of 0 to 250 msec durations), expected to produce no awareness, and longer trains (of 300 to 750 msec), many of which should be sufficient for awareness. Subjects reported their level of awareness after each trial. To demonstrate that a possible unconscious (nonconscious) mental event occurred, each stimulus was delivered during one of two lighted intervals (L_1 and L_2) and subjects were asked to make a forced choice as to whether a stimulus was present in L_1 or in L_2, regardless of whether they felt or were aware of any sensation from it. To show that detection had occurred the correct choices would have to exceed the 50 per cent correct choices expected by chance alone. Statistical analysis of the thousands of tests in nine suitable subjects showed, first, that correct detection of the stimulus in L_1 vs. L_2 occurred even when subjects were completely unaware of any sensation and were guessing. With train durations less than 150 msec there were correct answers in 57 per cent of the trials; i.e. for the 50 per cent incorrect choices expected by chance there was actually a 14 per cent probability of a correct choice, with strong significance. Correct choices increased with longer trains that produced no awareness; for example, with durations of 150 to 260 msec there were correct choices in 75 per cent of trials, giving a probability of 50 per cent correct for otherwise expected incorrect responses. The second finding was that to go from being correct-without-awareness to correct-with-awareness (i.e. to an awareness of the most minimal and uncertain kind) required, on average, an *additional* stimulus duration of 375 msec.[1]

Further fundamental implications of 'time-on' theory are discussed in Libet, 1989, 1992c, 1993b.

Is there a neural delay for an endogenous conscious experience, as exemplified by voluntary actions?

One type of endogenous conscious event that could be accessible to experimental study of the question is the self-initiation of a fully voluntary act. It had been shown (Kornhuber and Deecke, 1965, and many others thereafter) that a slow negative potential, the 'readiness potential' (RP), is recordable on the scalp at the vertex, with an onset of about one second before a 'self-paced' voluntary act. This 'readiness potential' indicated that cerebral processes specifically related to these voluntary acts begin well before the final cerebral commands to the moto-neurons for action. My question then became – when is the subject aware of his/her intention to act, in relation to the onset of RP and to the expression of the voluntary process by the muscles (as seen in the recorded electromyogram, EMG)?

Because of our focus on a fully endogenous mental event we altered the conditions of the original RP studies (Libet *et al.*, 1982, 1983) so as to virtually eliminate the possibility of external cues or limitations which were prevalent in the other RP studies of self-paced movements. Our subjects were free to perform a quick flexion of wrist and fingers at any time of their own spontaneous wish to do so, or not to perform the act at all if they felt so inclined in any given time period. Even under these conditions subjects reported after a series of some forty trials that they had 'preplanned' to act within the next second or so. In those series the RPs began more than one second before the EMG and resembled the RPs reported by others for 'self-paced' actions; these RPs were labelled 'RPI' by us. In most series the subjects reported no preplanning in any of the forty trials; the average RP in these series ('RPII') had an average onset of about −550 msec, i.e. 550 msec before the muscle EMG appeared.

Measurement of the time (W) at which a subject is first aware of the intention or wish to perform the voluntary act seemed initially to be a hopeless goal, since it had to rely on an introspective report of that timing. However, I hit on the possibility that the subject could monitor the 'clock-time' associated with that awareness but report that clock-time later, after the voluntary act had taken place. The clock was a moving spot on a cathode ray oscilloscope, circling the periphery of the face like the sweep-second hand of a real clock but doing so in 2.56 seconds rather than the usual 60 seconds. We developed a test of the accuracy of such a report that showed the latter was only about 50 msec off. In that test the subject was given a weak stimulus to the hand, at random times on the 'clock', while he/she was relaxed and not moving; the subject then reported the clock position at the time the skin stimulus was felt. Also, the reliability of the W reports turned out to be surprisingly acceptable (± 20 msec SE for each set of 40 Ws in each series of 40 voluntary acts; see Libet et al., 1983).

Timings of brain activity and conscious intention

The resultant average timings found for the onset of RPII and of W were −550 and −200 msec, respectively (see Figure 5.4). These results led to the following experimental conclusions. First, development of the *awareness* of the intention or wish 'to act now' required a substantial duration of cerebral activity (350 msec or more); this is in accord with the postulated neural delay for an endogenous conscious event. Second, *initiation* of the voluntary process is developed unconsciously, well before there is any awareness of intention to act. Third, although a cerebral volitional process begins substantially before the awareness W, W nevertheless does appear 150 to 200 msec before the final motor act. This third observation is important in that it leaves open a potential role for the conscious process in the volitional outcome. The interval between W and EMG provides time in which the conscious process could interfere with or 'veto' the consummation of the voluntary act. Since the motor cortex begins to fire commands to the lower motoneurons at about −50 msec, there is at least 100 msec during which activation of the motor cortex could be interfered with or blocked. We were able to demonstrate that a conscious veto can be effectively introduced by the subject in the 100 to 200 msec period before the prearranged time for a motor act to be performed. It has been argued that the appearance of the conscious veto would itself require a prior period of unconscious neural development, just as for conscious intention; in such a case even this conscious control event would have an unconscious initiating process (Doty, 1985; Velmans, 1993a). However, conscious control of an event appears here after awareness of the impending voluntary action has developed. Conscious control is not a new awareness; it serves to impose a change on the volitional process and it may not be subject to the requirement of a preceding unconscious cerebral process found for awareness. In such a view, a potential role for free will would remain viable in the conscious control, though not in the initiation, of a voluntary act. These findings taken together have a fundamental bearing on the issues of voluntary action, free will and individual responsibility for conscious urges and actions (see Libet, 1985, 1992c).

OTHER PHILOSOPHICAL ISSUES FOR POSSIBLE EXPERIMENTAL STUDY

One of the most mysterious and seemingly intractable problems in the mind–brain relationship is that of the *unitary and integrated nature of conscious experience* (issue A). This phenomenon is somehow a product of a brain with an estimated 100 billion neurons, each of which may have thousands of inter-

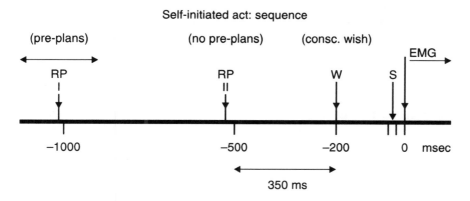

Figure 5.4 Diagram of sequence of events, cerebral and subjective, that precede a fully self-initiated voluntary act. Relative to 0 time, detected in the electromyogram (EMG) of the suddenly activated muscle, the readiness potential (RP) (an indicator of related cerebral neuronal activities) begins first, at about –1050 ms when some preplanning is reported (RP I), or about –550 ms with spontaneous acts lacking immediate preplanning (RP II). Subjective awareness of the wish to move (W) appears at about –200 ms, some 350 ms after the onset even of RP II but well before the act (EMG). Subjective timings reported for awareness of the randomly delivered S (skin) stimulus average about –50 ms relative to actual delivery time

Source: Libet, 1989: 333, by permission of Cambridge University Press

connections with other neurons. There is increasing evidence that many functions of the cerebral cortex are localized, apparently organized into specialized columns of neurons. In spite of the enormously complex array of structures and functions, whatever does reach awareness is experienced as unified and integrated. A second apparently intractable question is issue B – *can the conscious mental process actually influence or control some activities of the cerebral neurons?* (See the introductory page of this chapter.)

Both of these issues have been the subjects of many philosophical analyses and proposals since Descartes and earlier, but this is not the place to review all that. Rather, our approach as scientific investigators should be to inquire whether experimentally testable hypotheses can be generated in attempting to deal with these two issues. On issue A, Eccles (Popper and Eccles, 1977: 362) has proposed, based on a dualist–interactionist view, that 'the experienced unity comes not from a neurophysiological synthesis but from the proposed integrating character of the self-conscious mind'. This view had, in principle, been expressed by Sherrington (1940), and also by Sperry (1952, 1980) and Doty (1984). For Sperry and Doty, however, the mind doing the integrating was viewed in monistic terms, as an emergent property of brain processes. On issue B, both Eccles and Sperry have proposed that the 'mental sphere' could influence neuronal function, but in dualistic vs. monistic terms, respectively. The view held probably by most neuroscientists (and perhaps modern philosophers) is a monist–deterministic one, in which conscious mental experience is simply an 'inner aspect' of brain function (identity theory); it is fully determined by knowable physicochemical processes in the brain, and its apparent ability to influence brain function is a subjective illusion with no actual causal powers. All of these views are in fact philosophical theories. Although each has explanatory power and each can be shown to be compatible with (not falsified by) the available evidence, none has been subjected to appropriate or adequate experimental testing in a format that could potentially falsify it.

A recent neurophysiological observation may offer one possible route to investigating issue A, i.e. experiential integration or, as it is often referred to, the 'binding problem'. This is the discovery of widespread synchronization of oscillatory neuronal electrical potentials in response to a visual image (Gray and Singer, 1989; Singer, 1990). It has led to some speculation that a 'correlation' model (based on the widely occurring synchronization of some activities) might represent the neural coding for a unified mental image in an otherwise chaotic background. This speculation is still to be tested. I would, however, note that any experimental test should be careful to distinguish between 'binding' at a cognitive level (that may or may not involve conscious experience) and the binding that refers to unity experienced in awareness. A meaningful response to a visual image that contains forms, colours, shades of intensity, etc. requires an integration of these properties for either kind of binding, with or without awareness. A test for cognitive binding using a behavioural response in a monkey may not distinguish conscious from unconscious mental functions.

I have recently proposed that we may view subjective experience as if it were a field, produced by appropriate though multifarious neuronal activities of the brain. This conscious mental field would have the attribute of a unitary, integrated experience or awareness, and it would also have a causal ability to affect or alter neuronal function. The arguments in support of this theoretical field approach to the problem of experiential unity are beyond the scope of the present chapter. Details of the theory, along with a suggested experimental test of it, are given in Libet (1993b, 1994). The point of mentioning this field theory here is simply to note that it is possible to formulate a theory and design an experimental test of it even when the theory deals with the profound issues of conscious unity and with the question of whether the conscious function can actually influence brain function.

NOTE

1 (a) A statistical model produced the mean train duration for all trials in which there was correct detection but no awareness at all; this was compared (b) to the mean train duration for all trials in which there was both correct detection *and* awareness (of something, i.e. at the uncertain level of awareness). Note that responses in both groups were all correct, with only the minimal, uncertain awareness added in group (b). The mean train duration in group (b) was 375 msec greater than that in group (a). This additional value of 375 msec (required to bring in awareness) was equal to twelve times its own standard error (SE). Such a relation of a measured quantity to its SE is termed z; a value of 12 for z indicates a very high significance for the 375 msec difference between train durations in group (a) and those in group (b).

REFERENCES

Adrian, E.D. (1952) 'What happens when we think', in P. Laslett (ed.) *The Physical Basis of Mind*, Oxford: Blackwell.

Bremer, F. (1937) 'L'activité cérébrale au cours du sommeil et de la narcose. Contribution a l'étude du mécanisme du sommeil', *Bullétin de Académie Royale Médecin Belgique* 2: 68–86.

Dennett, D.C. and Kinsbourne, M. (1992) 'Time and the observer: the where and when of consciousness in the brain', *Behavioral and Brain Sciences* 15: 183–201.

Doty, R.W. (1984) 'Some thoughts and some experiments on memory', in L.R. Squire and N. Butters (eds) *Neuropsychology of Memory*, New York: Guilford.

—— (1985) 'The time course of conscious processing: vetoes by the uninformed?', *Behavioral and Brain Sciences* 8: 541–542.

Gazzaniga, M.S. (1993) 'Brain mechanisms and conscious experience' in Ciba Foundation Symposium 174, *Experimental and Theoretical Studies of Consciousness*, Chichester: Wiley.

Gray, C.M. and Singer, W. (1989) 'Stimulus-specific neuronal oscillations in orientation columns of cat visual cortex', *Proceedings of the National Academy of Science USA* 86: 1698–1702.

Ingvar, D. and Phillipson, L. (1977) 'Distributions of cerebral blood flow in the dominant hemisphere during motor ideation and motor performance', *Annuals of Neurology* 2: 230–237.

Kornhuber, H. and Deecke, L. (1965) 'Hirnpotentialänderungen bei Willkürbewegungen und passiven Bewegungen des Menschen: Bereitschaftspotential und reafferente Potentiale', *Pflügers Archiv für die gesamte Physiologie des Menschen und Tiere* 284: 1–17.

Libet, B. (1966) 'Brain stimulation and the threshold of conscious experience', in J.C. Eccles (ed.) *Brain and Conscious Experience*, Berlin: Springer-Verlag.

—— (1973) 'Electrical stimulation of cortex in human subjects, and conscious sensory aspects', in A. Iggo (ed.) *Handbook of Sensory Physiology*, vol. 2: *Somatosensory System*, New York: Springer-Verlag.

—— (1985) 'Unconscious cerebral initiative and the role of conscious will in voluntary action', *Behavioral and Brain Sciences* 8: 529–566.

—— (1987) 'Consciousness: conscious subjective experience', in G. Adelman (ed.) *Encyclopedia of Neuroscience*, Boston, MA: Birkhauser.

—— (1989) 'Conscious subjective experience vs. unconscious mental functions: a theory of the cerebral processes involved', in R.M.J. Cotterill (ed.) *Models of Brain Function*, Cambridge: Cambridge University Press.

—— (1992a) 'Introduction to slow synaptic potentials and their neuromodulation by dopamine', *Canadian Journal of Physiology and Pharmacology* 70: S3–S11.

—— (1992b) 'Models of conscious timing and the experimental evidence', *Behavioral and Brain Sciences* 15: 213–215.

—— (1992c) 'The neural time-factor in perception, volition and free will', *Revue de métaphysique et de morale* 97(2): 255–272.

—— (1993a) 'The neural time factor in conscious and unconscious events', in Ciba Foundation Symposium 174, *Experimental and Theoretical Studies of Consciousness*, Chichester: Wiley.

—— (1993b) *Neurophysiology of Consciousness*, Boston, MA: Birkhauser.

—— (1994) 'A testable field theory of mind–brain interaction', *Journal of Consciousness Studies* 1: 119–126.

Libet, B., Alberts, W.W., Wright, E.W., Delattre, L., Levin, G. and Feinstein, B. (1964) 'Production of threshold levels of conscious sensation by electrical stimulation of human somatosensory cortex', *Journal of Neurophysiology* 27: 546–578.

Libet, B., Alberts, W.W., Wright, E.W. and Feinstein, B. (1967) 'Responses of human somatosensory cortex to stimuli below threshold for conscious sensation', *Science* 158: 1597–1600.

Libet, B., Alberts, W.W., Wright, E.W., Lewis, M. and Feinstein, B. (1975) 'Cortical representation of evoked potentials relative to conscious sensory responses and of somatosensory qualities in man', in H.H. Kornhuber (ed.) *The Somatosensory System*, Stuttgart: Thieme Verlag.

Libet, B., Gleason, C.A., Wright, E.W. and Pearl D.K. (1983) 'Time of conscious intention to act in relation to onset of cerebral activities (readiness-potential); the unconscious initiation of a freely voluntary act', *Brain* 106: 623–642.

Libet, B., Pearl, D.K., Morledge, D.M., Gleason, C.A., Hosobuchi, Y. and Barbaro, N.M. (1991) 'Control of the transition from sensory detection to sensory awareness in man by the duration of a thalamic stimulus. The cerebral time-on factor', *Brain* 114: 1731–1757.

Libet, B., Wright, E.W. Jr., Feinstein, B. and Pearl, D.K. (1979) 'Subjective referral of the timing for a conscious sensory experience: a functional role for the somatosensory specific projection system in man', *Brain* 102: 191–222.

Libet, B., Wright, E.W., Feinstein, B. and Pearl, D.K. (1992) 'Retroactive enhancement of a skin sensation by a delayed cortical stimulus in man: evidence for delay of a conscious experience', *Consciousness and Cognition* 1: 367–375.

Libet, B., Wright, E.W. and Gleason, C.A. (1982) 'Readiness-potentials preceding unrestricted "spontaneous" vs. pre-planned voluntary acts', *Electroencephalography and Clinical Neurophysiology* 54: 322–335.

Moruzzi, G. and Magoun, H.W. (1949) 'Brain stem reticular formation and activation of the EEG', *Electroencephalography and Clinical Neurophysiology* 1: 455–473.

Nagel, T. (1979) *Mortal Questions*, Cambridge: Cambridge University Press.

Ojemann, G.A. (1982) 'Models of the brain organization for higher integrative functions derived with electrical stimulation techniques', *Human Neurobiology* 1: 243-299.

Penfield, W. (1958) The *Excitable Cortex in Conscious Man*, Liverpool: Liverpool University Press.

Popper, K.R. and Eccles, J.C. (1977) *The Self and its Brain*, Heidelberg: Springer.

Posner, M. (1993) 'Seeing the mind', *Science* 262: 673–674.

Raab, D.H. (1963) 'Backward masking', *Psychological Bulletin* 60: 118–129.

Serota, H.M. and Gerard, R.W. (1938) 'Localized thermal changes in the cat's brain', *Journal of Neurophysiology* 1: 115–124.

Sherrington, C.S. (1940) *Man on his Nature*, Cambridge: Cambridge University Press.

Singer, W. (1990) 'Search for coherence: a basic principle of cortical self-organization', *Concepts in Neuroscience* 1: 1–26.

Sperry, R.W. (1952) 'Neurology and the mind–brain problem', *American Scientist* 40: 291-312.

—— (1980) 'Mind–brain interaction: mentalism yes; dualism no', Neuroscience 5: 195–206.

—— (1985) *Science and Moral Priority*, Westport, CN: Praeger.

Sperry, R.W., Gazzaniga, M.S. and Bogen, J.E. (1969) 'Interhemispheric relationships: the neocortical commissures: syndromes of hemisphere disconnection', in P.J. Vinken and G.W. Bruyn (eds) *Handbook of Clinical Neurology*, vol. 4, Amsterdam: North Holland.

Taylor, J.L. and McCloskey, D.I. (1990) 'Triggering of pre-programmed movements as reactions to masked stimuli', *Journal of Neurophysiology* 63: 439–446.

Velmans, M. (1991a) 'Is human information processing conscious?', *Behavioral and Brain Sciences* 14: 651–669.

—— (1991b) 'Consciousness from a first-person perspective', *Behavioral and Brain Sciences* 14(4): 702–726.

—— (1993a) 'Discussion' in Ciba Foundation Symposium 174, *Experimental and Theoretical Studies of Consciousness*, Chichester: Wiley.

—— (1993b) 'Consciousness, causality and complementarity', *Behavioral and Brain Sciences* 16(2): 409–416.

Chapter 6

Dissociable aspects of consciousness

Andrew W. Young

'Where am I?' A question repeated in a thousand B-movies, as our hero comes round, rubbing the back of his head where the bad guy slugged him with the butt of his revolver. The scene works because all of us know that loss of consciousness is a common consequence of closed head injury. The disorientation and the inevitable follow-up, 'What happened?', show that the scriptwriters knew a few clichés about post-traumatic amnesia too.

In neurological clinics, the durations of unconsciousness and post-traumatic amnesia are recognized as useful pointers to the severity of the underlying brain injury. In addition, doctors have developed guidelines for assessing a patient's level of consciousness at any given time. The most widely adopted terminology distinguishes different overall impairments ranging from delirium via stupor and coma to vegetative state (Bates and Cartlidge, 1994). Formal assessments are often based on the Glasgow Coma Scale (Teasdale and Jennett, 1974), which looks separately at three easily determined behavioural indices; eye opening, verbal responses and motor responses. Each of these is rated on a scale measuring an increasing degree of dysfunction; for example, eye opening may occur spontaneously, in response to speech, in response to pain, or not at all. The advantage of this scale is that it covers a wide range, from full consciousness to deep coma, simply and reliably. However, even in patients who are obviously awake, significant disorientation or other cognitive changes can be observed. A quick evaluation of the cognitive status of patients who are clearly awake can be achieved with the Mini-Mental State examination (Folstein *et al.*, 1975).

The idea of levels of consciousness is easy to grasp because we are all used to being awake, drowsy or asleep. Wakefulness and arousal are influenced by the brain stem reticular formation, and especially noradrenergic neurons in the locus coeruleus (Carlson, 1991). To keep us awake, neurotransmitters are sprinkled into the synapses of huge numbers of neurons in the cerebral cortex by ascending pathways with very widespread projections. Going to sleep involves a set of physiological changes which need to be properly coordinated with each other. In some sleep disorders the relevant processes get out of step, as in cataplexy, which can make an awake person wilt and fall to the ground for a few minutes when the inhibition of motor neurons that should be part of deep sleep occurs during the day.

Such facts make it abundantly clear that consciousness is a product of brain activity. However, we also know that consciousness is not a direct result of *any* neuronal activity, because there are plenty of things the neurons in our central nervous systems do of which we are not aware, like adjusting the size of the eye's pupil to the prevailing illumination, or which carry on automatically but can be subject to occasional conscious intervention, like breathing. In general, these automatic activities do not require the activity of neurons in the cerebral cortex. Even for the cerebral cortex, though, neuronal activity is not in itself sufficient to produce consciousness; studies of the brain's electrical activity show that when we are in deep sleep, cortical neurons still do *something*, but that something is different from how they function when we are awake (Carlson, 1991).

Two points stand out from this brief introduction. First, consciousness is not an all or none phenomenon; we must be able to account for different forms or levels of consciousness. Second, the transition from unconsciousness to consciousness is, in neural terms, more than simply a change from neuronal inactivity to neuronal activity; it is as much a change in what the neurons are doing.

A third point has been more difficult to establish, but dominates recent neuropsychological investigations of consciousness. This is that, although changes in level of consciousness are commonly observed after brain injury, one can also find changes that selectively affect different aspects of consciousness. Investigations of these impairments show that consciousness does not equate with the integrated functioning of the whole brain; instead, it can be affected in different ways by injuries to different parts of the brain. In this chapter, I will discuss illustrative examples and examine the conclusions that follow.

THE SPLIT-BRAIN CASES

The brain's cerebral cortex consists of left and right hemispheres which are linked by nerve tracts known as the cerebral commissures; of these, the corpus callosum is the most extensive, and there is a much smaller anterior commissure. Operations which involve severing one or both of these commissures, with the intention of relieving otherwise intractable epileptic seizures, have been reported since the 1940s; this is now known as the split-brain operation. The findings and implications of this operation have been widely discussed in many scientific papers, in textbooks and in the popular press. Some of these discussions have been speculative and even misleading, but an accessible and balanced introduction to the area can be found in Springer and Deutsch (1993), while Farthing (1992) gives a detailed discussion of issues concerning consciousness and the split brain. I will only summarize some of the key points here.

Initial findings from the 1940s series of patients revealed little in the way of overall changes in perceptual, intellectual and motor abilities after the operation. However, ingenious testing methods introduced with the series of operations begun in the 1960s produced dramatic results. These new testing procedures depended upon the fact that, broadly speaking, each cerebral hemisphere receives input from the opposite side of space and controls fine movements of the opposite side of the body. In the case of vision, for example, the optic nerve fibres coming from the retina at the back of each eye divide, so that stimuli falling to the left of the point of fixation are projected to the visual cortex of the right cerebral hemisphere, and stimuli falling to the right of fixation are projected to the visual cortex of the left cerebral hemisphere. With the cerebral commissures severed, information about what each hemisphere sees cannot then be relayed to the other hemisphere, at least at cortical level. By presenting stimuli left or right of fixation to a split-brain patient, one is then in principle able to test each hemisphere's independent functional capabilities. This procedure was initially limited by the need to keep presentation times sufficiently brief to prevent the eye movements which would allow both hemispheres to see what had been presented, but later work has also incorporated techniques that can allow prolonged lateralized input.

Split-brain research has persistently shown that almost all verbal reports originate from the left hemisphere. Thus an object presented in a split-brain patient's right visual field (i.e. right of fixation), and hence to the left cerebral hemisphere, is readily named, but the same object cannot be named if it is presented in the left visual field. This left hemisphere dominance for speech had been known since the nineteenth century. What was much more interesting were findings that although the split-brain patients' right hemispheres were mostly mute, they were certainly not blind. For example, patients could point to an object that had been presented in the left visual field, if allowed to use the left hand for the response. Here, the right hemisphere is able to demonstrate nonverbally what it has seen, since it has primary control of fine motor movements of the left hand. Similarly, if an object (such as a spoon or a brush) had been felt behind a screen using the left hand, it could not be named, yet the patient could show by moving the left hand how he or she would use it. Notice in both examples that although the right hemisphere is mute in terms of its ability to produce speech, it seems to show at least some rudimentary language comprehension, since left hand responses have been made to simple instructions.

Although the split-brain results are intriguing, there are several reasons why they must be treated with caution. One concerns the possibility of cross-cueing. For example, if the patient were to make slight left hand brushing movements when a picture of a brush was presented in the left visual field (i.e. to the right hemisphere), this might give the left hemisphere a cue to the object's possible identity, allowing a verbal guess. Such strategies can become quite subtle, and care is needed to exclude them wherever possible.

More serious problems centre on the fact that the split-brain operation is carried out to relieve otherwise intractable epilepsy; all of the patients therefore have longstanding neurological disorders, and some have additional damage from head injuries sustained during fits. This problem is compounded by the fact that the studies necessarily tend to rely on data from only a few patients. It then becomes crucial to know what additional brain damage these particular patients have, other than that due to the operation itself. This is not easy to establish, making it unclear how the results can be generalized to the normal brain. An example can be seen in Gazzaniga's (1983) claim that previous studies had *overestimated* the language comprehension abilities of the right hemisphere by relying on a group of patients with pre-surgical left hemisphere damage. In reply, Zaidel (1983) pointed out that the two patients he had worked with were relatively free from extra-callosal damage but that, if anything, they had greater right than left hemisphere damage, and might thus *underestimate* right hemisphere comprehension abilities. This type of dispute has proved very difficult to resolve.

The main issue relating to consciousness after the split-brain operation concerns whether the surgically disconnected cerebral hemispheres are each separately conscious. If one asks a split-brain patient whether she or he experiences dual consciousness in everyday life, the answer is a clear 'no'. Unfortunately, there are different ways one can interpret this answer. The most obvious way is to argue that since the answer comes from the left hemisphere, it does not tell us whether or not the disconnected right hemisphere has a separate consciousness that cannot be accessed by the left hemisphere. As Farthing (1992) points out, we then have a special case of the *other-minds* problem. The issues involved in establishing whether or not the isolated right hemisphere is conscious become no different to those involved in determining whether animals are conscious, or preverbal infants. It is a matter of deciding what is to count as an appropriate criterion. For many people, the presence of the ability to give apparently volitional answers to simple questions by left hand responses constitutes sufficient evidence, and this is bolstered by anecdotes that split-brain patients (very) occasionally find their left and right hands trying to do different things. There is also evidence of emotional reactions from the right hemisphere; such as a lady who blushed and giggled when a nude photograph was shown in her left visual field, but could not explain why, or a man who gave a prompt 'thumbs down' signal to a picture of Hitler (Sperry *et al.*, 1979).

A more subtle possibility, though, is that the disconnected cerebral hemispheres largely continue to function as a unified system. In everyday life, where the special testing procedures used in the laboratory studies do not apply, both hemispheres will continue to have similar experiences because of their co-existence within the same body. In addition, there is some scope for the integration of their activities through subcortical structures (Sergent, 1987). On this view, the patients' stated experience of unified consciousness is not merely a consequence of the left hemisphere's limited viewpoint. Several observations consistent with this general claim have been noted. For example, Weiskrantz (1988: 192) reported that split-brain patients he tested maintained that they 'saw' visual stimuli presented to their right hemispheres, even though they could not always identify them verbally.

An important series of findings come from case PS, who showed more extensive right hemisphere language abilities than most split-brain patients, and was able to spell out words with his left hand by arranging Scrabble letters

(Gazzaniga and LeDoux, 1978). Very clear evidence of right hemisphere consciousness was obtained; when responding by left hand spelling to questions using key words presented only in the left visual field, PS could give his name, his girlfriend's name, his mood, his hobby and so on. This shows that a person *can* have some degree of dual consciousness, at least in these admittedly exceptional circumstances. However, Gazzaniga has taken the view that this separate right hemisphere consciousness in PS can be attributed to its relatively developed language abilities. In the split-brain patients who lack right hemisphere language, Gazzaniga considers that the right hemisphere is not conscious and is incapable of carrying out cognitive tasks other than perceptual recognition.

FORMS OF CONSCIOUSNESS

A lot of the discussion about consciousness in split-brain patients seems to come down to an argument about what is the essence of consciousness. For some, propositional language is essential, so the right hemisphere is both mute and nonconscious; for others, flexibility of response or ability to experience emotion and act intentionally are more important, and the split-brain operation creates a person with some degree of dual consciousness.

But why should we assume that consciousness is a unitary phenomenon, requiring a unitary explanation? It seems more reasonable to begin by supposing that, like many complex biological phenomena, consciousness involves different aspects which will need to be accounted for in different ways. When seen in this way, there is no reason to seek *the* solution to *the* problem of consciousness; instead, it is essential to be clear about which aspect of consciousness is being discussed (see Velmans, Chapter 1 above).

A useful start has been made by Block (1995), who distinguishes phenomenal consciousness from access consciousness. Phenomenal consciousness is the experience of seeing, hearing, touching, etc., whereas access consciousness involves bringing stored information to mind, such as when recognizing an object or a face, remembering something that happened in the past and so on. For Block (1995), phenomenal consciousness refers to what it is like to have a certain kind of experience, whereas the hallmark of access consciousness is the availability of a piece of information for use in reasoning, speech and action.

A further important distinction concerns the difference between direct experience and reflexive consciousness; the difference is between seeing a pink elephant and knowing that it is *me* who is seeing that pink elephant (Marcel, 1993). This reflexive consciousness forms part of our consciousness of ourselves, but self-consciousness also involves the possession of a concept of the self and the ability to use this concept in thinking about oneself.

MEMORY AND CONSCIOUSNESS

The experience of remembering is a good example of what Block (1995) calls access consciousness. Amnesic patients, who often cannot remember what they were doing a few hours or even minutes ago, are therefore experiencing a severe impairment of access consciousness. In such cases, performance can be at chance levels in direct tests of memory. Direct tests would include recalling the items from a list learned earlier, picking them out from a list of previously learned items and new distractors and so on. However, the performance of amnesics is often less severely impaired if memory is tested indirectly, using tasks that do not require one to know that something has been remembered (Schacter, 1987).

The path-breaking studies were carried out by Warrington and Weiskrantz (1968, 1970), who asked amnesic patients to identify fragmented pictures or words, and showed that subsequent identification of the same stimuli was facilitated. For amnesics, just as much as for normal people, it becomes easier to recognize a fragmented picture of an object if you have already had to recognize the same object before. This type of finding can be obtained even when the amnesic patients fail to remember having taken part in any previous testing sessions! Hence amnesics show a form of nonconscious memory, in which their performance can be affected by previous experiences they may completely fail to remember overtly.

As well as highlighting the difference between conscious and nonconscious forms of memory, amnesia shows the importance of consciously accessible memories to maintaining our sense of self and orientation in the world. This can be seen very clearly through case CW, who suffered herpes simplex encephalitis in 1985 (Wilson et al., in press; Wilson and Wearing, 1995). This is a viral infection that attacks the brain's temporal lobes, and can lead to severe memory impairments.

Before his illness, CW had been an exceptionally talented musician with a most promising career. He was a specialist in early music, and an authority on the sixteenth-century composer Lassus. He was chorus master with the London Sinfonietta and had joined the staff of the BBC in 1983.

Afterwards, CW was able to remember little about his adult life other than his wife and his being a musician who had worked for the BBC. When asked to give as many names as possible of famous musicians, he could think of only four in one minute: Mozart, Beethoven, Bach and Haydn. He remembered no famous painters or artists, and only one writer (Dickens). On the Rivermead Behavioural Memory Test (Wilson et al., 1985) CW's screening score was 0/12, and he was also very poor on other tests of remembering visual or verbal material. Wilson, an exceptionally experienced clinical neuropsychologist, considered him the most densely amnesic patient she had ever seen (Wilson and Wearing, 1995).

Memory researchers often draw a distinction between our memory for specific episodes that have happened to us (e.g. remembering your holiday last year) and semantic memories, where the item is known from so many sources that it is no longer linked to any specific episode (e.g. remembering that Paris is the capital of France; you know this is correct, but not where or how you first learned it). Clearly, CW's episodic memory was grossly impaired. However, people with amnesias often show relative sparing of semantic memory, but this was not found for CW, whose semantic memory was also markedly abnormal; for example, when asked to define 'eyelid' he said 'I don't know that word, it must be used by a great specialist.' When this semantic memory loss was investigated in detail, CW was found to show especially poor knowledge of semantic information for living things. This differentially severe deficit for living things has been noted in other studies of post-encephalitic patients (Warrington and Shallice, 1984).

Although memory is severely affected in cases of amnesia, other intellectual abilities may remain remarkably preserved. This was also true for CW, whose IQ of 106 was in the average range when tested within a year after his illness, though this was undoubtedly well below his premorbid level. His immediate memory span was normal; he could repeat six digits in the order given to him, or four in reverse order. Reaction time to press a button as quickly as possible whenever a red light appeared was normal. Even more strikingly, CW remained able to sight read music, transpose keys and extemporize, and he could still conduct his choir. None the less, his wife felt that his musical skills had deteriorated, but the changes would not be evident to non-musicians (Wilson and Wearing, 1995). In all of these examples, whatever deficits CW showed in relation to his likely premorbid level of functioning were relatively limited in comparison to his devastating amnesia.

A most striking feature of CW's case was that the world seemed to him to be in a state of flux. He made comments like 'You weren't wearing blue just now. No, no, it was yellow or pink but it certainly wasn't blue.' When playing patience with a pack of cards, he kept thinking that the cards were changing whenever he looked away from them, so he devised a system for writing down their positions, to try to work out what was going on. He also began to keep a diary of what was happening to him, carefully recording the time, the date and the observation that he was now fully conscious, as if he had just woken up after his long illness. Diary entries to this effect were made hundreds of times across more than nine years, and the same feelings were evident in CW's everyday life. When asked to carry out neuropsychological tests, he 'frequently became angry saying he had just woken up for the first time in months, he had not seen or heard anything until that moment, and hence could not possibly know the answers to the questions' (Wilson et al., in press).

In the words of his wife, CW's world

'now consists of a *moment* with no past to anchor it and no future to look ahead to. It is a blinkered moment. He sees what is right in front of him but as soon as that information hits the brain it fades. Nothing registers. Everything goes in perfectly well . . . he perceives his world as you or I do, but as soon as he's perceived it and looked away it's gone for him. So it's a moment to moment consciousness as it were . . . a time vacuum.'

(Wilson and Wearing, 1995: 15)

A major contribution to these strange experiences must have been CW's inability to remember things for any length of time. For CW, the extent of any active record of what had been happening was limited to a matter of seconds, or perhaps a few minutes. Without any clear record of anything earlier than this, CW concluded that he had just emerged from a long period of unconsciousness.

However, Wilson *et al.* (in press) think that CW's amnesia was not in itself sufficient to account for his continual belief that he had just woken up. They point out that other amnesic patients do not make the same claim. For example, the amnesic patient HM described his experience thus: 'Every day is alone in itself, whatever enjoyment I've had and whatever sorrow I've had' (Milner *et al.*, 1968: 217). Although this shows some similarities to CW's predicament, HM did not think he had just woken up and seemed to appreciate a more considerable time span. However, his retrograde amnesia and loss of personal knowledge were not as severe as CW's, since HM could recall many things from his early life.

More importantly, Wilson *et al.* (in press) point out that CW was impervious to evidence which was inconsistent with his claim to have just woken up, such as the numerous timed and dated entries from his diaries. They also note that when the alternative hypothesis that he had suffered profound memory loss was put to him, CW denied it and showed signs of anxiety and agitation. Wilson *et al.* (in press) therefore saw CW's constant claim that he had just awoken as a delusion representing his attempt to provide a personally acceptable solution to his strange and dramatic experiences; 'It seems likely that the belief has become strengthened and proceduralised by repeated exercise, to a point at which it blocks out the awful alternative' (Wilson *et al.*, in press).

Whatever the exact interpretation, CW's case shows dramatically how important our memories are to orientation in time and place. Although fully conscious, CW often had no adequate idea of who he was, where he was, or why he was there. Without memory, he was in a state graphically described by Wilson and Wearing (1995) as a 'prisoner of consciousness'.

VISUAL EXPERIENCE

Some of the most dramatic findings of impairments affecting different aspects of consciousness come from studies of vision after brain injury. The best known of these involve investigations of responses to visual stimuli presented in what are apparently blind parts of the visual field (Weiskrantz, 1986, 1990; Weiskrantz *et al.*, 1974).

A consequence of brain injury involving the primary visual cortex (area V1) can be a loss of vision for part of the visual field, known as a scotoma. To test for a visual field defect the person is usually asked to report what is seen when stimuli are presented at different locations. Such work has shown that there is an orderly mapping of the area of lost vision onto the damaged part of area V1. However, it turns out that for some patients, accurate responses to visual stimuli presented in the scotoma can be elicited with tasks in which they are encouraged to make guesses about what has been presented. Weiskrantz's term 'blindsight' neatly sums up the paradoxical result of responses to stimuli which people insist that they do not see.

A substantial number of studies of this type have now been reported; we will begin by looking at responses to stimulus location by DB, the most extensively investigated case.

Responses to stimulus location in blindsight

DB underwent an operation in 1973 to remove an arteriovenous malformation from his right occipital lobe. This necessitated the removal of most of area V1 from the right cerebral hemisphere. Since the optic nerves project mainly to V1, the operation left DB with a substantial blind region in his field of vision. Initially, this scotoma occupied almost the entire left half of his field of vision, but over the next few years it gradually contracted until only the lower left quadrant was involved. Thus DB did not report seeing stimuli falling anywhere in the region to the lower left of the point he was fixating, and for some time he also did not report seeing stimuli in most of the area to the upper left of fixation.

Weiskrantz et al. (1974) began by replicating a surprising finding made by Pöppel et al. (1973). They presented brief (three-second) flashes of light at different horizontal positions within DB's scotoma, and asked him to move his eyes to look to where he guessed each flash had occurred. Even though DB denied seeing the flashes, there was a clear correspondence between his eye movements and the actual target position for targets presented up to 25 degrees from fixation.

This result showed that DB was still getting some information about the location of the light flashes. Even more accurate responses were obtained when Weiskrantz et al. (1974) asked DB simply to point to where he guessed each flash had been. However, performance for DB's 'blind' field was somewhat below what he could achieve using the part of his field that still had normal vision.

Fact or artefact?

Location is by no means the only visual characteristic that can be processed without corresponding visual experience. Other studies of blindsight have shown discrimination of orientation and movement, and by asking DB to guess whether a presented stimulus was a grating of vertical dark and light bars Weiskrantz et al. (1974) were even able to determine his visual acuity (in terms of the narrowest grating that could be detected). Gratings with bar widths of 1.5 minutes of arc could be detected in the sighted part of his field of vision, and a rather less acute but still impressive 1.9 minutes in the blind field.

Studies of blindsight raise a number of issues. High among these is whether we should accept the findings as scientific fact, or consider them artefacts reflecting explanations that do not demand the existence of some form of pre-served or residual visual capacity in the apparently blind area.

One potential problem is that there are differences between individual patients; Weiskrantz (1980) could find no evidence of residual visual function for eight out of twenty-two cases he was able to examine. These individual differences between patients need to be explored and explained, but they do not imply that the basic findings of preserved responses to location in the blind field for some patients are unsound. However, a widely discussed hypothesis is that the performances of patients who show blindsight might be mediated through light scattered onto parts of the retina unrelated to the scotoma, as a result of reflection off structures external or internal to the eye. Campion *et al.* (1983) criticized many of the early studies for failure to eliminate this possibility.

The simplest way to address this issue is to use the ophthalmological blind spot as a control. The blind spot occurs where the optic nerve leaves the retina. Performance based on cueing from scattered light would be unaffected by the absence of visual receptor cells in this area, whereas genuine blindsight would disappear when stimuli fall on the receptorless blind spot. Weiskrantz (1986) reported exactly this pattern of no blindsight in the blind spot for DB.

Studies of blindsight, then, have shown that the processing of visual stimuli can take place even when there is no phenomenal awareness of seeing them. Although explanations based on various types of artefact have been suggested, studies including careful control conditions have ruled these out. There are strong grounds for thinking it is a genuine phenomenon.

Responses to stimulus wavelength in blindsight

Much of the discussion of the brain mechanisms responsible for blindsight has centred around whether they involve spared areas of visual cortex, or are mediated subcortically by visual pathways which project directly to midbrain structures. Although mapping blindsight effects onto the midbrain seems to reassure those who want to argue that cortical equals conscious, detailed study of the visual pathways underlying these effects has shown clear involvement of visual cortex outside area V1 (Cowey and Stoerig, 1991, 1992). This can happen because the primary visual pathway through area V1 is not the only visual pathway with cortical projections; there are other routes to the cerebral cortex which bypass V1.

An important example comes from Stoerig and Cowey's (1989, 1991) work on wavelength sensitivity. Changes in wavelength are perceived by normal people as changes in colour. To achieve this, the retina contains three types of cone, each of which is maximally sensitive to light of a different wavelength. Outputs from these three types of cone are converted into colour-opponent signals for red–green and blue–yellow dimensions, and a separate luminance response. This anatomical arrangement means that for normal daytime vision, which is mediated by the cone receptors, we are more sensitive to light of certain wavelengths than others. Moreover, because of the colour-opponent mechanisms, the peak sensitivities do not correspond to the absorbence peaks of the cones themselves.

Stoerig and Cowey (1989, 1991) therefore measured thresholds for detecting stimuli of different wavelengths presented in subjectively blind parts of the visual field. They found that, although these thresholds were lower than normal, they showed the characteristic shape discontinuities which indicate the involvement of opponent cone mechanisms.

The importance of this finding is that colour opponency has not been found in the visual pathways going to the midbrain; it is thought to be a feature of the cortical pathways. Hence Stoerig and Cowey's (1989, 1991) results imply that parts of the visual cortex can be involved in visual functions without corresponding visual experience.

Blindsight and phenomenal experience

Although blindsight patients can produce accurate responses under conditions in which they insist that they see nothing at all, matters are actually rather more complicated. Usually, some degree of practice is needed before blindsight can be demonstrated; the patients seem to be able to learn to attend to something, yet that something is not usually described as being like a visual experience. Soon after surgery, DB was not aware of stimuli in his blind field at all, except that in some regions moving stimuli could produce peculiar radiating lines. Later, though, he started to say that he 'knew something was there', and roughly where it was, but that he did not in any sense 'see' it (Weiskrantz, 1980: 374).

One possibility is that blindsight patients might actually be conscious of the stimuli to which they respond, but that this consciousness is no longer accessible to the language system used in answering questions about what was seen. If this were the case, blindsight would be a variant of what has been found for split-brain patients, whose right visual cortex has been surgically disconnected from the left hemisphere's language centres. However, Weiskrantz (1988) has pointed out that the responses of split-brain patients to visual stimuli projected to the right cerebral hemisphere are unlike those of blindsight patients. Parameters such as stimulus size have a marked effect on demonstrations of blindsight, but the same variations do not affect responses from the surgically disconnected right hemisphere. In addition, we have already noted that Weiskrantz (1988) found that split-brain patients did often claim to see visual stimuli presented to the right hemisphere, even though they could not always identify them verbally. It thus seems that the explanation of blindsight is not merely loss of access to verbal capacities.

The various facts summarized so far might lead one to suppose that area V1 is the unique source of phenomenal visual experience, but this also does not seem to be correct; the full picture is going to be more complicated, and more interesting. Relevant findings come from studies which have looked at circumstances under which people *can* have conscious visual percepts of stimuli presented in regions of defective vision.

Pioneering work was reported by Torjussen (1978), who found that patients with right hemianopias reported seeing all of a circle when it was presented so as to fall half in the blind and half in the sighted region, yet they reported nothing if a semicircle was presented in the blind visual field, and just a semicircle if this was presented in the sighted region. Torjussen's findings are particularly significant because they show that the interaction between the stimuli in the blind and sighted parts of the visual field can affect what people report that they see in the blind region. Notice that presenting a semicircle in the blind field alone was insufficient for it to be perceived, yet essentially the same stimulus was reported as having been seen when it formed part of a complete figure which extended into the sighted field.

A different type of example comes from case GY, a man who had sustained injuries in a road accident when a child; these severely damaged the primary visual pathway in the left cerebral hemisphere, including total destruction of area V1 (Barbur et al., 1993). GY had been investigated in previous work on blindsight (Barbur et al., 1980), when it was noted that flashed or rapidly moving targets presented to his impaired right visual field did elicit a form of visual sensation, whereas static or slowly moving targets were reported as unseen. The blindsight work had concentrated on these subjectively unseen stimuli, but Barbur et al. (1993) turned their attention to GY's relatively preserved (though by no means perfect) perception of movement. By measuring cerebral blood flow when GY was asked to judge the direction of a rapidly moving stimulus, they found increased activity in parts of the remaining visual cortex in the left hemisphere.

This demonstration of a form of conscious perception of movement without area V1 shows that V1 is not essential to all visual experience. It appears more likely that visual experience is associated with activity of the cortical areas which are particularly specialized for that type of activity; in this case, an area outside V1 which is specialized for the perception of movement. However, there is a clear contrast between the involvement of visual areas outside V1 in GY's conscious perception of movement and the evidence of involvement of visual areas other than V1 in blindsight (Cowey and Stoerig, 1991, 1992). At present, this only serves to deepen the mystery of why some types of cortical activity seem to generate a conscious visual experience and some don't. A similar paradox is evident in work on responses to wavelength in achromatopsia.

Responses to wavelength in achromatopsia

Achromatopsic patients experience the world in shades of grey, or in less severe cases colours can look very washed out. This is quite different to the forms of colour-blindness produced by deficiencies in one of the three types of cone receptor in the retina, for which there is still experience of colour but certain colours are not discriminated from each other. Instead, severe achromatopsias produced by cortical injury are described by the patients themselves in terms which suggest they are experienced as more like watching black and white television. Hence achromatopsia provides an interesting example of loss of one aspect of visual experience: colour.

Heywood *et al.* (1991) measured the sensitivity to light of different wavelengths for an achromatopsic patient who had no experience of colour, MS. In this test, MS described all the stimuli he saw as 'dim white' or 'grey', despite the differences in wavelength. Similarly, other work established that MS could not match or name colours, and he performed at random when asked to arrange colour patches by hue. However, although MS showed a general overall loss of sensitivity, Heywood *et al.* (1991) found that the wavelengths he could see best were none the less the same as for a normal observer. As we noted for the blindsight work, these differences in sensitivity across wavelength derive from opponent cone mechanisms; so this result demonstrated the presence of opponent cone mechanisms despite MS's complete loss of colour experience.

Heywood *et al.*'s (1991) findings show the same pattern as was found for blindsight cases by Stoerig and Cowey (1989, 1991). Yet the patients with blindsight deny seeing the presented lights at all, and must guess in the sensitivity test, whereas MS was well aware of whether or not he could see a light, but did not know what colour it was. Again, this highlights the fact that we don't really know why responses to wavelength should be preserved in both types of case, which are otherwise so different. It is not simply a matter of visual experience versus no visual experience, as in the original studies of blindsight. Instead, loss of part of our normal visual experience can be highly selective; in this case for colour, which was no longer seen by MS even though much of the mechanism for dealing with wavelengths by opponent channels continued to function. Further work with MS produced many more demonstrations of this, including the important finding that he could still use differences in wavelength to extract information about shape (Heywood *et al.*, 1994). In this sense, achromatopsia can involve a restricted defect of phenomenal consciousness.

COVERT RECOGNITION OF FAMILIAR FACES

Selective deficits are not unique to phenomenal consciousness. A highly specific deficit of what Block (1995) calls access consciousness can be found in prosopagnosia, a neurological deficit affecting the recognition of familiar faces. Even the best-known faces may not be recognized, including famous people, friends, family and the patient's own face when looking in a mirror. In contrast, recognition from nonfacial cues (such as voice, name, and sometimes even clothing or gait) is usually successful.

These failures of face recognition have been very circumscribed in a few rare cases. One of De Renzi's (1986) patients could find his own belongings when they were mixed in with similar objects, identify his own handwriting, pick out a Siamese cat among photographs of other cats, recognize his own car without reading the number plate and sort domestic coins from foreign coins. In all of these tasks he was therefore able to identify individual members of visual categories with high inter-item similarity, yet he could not recognize the faces of relatives and close friends. Just as strikingly, the deficit can affect mainly *human* faces; when McNeil and Warrington's (1993) prosopagnosic patient took up farming, he was able to learn to recognize his sheep and correctly identified several of them from photographs of their faces!

Although prosopagnosic patients no longer recognize familiar faces overtly, there is substantial evidence of covert recognition from physiological and behavioural measures (Young, 1994). Bauer's (1984) study was the first to demonstrate this convincingly. He measured skin conductance while a prosopagnosic patient, LF, viewed a familiar face and listened to a list of names. When the name matched the face LF was looking at, there was a greater skin conductance change than when someone else's name was read out. Yet if LF was asked to choose which name in the list was correct for the face, his performance was at chance level. There was thus a marked difference between overt recognition, which was at chance level for LF, and some form of preserved covert recognition, as evidenced by his skin conductance responses.

Other indices of covert recognition in prosopagnosia include priming techniques. For example, subjects may be shown a face prime and then asked to classify a following target name as familiar or unfamiliar. Studies of this type have demonstrated that responses to the target name are facilitated if the prime is the same person as the target (e.g. if Ronald Reagan's face is used as the prime preceding the name 'Ronald Reagan') or a close associate (e.g. if Nancy Reagan's face is used as the prime preceding the name 'Ronald Reagan'). This is found for prosopagnosic patients even though they do not recognize the face primes overtly (de Haan et al., 1992; Young et al., 1988).

However, the loss of overt recognition of familiar faces found in prosopagnosia need not be absolute. Sergent and Poncet (1990) noticed that their patient, PV, could sometimes achieve overt recognition of faces if several members of the same semantic category were presented together. This effect has been replicated with other cases (de Haan et al., 1991; Diamond et al., 1994; Sergent and Signoret, 1992). However, it only happens when the patients can determine the category themselves; otherwise, they continue to fail to recognize the faces overtly even when the occupational category is pointed out. This shows that the phenomenon involves genuine recognition, not guessing based on inferences about the members of a given category (i.e. the patients do not depend on reasoning that if they're singers, the blonde one could be Madonna, etc.).

Such findings in prosopagnosia suggest that activation must cross some form of threshold before it can result in conscious awareness of recognition of the face. This can be simulated with a computer model in which excitation can be continuously passed from one functional unit to another, but a separate threshold is set to determine any explicit output. Burton et al. (1990) had proposed a simulation of this type which could encompass several findings related to normal face recognition. The prosopagnosic pattern of preserved priming effects, without explicit classification of face inputs, can be simulated with this model simply by halving the connection strengths between two of its pools of functional units (Burton et al., 1991). The effect of damaging the model in this way is that sufficient activation can still be passed around the system to mediate priming effects, but insufficient to cross the threshold for explicit output.

We can thus understand one way in which covert responses might be preserved when there is no overt discrimination, and this seems highly relevant to understanding access consciousness. However, although it represents a step forward, what has actually been established is that this is one form of possible mechanism, not that it is the only or the correct answer. Even if it proves to be a valid simulation of one aspect of the problem, this is not the same as solving it. A moment's reflection is all that is needed to see that the units in a computer program do not become conscious when their activation passes an arbitrary threshold.

INSIGHT AND LACK OF INSIGHT

There are other impairments which show that the boundary between being conscious or not conscious of something is not always clearly marked. Unilateral neglect is a good example; in some ways it seems more like a distortion than a loss of awareness. Patients with unilateral neglect fail to respond to stimuli located opposite the side of their brain lesion. The condition is more common after lesions of the right cerebral hemisphere, when left-sided stimuli are neglected.

Neglect has often been discussed as if the fact that patients do not respond to left-sided stimuli implies that they are not aware of them. In an ingenious experiment, Marshall and Halligan (1988) showed a drawing of a house in which bright red flames were emerging from the left hand side to PS, a patient with left-sided neglect. Although she correctly identified the drawing as a house, PS failed to report that it was on fire, and asserted that this drawing was the same as another drawing that had no flames. Yet when asked which house she would prefer to live in, PS consistently tended to choose the non-burning one, even though she considered the question silly because in her view the two pictures were the same. The information that the house was on fire was apparently registered only at a nonconscious level.

In later trials, PS was shown a drawing in which flames emerged from the right hand side of the house, which she immediately commented upon. Subsequently, she finally noticed the fire in the house with the left-sided flames, exclaiming 'Oh my God, this one's on fire!' Thus the failure of conscious recognition of the left-sided flames could be overcome by appropriate cueing.

A number of similar findings implying semantic processing of neglected stimuli have been reported, including elegant studies of priming effects (Berti and Rizzolatti, 1992; McGlinchey-Berroth et al., 1993). However, other studies have described phenomena which highlight the complex and paradoxical nature of the breakdown of perceptual awareness in neglect, suggesting the need for caution in the interpretation of this disorder. Bisiach and Rusconi (1990) repeated Marshall and Halligan's (1988) experiment with four neglect patients; none of them was initially aware of the left-sided flames, and two showed a consistent preference, but for the burning house! Moreover, when asked to trace her finger around the outlines of the houses, one of these patients accurately traced the left-sided flames in one of the drawings. To do this, she must have looked at the left side of each drawing, yet afterwards she still thought that the two pictures were the same. Similar observations were reported by Young *et al.* (1992), who were asking neglect patient BQ to identify both halves of chimaeric faces made from the left and right sides of different people. Even when BQ had looked at and accurately described the facial features on the left side of a chimaeric, she would identify only the right side.

It is thus unlikely that the perceptual alterations found in cases of neglect will map directly onto straightforward aware versus unaware or conscious versus nonconscious dichotomies. Instead, the patients can show that they are conscious of something on the left at one moment, and then proceed to ignore it a few seconds later. One gets the feeling that their experiences may be akin to that of someone watching a particularly good conjuring trick, who knows where her watch is at one moment but not the next.

A curious feature of unilateral neglect, which can exasperate relatives, is that patients may show very little insight into their problems. Loss of insight is termed 'anosognosia' by neurologists, and can be found in a variety of different settings. In the nineteenth century, Anton and others had described patients who denied various forms of disability including paralysis, blindness or deafness (Förstl *et al.*, 1993).

Anton emphasized that unawareness of impairment can occur without generalized intellectual impairment (Förstl *et al.*, 1993); it need not involve any global change of consciousness. This is made very clear by reports of patients who are unaware of one of their problems yet perfectly well aware of another. Paralysis of one side of the body (hemiplegia) and blindness for half the field of vision (hemianopia) are relatively common consequences of brain injury, yet there can be dissociations between anosognosia for hemiplegia and anosognosia for hemianopia (Bisiach *et al.*, 1986); some patients deny their visual problems yet agree that one side of their body is paralysed, and vice versa. The fact that anosognosia can be specific to particular disabilities shows that it does not result from a general change in the patient's state of consciousness. It seems to reflect an underlying defect in the ability to monitor what one is doing, but like other impairments of consciousness these monitoring problems can be highly selective.

IMPLICATIONS

We have seen that some of the problems caused by brain injury involve the disruption of different forms of consciousness or awareness. In each case, there is no general perturbation of consciousness, but one aspect is affected, often in a highly selective way. Any adequate theory of consciousness will need to be able to accommodate this basic point. A similar claim was made by Searle (1992), who used the fact that different features of consciousness can be stripped away in pathological forms as a criterion for identifying structural features of normal, everyday consciousness.

These neuropsychological findings have important implications for our understanding of consciousness. For example, they show the incorrectness of the assumption that conscious awareness is integral to the operation of perceptual mechanisms. Instead, visual stimuli can be located even though they are not consciously perceived, differences in wavelength can be processed without the experience of seeing colour, the identities of faces which are not consciously recognized can influence responses to people's names and so on.

Anatomical studies of the visual system have revealed an intricate arrangement, involving distinct areas in the cerebral cortex and several parallel cortical and subcortical visual pathways (Weiskrantz, 1990; Zeki, 1993). In general, it seems that the task of seeing is devolved to separate processing streams containing components that have become specialized for particular purposes, such as seeing colour, form or movement. This holds not only for basic aspects of vision, such as the perception of lightness and orientation, but also for higher order visual abilities involved in the perception and recognition of complex shapes, such as faces (Perrett et al., 1992).

These specialist areas in the brain have been shaped by evolution, and during evolution specialization can carry costs as well as benefits. Hence the optimal balance of costs and benefits is likely to allow scope for some cross-talk between specialist areas, and we are not talking about the degree of dedicatedness found, say, in the components of a radio. None the less, it is remarkable just how much of the processing of particular types of stimulus, such as colours or faces, may continue when the corresponding conscious experience is missing.

Perception, action and intention

A striking feature of these disorders is how consciousness is intimately linked to intentional action. To demonstrate blindsight, patients have to be encouraged to guess; they do not behave as if they are seeing the stimulus. Similarly, prosopagnosic patients do not act as if they recognize faces in everyday life. An amusing example of what can at times be a deeply embarrassing problem comes from Newcombe et al.'s (1994) description of a retired mathematician who had been prosopagnosic all his life:

> At the age of 16 years, while on holiday, he stood in a queue for 30 min next to a family friend whom he had known all his life, without any experience of familiarity. The friend complained – mildly – to his parents and his father reacted strongly to this apparent discourtesy. Soon after, cycling from the village to his home, he saw a man walking toward him. In his own words: 'Mindful of my father's recent forceful comments, I decided to play it safe. As we passed, I said "Good morning, Sir." My father said later that I had never addressed him as politely before or since.'
>
> (Newcombe et al., 1994: 108)

This holds even for the cases with covert recognition. PH, who cooperated with my colleagues in an investigation which lasted for many years, did not act as if he could recognize us, even though he showed covert recognition of our faces (de Haan *et al.*, 1987).

To see why certain types of consciousness have become intimately linked with intentional actions, one needs to consider the delicate balance between speed of response and flexibility of response. The purpose of perceptual systems is to create representations of external events that can permit effective action in the world that an organism inhabits. Any degree of flexibility of response requires sophisticated representations of events, which take time to create. Hence flexibility of response comes at the cost of loss of speed. Some types of covert effect can thus be seen to reflect automatic components built in to the visual system to reduce some of this loss of speed; for example, by predicting what is likely to follow and setting up preparatory responses.

One way to balance the competing demands of flexibility and speed is to allow most actions to run off under automatic control, and to involve mechanisms which can allow greater choice only when these are needed. This is also a convenient solution because nervous systems must evolve, and one way to do this is to add extra levels of control to mechanisms that are already sufficient for many purposes.

A compelling demonstration comes from the dissociation of action and conscious perception found in case DF, who had suffered carbon monoxide poisoning, leaving her with gross perceptual impairments. DF was severely impaired at judging the orientation of a slot when she was asked to do this by rotating a second slot to match the inclination of the original (Milner *et al.*, 1991). Yet when DF was asked to put her hand into the slot, she immediately positioned it correctly. DF also shaped her fingers appropriately for the size of an object she was about to pick up, even though her ability to make overt size judgements was poor (Goodale *et al.*, 1991).

Note that it was only certain types of action which were preserved for DF. In general, her accurate responses involved well-practised everyday movements that can be run off without conscious control, whereas inaccurate responses arose in tasks that need continual conscious intervention. This is exactly as would be expected from the general position outlined here.

THE CARTESIAN THEATRE

Findings of selective neuropsychological impairments of different aspects of consciousness highlight the danger of thinking that the subjective unity of conscious experience implies that a unitary brain system is involved. Subjective unity is then taken to imply that there is a place in the brain where 'it all comes together'; Dennett and Kinsbourne (1992) called this the Cartesian Theatre, because Descartes had proposed a single interface between mind and brain.

Mounting numbers of neuropsychological dissociations are making the assumptions behind the Cartesian Theatre look increasingly unlikely, and Dennett and Kinsbourne (1992) have shown that it also has serious philosophical problems.

An alternative hypothesis is that the contents of consciousness correspond to the information that is made available to executive mechanisms to coordinate and integrate what would otherwise be independent processing streams (Baars, 1988; Morris and Hampson, 1983). However, the principal assumption of a single locus for consciousness remains; both Baars (1988) and Morris and Hampson (1983) think that there is a unified executive system.

Even this does not seem very convincing. Marcel (1993) drew attention to reports by Bisiach and Geminiani (1991) of inconsistencies between denial as evidenced in the actions and verbal reports of anosognosic patients. For example, a patient with left-sided paralysis following a right hemisphere stroke may bemoan his paralysis yet keep trying to get out of bed and walk, while another patient denies having any deficit on verbal interrogation yet makes no attempt to get out of bed. In his 1898 paper, Anton had noted the same phenomenon, commenting that 'such patients pay little attention to the loss of sensation or motor functions. They try to walk in spite of their paresis, and they fall, only to repeat the same attempt after a short time' (Förstl et al., 1993: 3). Anton made a parallel to the problems encountered in cases of hysteria, and Marcel (1993) also likened them to dissociative states; part of the patient's mind seems to know the pertinent facts, but another part doesn't. This undermines the idea of a fully unified self that is experiencing what is happening, and suggests that our sense of a single conscious self may be built on weak foundations which are easily disrupted under unusual or pathological circumstances.

CODA

So where are we after this brief reconnaissance of some of the dissociable aspects of consciousness revealed in neuropsychological studies? Clearly, impairments of consciousness can be highly selective, both to certain forms of consciousness (phenomenal consciousness, access consciousness, etc.) and to certain types of content (movement, colour, face recognition and so on). These facts must be explained by any adequate account, though it is also becoming clear that matters are further complicated because the boundary between what is consciously available and what is not consciously available to patients is not always sharply demarcated or under all circumstances impassable.

The problems of consciousness have puzzled people for many centuries, and were at times considered too deep for psychology even to attempt to face. Yet the neuropsychological evidence now seems to offer important pointers to some features of the answers. Much remains to be explored, but careful case studies are helping us to make progress with these very difficult questions.

REFERENCES

Baars, B.J. (1988) *A Cognitive Theory of Consciousness*, Cambridge: Cambridge University Press.

Barbur, J.L., Ruddock, K.H. and Waterfield, V.A. (1980) 'Human visual responses in the absence of the geniculo-calcarine projection', *Brain* 103: 905–928.

Barbur, J.L., Watson, J.D.G., Frackowiak, R.S.J. and Zeki, S. (1993) 'Conscious visual perception without V1', *Brain* 116: 1293–1302.

Bates, D. and Cartlidge, N. (1994) 'Disorders of consciousness', in E.M.R. Critchley (ed.) *The Neurological Boundaries of Reality*, London: Farrand.

Bauer, R.M. (1984) 'Autonomic recognition of names and faces in prosopagnosia: a neuropsychological application of the guilty knowledge test', *Neuropsychologia* 22: 457–469.

Berti, A. and Rizzolatti, G. (1992) 'Visual processing without awareness: evidence from unilateral neglect', *Journal of Cognitive Neuroscience* 4: 345–351.

Bisiach, E. and Geminiani, G. (1991) 'Anosognosia related to hemiplegia and hemianopia', in G. P. Prigatano and D. L. Schacter (eds) *Awareness of Deficit after Brain Injury: clinical and theoretical issues*, Oxford: Oxford University Press.

Bisiach, E. and Rusconi, M.L. (1990) 'Break-down of perceptual awareness in unilateral neglect', *Cortex* 26: 643–649.

Bisiach, E., Vallar, G., Perani, D., Papagno, C. and Berti, A. (1986) 'Unawareness of disease following lesions of the right hemisphere: anosognosia for hemiplegia and anosognosia for hemianopia', *Neuropsychologia* 24: 471–482.

Block, N. (1995) 'On a confusion about a function of consciousness', *Behavioral and Brain Sciences* 18: 227–287.

Burton, A.M., Bruce, V. and Johnston, R.A. (1990) 'Understanding face recognition with an interactive activation model', *British Journal of Psychology* 81: 361–380.

Burton, A.M., Young, A.W., Bruce, V., Johnston, R. and Ellis, A.W. (1991) 'Understanding covert recognition', *Cognition* 39: 129–166.

Campion, J., Latto, R. and Smith, Y.M. (1983) 'Is blindsight an effect of scattered light, spared cortex, and near-threshold vision?', *Behavioral and Brain Sciences* 6: 423–486.

Carlson, N.R. (1991) *Physiology of Behavior*, 4th edn., Boston, MA: Allyn and Bacon.

Cowey, A. and Stoerig, P. (1991) 'The neurobiology of blindsight', *Trends in Neurosciences* 14: 140–145.

—— (1992) 'Reflections on blindsight', in A.D. Milner and M.D. Rugg (eds) *The Neuropsychology of Consciousness*, London: Academic Press.

de Haan, E.H.F., Bauer, R.M. and Greve, K.W. (1992) 'Behavioural and physiological evidence for covert face recognition in a prosopagnosic patient', *Cortex* 28: 77–95.

de Haan, E.H.F., Young, A. and Newcombe, F. (1987) 'Face recognition without awareness', *Cognitive Neuropsychology* 4: 385–415.

—— (1991) 'Covert and overt recognition in prosopagnosia', *Brain* 114: 2575–2591.

De Renzi, E. (1986) 'Current issues in prosopagnosia', in H.D. Ellis, M.A. Jeeves, F. Newcombe and A. Young (eds) *Aspects of Face Processing*, Dordrecht: Martinus Nijhoff.

Dennett, D.C. and Kinsbourne, M. (1992) 'Time and the observer: the where and when of consciousness in the brain', *Behavioral and Brain Sciences* 15: 183–201.

Diamond, B.J., Valentine, T., Mayes, A.R. and Sandel, M.E. (1994) 'Evidence of covert recognition in a prosopagnosic patient', *Cortex* 30: 377–393.

Farthing, G.W. (1992) *The Psychology of Consciousness*, Englewood Cliffs, NJ: Prentice Hall.

Folstein, M.F., Folstein, S.E. and McHugh, P.R. (1975) '"Mini-Mental State": a practical method for grading the cognitive state of patients for the clinician', *Journal of Psychiatric Research* 12: 189–198.

Förstl, H., Owen, A.M. and David, A.S. (1993) 'Gabriel Anton and "Anton's symptom": on focal diseases of the brain which are not perceived by the patient (1898)', *Neuropsychiatry, Neuropsychology, and Behavioral Neurology* 6: 1–8.

Gazzaniga, M.S. (1983) 'Right hemisphere language following brain bisection: a 20-year perspective', *American Psychologist* 38: 525–537.

Gazzaniga, M.S. and LeDoux, J.E. (1978) *The Integrated Mind*, New York: Plenum.

Goodale, M.A., Milner, A.D., Jakobson, L.S. and Carey, D.P. (1991) 'A neurological dissociation between perceiving objects and grasping them', *Nature* 349: 154–156.

Heywood, C.A., Cowey, A. and Newcombe, F. (1991) 'Chromatic discrimination in a cortically colour blind observer', *European Journal of Neuroscience* 3: 802–812.

—— (1994) 'On the role of parvocellular (P) and magnocellular (M) pathways in cerebral achromatopsia', *Brain* 117: 245–254.

Marcel, A. J. (1993) 'Slippage in the unity of consciousness', in Ciba Foundation Symposium no. 174, *Experimental and Theoretical Studies of Consciousness*, Chichester: Wiley.

Marshall, J.C. and Halligan, P.W. (1988) 'Blindsight and insight in visuo-spatial neglect', *Nature* 336: 766–767.

McGlinchey-Berroth, R., Milberg, W.P., Verfaellie, M., Alexander, M. and Kilduff, P.T. (1993) 'Semantic processing in the neglected visual field: evidence from a lexical decision task', *Cognitive Neuropsychology* 10: 79–108.

McNeil, J.E. and Warrington, E.K. (1993) 'Prosopagnosia: a face specific disorder', *Quarterly Journal of Experimental Psychology* 46A: 1–10.

Milner, A.D., Perrett, D.I., Johnston, R.S., Benson, P.J., Jordan, T.R., Heeley, D.W., Bettucci, D., Mortara, F., Mutani, R., Terazzi, E. and Davidson, D.L.W. (1991) 'Perception and action in "visual form agnosia"', *Brain* 114: 405–428.

Milner, B., Corkin, S. and Teuber, H.-L. (1968) 'Further analysis of the hippocampal amnesic syndrome: a 14 year follow-up study of H.M', *Neuropsychologia* 6: 215–234.

Morris, P.E. and Hampson, P.J. (1983) *Imagery and Consciousness*, London: Academic Press.

Newcombe, F., Mehta, Z. and de Haan, E.H.F. (1994) 'Category specificity in visual recognition', in M.J. Farah and G. Ratcliff (eds) *The Neuropsychology of High-Level Vision: collected tutorial essays*, Hillsdale, NJ: Lawrence Erlbaum.

Perrett, D.I., Hietanen, J.K., Oram, M.W. and Benson, P.J. (1992) 'Organization and functions of cells responsive to faces in the temporal cortex', *Philosophical Transactions of the Royal Society, London* B335: 23–30.

Pöppel, E., Held, R. and Frost, D. (1973) 'Residual visual function after brain wounds involving the central visual pathways in man', *Nature* 243: 295–296.

Schacter, D.L. (1987) 'Implicit memory: history and current status', *Journal of Experimental Psychology: Learning, Memory, and Cognition* 13: 501–518.

Searle, J.R. (1992) *The Rediscovery of the Mind*, Cambridge, MA: MIT Press.

Sergent, J. (1987) 'A new look at the human split brain', *Brain* 110: 1375–1392.

Sergent, J. and Poncet, M. (1990) 'From covert to overt recognition of faces in a prosopagnosic patient', *Brain* 113: 989–1004.

Sergent, J. and Signoret, J.-L. (1992) 'Implicit access to knowledge derived from unrecognized faces in prosopagnosia', *Cerebral Cortex* 2: 389–400.

Sperry, R.W., Zaidel, E. and Zaidel, D. (1979) 'Self recognition and social awareness in the deconnected minor hemisphere', *Neuropsychologia* 17: 153–166.

Springer, S.P. and Deutsch, G. (1993) *Left Brain, Right Brain*, 4th edn., San Francisco: W.H. Freeman.

Stoerig, P. and Cowey, A. (1989) 'Wavelength sensitivity in blindsight', *Nature* 342: 916–918.

—— (1991) 'Increment-threshold spectral sensitivity in blindsight. Evidence for colour opponency', *Brain* 114: 1487–1512.

Teasdale, G. and Jennett, B. (1974) 'Assessment of coma and impaired consciousness: a practical scale', *Lancet* 13 July: 81–83.

Torjussen, T. (1978) 'Visual processing in cortically blind hemifields', *Neuropsychologia* 16: 15–21.

Warrington, E.K. and Shallice, T. (1984) 'Category specific semantic impairments', *Brain* 107: 829–854.

Warrington, E.K. and Weiskrantz, L. (1968) 'New method of testing long-term retention with special reference to amnesic patients', *Nature* 217: 972–974.

—— (1970) 'Amnesia: consolidation or retrieval?', *Nature* 228: 628–630.

Weiskrantz, L. (1980) 'Varieties of residual experience', *Quarterly Journal of Experimental Psychology* 32: 365–386.

—— (1986) *Blindsight: a case study and implications*, Oxford: Oxford University Press.

—— (1988) 'Some contributions of neuropsychology of vision and memory to the problem of consciousness', in A.J. Marcel and E. Bisiach (eds) *Consciousness in Contemporary Science*, Oxford: Oxford University Press.

—— (1990) 'The Ferrier Lecture, 1989. Outlooks for blindsight: explicit methodologies for implicit processes', *Proceedings of the Royal Society, London* B239: 247–278.

Weiskrantz, L., Warrington, E.K., Sanders, M.D. and Marshall, J. (1974) 'Visual capacity in the hemianopic field following a restricted occipital ablation', *Brain* 97: 709–728.

Wilson, B., Cockburn, J. and Baddeley, A.D. (1985) *The Rivermead Behavioural Memory Test*, Bury St Edmunds: Thames Valley Test Company.

Wilson, B.A., Baddeley, A.D. and Kapur, N. (in press) 'Dense amnesia in a professional musician following herpes simplex virus encephalitis', *Journal of Clinical and Experimental Neuropsychology*.

Wilson, B.A. and Wearing, D. (1995) 'Prisoner of consciousness: a state of just awakening following herpes simplex encephalitis', in R. Campbell and M. Conway (eds) *Broken Memories*, Oxford: Blackwell.

Young, A.W. (1994) 'Covert recognition', in M.J. Farah and G. Ratcliff (eds) *The Neuropsychology of High-Level Vision: collected tutorial essays*, Hillsdale, NJ: Lawrence Erlbaum.

Young, A.W., Hellawell, D. and de Haan, E.H.F. (1988) 'Cross-domain semantic priming in normal subjects and a prosopagnosic patient', *Quarterly Journal of Experimental Psychology* 40A: 561–580.

Young, A.W., Hellawell, D.J. and Welch, J. (1992) 'Neglect and visual recognition', *Brain* 115: 51–71.

Zaidel, E. (1983) 'Language in the right hemisphere: convergent perspectives', *American Psychologist* 38: 542–545.

Zeki, S. (1993) *A Vision of the Brain*, Oxford: Blackwell.

Chapter 7

Somatic consequences of consciousness

Anees A. Sheikh, Robert G. Kunzendorf and Katharina S. Sheikh

In the introduction to *The Healing Heart* (Cousins, 1983), Dr Bernard Lown describes a seriously ill patient. He had suffered a heart attack which had severely damaged the cardiac muscle; he was experiencing chaotic arrhythmia that was hard to control and his breathing was laboured. The patient was being kept alive with oxygen and an intravenous drip of cardiac stimulant. On one of his rounds, Dr Lown mentioned to the attending staff that the patient's heart had a 'wholesome, very loud third sound gallop'. This condition indicates that the heart is straining and is on the brink of a failure. However, following this conversation the patient 'miraculously' improved and was discharged from the hospital. When asked by Dr Lown about his recovery, he responded:

> I was sure the end was near and you and your staff had given up hope. However, Thursday morning when you entered with your troops, something happened that changed everything. You listened to my heart; you seemed pleased by the findings and announced to all those standing about my bed that I had a wholesome gallop. I knew that the doctors, in talking to me, might try to soften things. But I know they wouldn't kid each other. So when I heard you tell your colleagues I had a wholesome gallop, I figured I still had a lot of 'kick' to my heart and could not be dying. My spirits were, for the first time, lifted and I knew I would recover.
>
> (Cousins, 1983: 16)

There is abundant anecdotal evidence demonstrating somatic or physiological consequences of conscious mental processes. Furthermore, an impressive body of empirical research has accumulated over the last two decades which demonstrates quite convincingly that conscious processes, in one form or another, are clearly capable of leading to measurable physiological changes and should be considered significant determinants of disease and health. This chapter first briefly traces the history of thought in the field of psychosomatics and then outlines research dealing with physiological or somatic consequences of meditation, imagery, biofeedback and hypnosis, which obviously involve conscious mental processes. The concluding section further emphasizes the role that consciousness plays in bringing about extensive physiological changes.

PSYCHOSOMATICS: A BRIEF HISTORICAL REVIEW

Although the term 'psychosomatic' was introduced by Heinroth, a German psychiatrist, in 1818, modern psychosomatic medicine came into being in the early 1930s as a result of an integration of two concepts of ancient Greek origin – *psychogenesis* and *holism* (Lipkowski, 1986a, 1986b).

The concept of psychogenesis refers to the belief that psychological factors are capable of causing bodily diseases. Starting with the ancient Greeks, numerous writers have asserted this position. For example, Archer, a seventeenth-century English physician, said:

> The observation that I have made in practice of physik these several years hath confirmed me in this opinion, that the original, or cause, of most mens and womens sickness, disease and death is first, some great discontent which brings a habit of sadness of mind.
>
> (Archer, 1673: 121)

Similarly, Benjamin Rush (1811), a famous American physician and author of the first American textbook of psychiatry, emphasized that the 'actions of the mind' caused many diseases and could be used as therapeutic agents. More recently, Freud and his followers made further contributions to the concept of psychogenesis.

The concept of holism was first introduced by Smuts in 1926, but its lineage dates back to ancient Greece. It is derived from the Greek word *holos*, meaning whole. 'It refers to the postulate that mind and body constitute an indivisible unity, or whole, and that the study and treatment of the sick need to take into account the whole person rather than isolated parts' (Lipkowski, 1986a: 4). For example, Plato, in *Charmides*, subtitled *The Mistake of Physicians*, suggests:

> And this is the reason why the cure of many diseases is unknown to the physicians of Hellas, because they are ignorant of the whole which ought to be studied also; for the part can never be well unless the whole is well. It is the greatest mistake in the treatment of disease that there are physicians who treat the body and physicians who treat the mind, since both are inseparable.
>
> (quoted in Freyhan, 1976: 381)

In 1637 the French philosopher René Descartes proposed the radical view that the body was separate from the mind. The body was regarded as a machine controlled by mechanistic laws, and the mind as an 'immaterial substance'. Although Descartes had left the possibility of mind–body interaction open, his ideas were profoundly influential in fostering biological determinism in medical theory and research (McMahon and Sheikh, 1989).

However, in spite of Descartes' far-reaching influence, the holistic notions survived and kept appearing in the works of many writers. Two significant twentieth-century examples include Cannon's (1915) concept of homeostasis which presented a somatic basis for the holistic notion and Adolf Meyer's (1957) psychobiology that asserted that 'mind and body were two distinct yet integral aspects of the human organism, a psychobiological unit, as a whole' (Lipkowski, 1986a: 5).

In the early 1930s, in reaction to Cartesian dualism and biological reductionism, the concepts of psychogenesis and holism appeared in a reformist movement called psychosomatic medicine. 'While core assumptions were of ancient lineage, that movement had a crucial new feature: it initiated a systematic scientific study of the interaction of psychological and biological factors in health and disease' (Lipkowski, 1986a: 5).

In 1939 the first issue of the journal *Psychosomatic Medicine* appeared and it formally sanctioned the scientific investigation of psychosomatics in medical thinking and research. This development apparently was overdue, for within two decades the psychosomatic movement was noticed internationally. By the early 1960s a dozen journals on this topic had appeared in the industrialized countries and since then membership of professional societies for psychosomatic research has undergone exponential growth (McMahon and Koppes, 1976; McMahon and Sheikh, 1989).

It has become increasingly clear that persons, not cells or organs, have diseases, and that human beings do not merely consist of 'self-contained organs carrying out specialized metabolic processes in isolation uninfluenced by external events' (Weiner, 1977: 8). Social and psychological variables now appear to play an important role in the predisposition for, and inception and maintenance of, diseases (Gatchel and Blanchard, 1993; Schwab, 1978; Sheikh *et al.*, 1979; Shontz, 1975; Weiner, 1977; Wittkower, 1977). Also, several personality factors (i.e. inability to release emotions) that characterize psychosomatic cases have been noted (Shontz, 1975; Gatchel and Blanchard, 1993).

Many theorists seem to agree that certain stimulus situations, overt or covert, elicit a variety of internal conditions, which if sufficiently intense and prolonged will lead to structural or somatic alterations. A number of theories have been proposed concerning which structure will undergo alterations (Lachman, 1972; Sheikh *et al.*, 1979).

According to *constitutional vulnerability (weak link) theories*, stressful stimulation damages the most vulnerable organ: the chain breaks at the weakest link. The elements that render a particular organ more vulnerable are genetic factors, injuries, diseases and other previous influences. Proponents of *organ response learning theories* hold that due to a previous connection between emotional stimulation and a reinforced response of an organ, further stressful cues lead to the same organ response. If these stressful situations are frequent, persistent and sufficiently intense, a malfunction of or damage to that organ may result. Partisans of *stimulus situation theories* contend that certain emotional stimulus situations cause specific physiological reactions and this leads to damage to the organ structure involved. An innate relationship between various patterns of stimulation and those of physiological reaction is often implied. Followers of *personality profile theories* maintain that various personality structures result in differing reaction tendencies, and thus different individuals are predisposed to different kinds of psychosomatic pathologies. Lastly, *symptom symbol theories*, which originated in psychoanalytic conceptions, hold that the diseased organ or system has symbolic meaning for the patient (Sheikh *et al.*, 1979).

It should be noted that the proponents of almost all of the foregoing theories have implicitly, if not explicitly, recognized the part played by conscious mental processes in the development of diseases.

MEDITATION AND PHYSIOLOGY

Meditation is perhaps the oldest and the most celebrated way of demonstrating the psychophysiological effects of consciousness (Ramaswami and Sheikh, 1989). A common element of the meditative experience in both Eastern and Western traditions 'is an overwhelming and compelling consciousness of the soul's oneness with the . . . Divine Ground' (Ramaswami and Sheikh, 1989: 435), and many mystics in both traditions are firmly grounded in theism. Meditation is generally thought to consist of four stages: preparation, attention, reception and higher consciousness (Willis, 1979; Goleman, 1988).

Meditation is obviously a complex subject matter. However, many investigators, for the purpose of research, have defined it as a 'stylized mental technique from Vedic or Buddhist [or Sufi] traditions repetitively practiced for the purpose of attaining a subjective experience that is frequently described as very restful, silent, and of heightened alertness, often characterized as blissful' (Jevning *et al.*, 1992: 415). After comparing numerous meditation techniques, Benson came to the conclusion that the differences between various techniques are merely 'stylistic manners reflecting a core of four universal ingredients' (Lichstein, 1988: 33). These four elements in Benson's (1975) *secular* method include a quiet environment, an object to dwell upon, a passive attitude and a comfortable position. Benson suggests that the object to concentrate on be a mental device, such as silent repetition of the word *one*, that will 'lure one's attention away from worldly concerns' (Lichstein, 1988, p. 33).

While meditation has been practised for centuries, its scientific study started only a few decades ago. Although a wide variety of meditation techniques exists, most of the available research deals with one specific technique, transcendental meditation (TM). Also, much of this research contains serious methodological flaws. But, in spite of the methodological shortcomings and considerable inconsistency of findings, a review of the literature indicates meditation is not a neutral event in its consequences, that it is different from ordinary rest and sleep and that it can have definite physiological consequences. Davidson (1976), Delmonte (1985, 1986), Jevning *et al.* (1992), Lichstein (1988), Ramaswami and Sheikh (1989), Wallace and Benson (1972), West (1987) and Woolfolk (1975) provide excellent reviews of the psychophysiological effects of meditation. It is not within the scope of this chapter to provide a detailed review. For details, the reader should consult the forementioned sources.

In this brief review, various meditation techniques have been lumped together;

for the aim here is not to compare the effects of different techniques but to see if meditation in general has any physiological consequences.

Cardiopulmonary responses

Theresa Bross, a French cardiologist who travelled to India in 1935, was perhaps the first to study the physiology of meditation. According to her report, one of the subjects was able to stop his heart (see Jevning *et al.*, 1992; Pelletier and Garfield, 1976). But more than twenty years later, three frequently quoted researchers, Wenger *et al.* (1961, 1963), were unable to find consistent changes in heart rate as a function of meditation among yogis. Since then, many studies have demonstrated the conscious control of heart rate, blood pressure, cholesterol levels, angina pectoris and premature ventricular contraction through meditative experiences (see Jevning *et al.*, 1992; Lichstein, 1988; Norris, 1989; Ramaswami and Sheikh, 1989; Sudsuang *et al.*, 1991).

In one of the earliest systematic studies on the effects of meditation, Bagchi and Wenger (1957) observed a lowering of the rate of respiration during meditation. Similar results were reported by Wenger *et al.* (1961) and Anand *et al.* (1961a). Hirai (1960), Akishige (1968) and Sugi and Akutsu (1968) reported significant reduction in oxygen consumption during meditation. Subsequently, numerous other researchers have reported changes in respiration rate, oxygen consumption, lung volume and related pulmonary phenomena. In many cases, the changes are of even higher magnitudes and significance than previously determined (Farrow and Herbert, 1982; Jevning *et al.*, 1992; Kesterson and Clinch, 1989; Lichstein, 1988; Sudsuang *et al.*, 1991; Wallace, 1970; Wallace and Benson, 1972; Wallace *et al.*, 1971). Also, in some cases these changes are accompanied by reports of experiences of pure consciousness.[1] Jevning *et al.* (1992) think a probable explanation of this discrepancy is employment of more experienced subjects and, in some cases, use of longer meditation periods, in later research.

Electrodermal changes

Several reports of the physiological effects of meditation indicate a marked increase of galvanic skin response (GSR) and decreased spontaneous electrodermal response (EDR) (see Jevning *et al.*, 1992; Ramaswami and Sheikh, 1989). Farrow and Herbert (1982) discovered that markedly increased GSR seemed to accompany reports of experiences of pure consciousness provided by the subjects. Orme-Johnson (1973) noted that GSR habituated to aversive auditory stimuli in both meditators and controls, but more quickly in meditators. Researchers also discovered that the GSR of meditators was more stable during meditation than that of resting controls. West (1979) found that meditators had a significant reduction in spontaneous skin conductance responses. Together, these results point towards higher behavioural stability (Ramaswami and Sheikh, 1989).

Electroencephalographic effects

Beginning with Das and Gastaut (1955), numerous other researchers have reported electroencephalographic (EEG) changes during meditation (Akishige, 1968, 1970; Anand *et al.*, 1961a; Banquet, 1973; Davidson, 1976; Kasamatsu and Hirai, 1966; Lynch *et al.*, 1974; Wallace *et al.*, 1971). The most common results include increase in the occurrence of the alpha wave. The appearance of theta waves has also been reported. In a recent review of physiological effects of transcendental meditation, Jevning *et al.* (1992) report a number of other EEG changes. These include high voltage theta burst activity, increased frontal alpha coherence and fast beta. They note that EEG coherence seems to correlate with subjective experiences of pure consciousness.

Researchers have also noted that external alpha-blocking stimulation, such as strong light, banging noise, or touching with a hot glass tube, did not block the alpha pattern when yogis were in *samadhi*,[2] while in a nonmeditating state the alpha was blocked (Anand *et al.*, 1961a, 1961b). Kasamatsu and Hirai (1966) in their EEG study employed forty-eight Japanese priests and their disciples with meditation experience ranging from one year to more than twenty years. At the beginning of meditation, fast alpha activity was noted. The alpha amplitude then increased, whereas the alpha frequency decreased. Also, EEG changes among Zen monks seem to positively correlate with subjective reports of deep meditation and the state of transcendence (Kasamatsu and Hirai, 1966; Banquet, 1973). Furthermore, the longer the subjects had spent in Zen training, the more the EEG changed. 'There was also a close relationship between degree of EEG changes and the Zen master's ratings of his disciples' mental status' (Ramaswami and Sheikh, 1989: 454).

Other physiological effects of meditation

Numerous other effects of meditation have been reported in the literature. These include the decline of adrenocortical activity (Bevan, 1980; Jevning *et al.*, 1978), decreased cortisol secretion (Subrahmanyam and Potkodi, 1980), increased urinary metabolite serotonin (Bujatti and Riederer, 1976), increased total protein level and decreased reaction time (Sudsuang *et al.*, 1991). In several clinical studies, it has been noted that meditation can play a significant role in the amelioration of a variety of health problems, such as asthma, insomnia, muscular dysfunction, severe migraine and cluster headaches, abuse of nonprescribed drugs, and cancer (Lichstein, 1988; Jevning *et al.*, 1992).

IMAGERY AND PHYSIOLOGY

Recently, mental imagery has become one of the most significant issues in cognitive and health psychology (Sheikh, 1983, 1984). While interest and research in imagery have mounted, a consensus concerning the nature and function of images is still lacking. However, whether images represent a direct encoding of perceptual experiences (Paivio, 1971), an artefact of propositional structuring (Pylyshyn, 1973), or a constructive and reconstructive process (Kosslyn, 1980) has not been of any real concern to the majority of clinicians and experimenters. They assume that everyone experiences mental representations of objects and events, and these representations constitute their subject matter. A definition of imagery such as the one by Richardson (1969: 2) is implicit in most of these approaches: 'Mental imagery refers to all those quasi-sensory or quasi-perceptual experiences of which we are self-consciously aware, and which exist for us in the absence of stimulus conditions that are known to produce their genuine sensory or perceptual counterparts.'

During the last two decades, a great deal of research has convincingly demonstrated that images can lead to definite somatic consequences (Kunzendorf and Sheikh, 1990; Sheikh and Kunzendorf, 1984; Sheikh et al., 1989). A brief review of this literature follows.

Imagery and heart rate

Studies of heart rate control through imaging had already been reported around the turn of the century (Tuke, 1872; Ribot, 1906). In the last two decades, several researchers obtained heart rate increases to imagined emotional and/or bodily arousal (Bauer and Craighead, 1979; Bell and Schwartz, 1975; Blizard et al., 1975; Boulougouris et al., 1977; Carroll et al., 1979, 1982; Craig, 1968; Gottschalk, 1974; Grossberg and Wilson, 1968; Jones and Johnson, 1978, 1980; Jordan and Lenington, 1979; Lang et al., 1980; Marks and Huson, 1973; Marks et al., 1971; Marzillier et al., 1979; Roberts and Weerts, 1982; Schwartz, 1971; Schwartz et al., 1981; Shea, 1985; Wang and Morgan, 1992; Waters and McDonald, 1973). Decreases in heart rate in response to relaxing images have also been reported (Arabian, 1982; Bell and Schwartz, 1975; Furedy and Klajner, 1978; McCanne and Iennarella, 1980; Shea, 1985). Furthermore, a number of studies have indicated a positive correlation between vividness of imagery and control of heart rate (Barbour, 1981; Carroll et al., 1979; Grossberg and Wilson, 1968; Lang et al., 1980). Also, biofeedback and imagery have been successfully combined in the treatment of various arrhythmias (Engel, 1979).

Imagery and blood pressure

Schwartz et al. (1981) and Roberts and Weerts (1982) reported that diastolic blood pressure rises in response to images of anger, but not to images of fear, whereas systolic blood pressure is raised by images of both anger and fear. Wang and Morgan (1992) noted an elevation in both systolic and diastolic blood pressure as a result of imagined exercise. In clinical research, long-lasting reductions in both systolic and diastolic blood pressure through relaxing images have been recorded (Ahsen, 1978; Crowther, 1983).

Imagery and blood flow

General blood flow is determined by vasoconstriction and vasodilatation. Several studies have indicated that vasomotor activity can be changed by imaging specific skin regions as feeling colder or hotter (Dugan and Sheridan, 1976; Kunzendorf, 1981, 1984; Ohkuma, 1985). The magnitude of these changes seems to be positively correlated with more prevalent visual and tactile images as assessed by scores on Kunzendorf's Prevalence of Imagery Tests (Kunzendorf, 1981).

Since heat images are capable of concentrating blood in localized tissues of the body, they may be the main underlying factor behind a number of other findings, such as the curing of warts through repeatedly imaging sensations of heat accompanying placebo ointments and dyes (Vollmer, 1946); the enlargement of breast size through repeated imaging of pulsation and warm feelings in the breast area (Willard, 1977); appearance of redness and swelling on skin through touching leaves that were imagined to be poisonous (Ikemi and Nakagawa, 1962), and redness and even blistering of the skin through imaginary burns (Paul, 1963). In contrast, it has been demonstrated that through images of inactivity haemophiliac dental patients (Lucas, 1965), as well as normal dental patients (Chaves, 1980), can reduce external bleeding. Although these studies used hypnosis as well as imagery, there is evidence that images alone are sufficient to lead to vaso-dilatation and vasoconstriction (see above).

Imagery and sexual response

Research shows that erotic images are sufficient to induce penile engorgement in men (Laws and Rubin, 1969; Smith and Over, 1987) and vaginal engorgement in women (Stock and Geer, 1982). It also appears that the degree of engorgement is positively correlated with imaging ability (Smith and Over, 1987; Stock and Geer, 1982). Research also indicates that erotic images frequently arise during sexual relationships and that they improve sexual responding (Hariton and Singer, 1974; Lentz and Zeiss, 1983–4; Pope et al., 1984). Moreover, erotic images seem to consistently induce arousal, whereas erotic pictures and X-rated films induce sexual arousal that tends to habituate (Smith and Over, 1987). In a recent study, Whipple et al. (1992) noted that orgasm from both self-induced imagery and genital self-stimulation led to significant and comparable increases in systolic blood pressure, heart rate, pupil diameter, pain detection threshold and pain tolerance threshold.

Imagery and body chemistry

A few studies have indicated that several changes in body chemistry can be induced through imaging. These include increase in free fatty acids accompanying anxious dream imagery (Gottschalk et al., 1966); alterations in cholesterol levels accompanying emotional and other images (Aya, 1967); increase in salivary flow through taste images (Barber *et al.*, 1964); and increase in gastric acid flow through taste images (Luckhardt and Johnston, 1924).

Imagery and ocular effects

Experimental research has shown that visual imagery can affect dilation of the pupil (Colman and Paivio, 1970; Paivio and Simpson, 1968; Simpson and Climan, 1971), the electrical activity of the retina (Kunzendorf *et al.*, 1995; Kunzendorf, 1984), and the reflex as well as voluntary movements of the eye (Zikmund, 1972; Richardson, 1978). Recently, Ruggieri and Alfieri (1992) studied the effects of perceiving and imagining near and far stimuli and discovered that processes of accommodation occur in both real and imagined conditions.

Imagery and electrodermal activity

A number of studies have shown that images of emotional and bodily arousal result in increased electrodermal activity in both normal and abnormal subjects (Bauer and Craighead, 1979; Drummond *et al.*, 1978; Gottschalk, 1974; Haney and Euse, 1976; Passchier and Helm-Hylkema, 1981). Also, image-induced galvanic skin response (GSR) seems to be positively correlated with vividness of imagery (Drummond *et al.*, 1978). In an applied investigation, Yaremko and Butler (1975) observed that, compared to ten pretest shocks, ten pretest images of electric shock produced faster electrodermal habituation to test shocks.

Imagery and electromyographs (EMGS)

Arousing images of stressful situations appear to increase frontalis EMG and subjectively experienced tension (Passchier and Helm-Hylkema, 1981) whereas relaxing images reduce these (Thompson and Adams, 1984). In line with William James' (1890) ideo-motor theory of the relationship between imaged activity and real behaviour, Lusebrink (1986–7) discovered that visual images of a pencil produced EMG activity in the right arm and visual images of the letter 'P' led to EMG activity in the lip. Similarly, Schwartz *et al.* (1974) noted that images of sadness and images of happiness, respectively, increased or decreased facial corrugator EMG activity. Also, Quintyn and Cross (1986) observed that images of movement were helpful in disinhibiting the 'frozen' body part in clients with Parkinson's disease.

Imagery and the immune system

It appears that a number of medical disorders result from overreaction or under-reaction of the immune system (Goldberg, 1985). Also, it is widely recognized that psychological and psychosocial variables play a significant role in immune-system functioning (Jemmott and Locke, 1984; Thackwray-Emmerson,

1988). Among the psychological variables affecting immune responses, mental images have been the focus of numerous researchers as well as clinicians, and their effects have been documented in both healthy subjects and cancer patients.

In healthy subjects, images of 'white blood cells attacking germs' increased neutrophil adherence (Schneider *et al.*, 1991), lymphocyte counts and salivary immunoglobulin A concentration (Jasnoski and Kugler, 1987; Olness *et al.*, 1989; Hall *et al.*, 1981), whereas images of an unresponsive immune system produced less neutrophil adherence (Schneider *et al.*, 1991) and lower lymphocyte stimulation of immune response (Smith *et al.*, 1985). Also, both image-induced increase and decrease in neutrophil adherence are positively correlated with vividness of induced images as judged by the subjects (Schneider *et al.*, 1991). Zachariae *et al.* (1990) combined relaxation and guided imagery procedure, instructing the subjects to imagine their immune system becoming very effective, and noted an increase in natural killer cell function in normal healthy subjects.

Pioneering work in the use of mental imagery with cancer patients was carried out by the Simontons as early as 1978 (Simonton *et al.*, 1978, 1980). They clinically tested the effects of imagery and relaxation with 159 patients who were diagnosed as having medically incurable cancer and were expected to die in a year. Of these, sixty-three were still alive two years later. Of the surviving patients, 22.2 per cent showed no evidence of cancer, 19.1 per cent were in remission and 31.8 per cent were stabilized. Unfortunately, they had no untreated control group.

Achterberg and Lawlis (Achterberg, 1984; Achterberg and Lawlis, 1979) and others have extended the Simonton work. In cancer patients, mental images of events such as tumours being absorbed or attacked by white blood cells have been demonstrated to increase the likelihood of remission (Achterberg, 1984, 1985; Gruber *et al.*, 1988; Norris, 1989; Pickett, 1987–8). Furthermore, the probability of remission seems to correlate positively with the imaging ability of the patients as assessed by image-CA, a technique developed by Achterberg and Lawlis (1979).

Attempts have also been made to utilize imagery in the treatment of various other medical problems, including the healing of burn wounds, ulcers, vaginitis, irritable bowel syndrome and rheumatoid arthritis (Gunville, 1991).

It is true that some of the studies reported in the section on imagery and physiology have serious methodological flaws, and several are merely clinical case studies. Also, negative findings are often not reported in the literature. Consequently one has to be cautious in drawing conclusions. However, it seems safe to conclude that imagery has immense potential to bring about a variety of physiological changes. As shown below, it may also be an important component in hypnosis and biofeedback. This field of inquiry deserves further attention from competent researchers.

BIOFEEDBACK, IMAGERY AND PHYSIOLOGY

Perhaps the first experiment employing biological feedback to the subject was carried out around the turn of the century by J.H. Bair (1901); however, formally, this field of study began about twenty-five years ago. Biofeedback training involves the

> continuous monitoring and amplifying of an ongoing biological process of a person, and the feeding back or displaying of this information to a person's . . . conscious awareness. This allows the individual to intentionally self-regulate the physiological activity being monitored by observing the effects of each self-regulation strategy.
>
> (Norris, 1989: 268)

During the last two decades, an enormous amount of experimental and clinical work has been conducted, and numerous physiological processes have thus been regulated or influenced. These include cardiovascular and cardiopulmonary changes, gastrointestinal motility, brain rhythms, striate muscle activity, blood flow to various parts of the body, blood glucose and insulin levels, and immune system functioning (Norris, 1989). There are many physiological disorders that biofeedback therapists have been able to treat with a considerable degree of success. These include migraine headaches, neurodermatitis, rheumatoid arthritis, asthma, tachycardia, arrhythmia, cardiospasm, hypertension, gastric ulcers, duodenal ulcers, ulcerative colitis, irritable bowel syndrome, inflammatory bowel disease, circulatory complications accompanying diabetes, vaginitis, burn wounds, diabetic foot ulcers, cerebral palsy, and functional bladder sphincter dyssynergia (Green and Green, 1977; Gunville, 1991; Ford, 1982, Norris, 1986; see also various issues of the journal *Biofeedback and Self-Regulation*).

A critical review of the biofeedback literature reveals that this technique is not equally effective for all subjects (King and Montgomery, 1980), and that individual differences in the effectiveness of biofeedback seem to be due to individual differences in imaging ability (Hirschman and Favaro, 1980; Ikeda and Hirai, 1976; Kunzendorf and Bradbury, 1983). Furthermore, the efficacy of biofeedback appears to be related not only to imaging ability, but also to the use of imagery during biofeedback (LeBouef and Wilson, 1978; Qualls and Sheehan, 1979; Schwartz, 1975; Takahashi, 1984).

Some researchers have explicitly compared the efficacy of biofeedback alone, biofeedback with imaging instructions, and imaging instructions without feedback. It appears that biofeedback with imaging instructions is more effective than biofeedback alone (Herzfeld and Taub, 1980; Ohkuma, 1985) and imaging alone may be more effective than biofeedback alone (Shea, 1985). It seems reasonable to conclude that the effects of biofeedback are partly reducible to autonomic effects of imagery.

HYPNOSIS AND PHYSIOLOGY

In recent years, interest in hypnosis as a scientific phenomenon has increased dramatically. Both experimental and clinical work has credited hypnosis with the capability of effecting a wide variety of physiological effects. For example, through hypnosis, allergic reactions have been inhibited, physiological reactions to cold stress have been minimized, labour contractions have been induced and inhibited in some women, some aspects of the narcotic withdrawal syndrome and of narcotic drug effects have been produced in postaddicts, water diuresis has been elicited in some hydrophenic females, ichthyosis has been mitigated, and wheals have even been produced in patients with a history of urticaria (see Barber, 1961, 1965, 1978, 1984). Increase in gastric acidity, metabolic rate and heart rate, reduction of blood calcium level, and alteration in spasticity of the bowels have also been noted (Gorton, 1959). Furthermore, attempts at preventing skin reactions produced by plants such as poison ivy (Ikemi and Nakagawa, 1962), at producing localized skin inflammation (Barber, 1970; Johnson and Barber, 1976), at stimulating the remission of warts (Johnson and Barber, 1978) and at stimulating growth of breasts (Williams, 1974; Willard, 1977) have been successful. Other somatic effects of hypnosis include changes in hypersensitivity of skin response (Black 1963; Black et al., 1963), immunomodulation (Hall et al., 1981), asthma and hayfever allergic symptoms (Mason and Black, 1958; Brown and Fromm, 1987), dog allergy (Perloff and Spiegelman, 1973), immune-related diseases (Margolis, 1983; Brown and Fromm, 1987), burn wounds (Barber, 1984), involuntary movements associated with Huntington's disease (Mold-awsky, 1984), blood flow and bleeding (Barber, 1984), irritable bowel syndrome and peptic ulceration (Whorwell, 1991).

There is evidence that, just like biofeedback and imagery, hypnosis and imagery are also closely related (Barber, 1978, 1984). It has been pointed out that suggestions employed in hypnosis generally direct the subject to imagine various situations (Honiotes, 1977; Weitzenhoffer and Hilgard, 1962). Hypnotic responsiveness and the ability to be absorbed in activities involving fantasy and imagination seem to be positively correlated (Barber, 1984; Hilgard, 1970; Sheehan, 1972). Sarbin (1976) has described the good hypnotic subject as being very similar to a child engaged in imaginative play and Crawford (in press) has confirmed that hypnosis and imagination are neurophysiologically related. Also, several researchers have concluded that hypnosis basically intensifies the subject's imaginative processes (Barber et al., 1974; Hilgard, 1965; Sarbin and Coe, 1972). Finally, research has shown that autonomic effects of hypnotic suggestion are mediated by mental imagery (Barber, 1984), that individual differences in the effectiveness of hypnosis are attributable to the imaging ability of the subjects (Spanos et al., 1988; Willard, 1977), and that although hypnotic images produce significant changes in physiological responses, waking images produce equivalent or even greater changes (Ikemi and Nakagawa, 1962; Shea, 1985; Spanos et al., 1988; Winer et al., 1965). It is interesting to note that the commission appointed by the king of France in the eighteenth century to investigate Mesmer's claims also concluded that his cures were primarily due to the excitement of the imagination of the patients (Sheikh *et al.*, 1979). Admittedly not all theorists in the field of hypnosis assign a preeminent role to imagery in hypnosis. For further details, the reader is referred to other sources (Lynn and Rhue, 1991).

CONCLUDING REMARKS

The foregoing review makes it abundantly clear that consciousness is not a mere epiphenomenon, a derivative of physiological processes, and in itself of no functional significance. As the Nobel prize-winning physicist Eugene Wigner, reflecting on the connection between consciousness and the physical world, observed, 'if mind could not affect the physical world but was only affected by it, this would be the only known example in modern physics of such a one-way interaction' (Dossey, 1982: 208).

It seems obvious that conscious mental activity can bring about far-reaching physiological changes and its role in health and disease has been grossly under-valued in medical communities. Dr Marcia Angell (1985: 1572) in the *New England Journal of Medicine* sums up the prevalent medical view: 'it is time to acknowledge that our belief in disease as a direct reflection of mental state is largely folklore.' It is apparent that we have not yet been able to escape the clutches of dualistic thinking. As Patricia Norris (1986) remarks, philosophy gets in the way of reality, and the research of the last three decades has not influenced the everyday practice of medicine. David McClelland describes the situation this way:

> Judging from my own experience, there will be resistance at every level to the notion that psychological variables play a key role in health, illness, and treatment. I have been told flatly by a world famous immunologist, for example, that psychological factors do not affect the immune system, despite, in my estimation, convincing evidence to the contrary. I have found it very difficult to get scientific papers . . . published in medical journals because reviewers have never heard of the variables . . . or simply find it impossible to believe that they could affect physiological processes. We must not assume that it is enough to demonstrate the importance of psychological variables in health areas to our own personal or scientific satisfaction. It will also require much effort to educate the medical and wider community to the role of psychological variables in health.
>
> (1985: 465–466)

Although we have been able to confirm the existence of events that a non-interactionist dualism prohibits, we have not been able to come out of its tenacious hold (McMahon, 1986). Perhaps it is so because no viable alternative models of human nature have been presented in any detail. For example, while it is obvious that there is a big leap involved from consciousness to physiology, we have been evading the question of the 'how' of physical symptom formation, and so far extremely limited attention has been given to the matter of transition from a purely mental concept, such as consciousness, to very specific somatic alterations (Kunzendorf, 1991; McMahon and Sheikh, 1989). As the eminent physicist Schrödinger observed, regarding the mind–matter issue: 'Science has never been able to adumbrate the causal linkage satisfactorily even to its most ardent disciples' (1945: 94).

It is commendable that recently a few open-minded scientists are beginning to look beyond the prevalent ideas concerning the relationship of mind and matter, and are trying to formulate new theories that would more adequately account for new observations (Dossey, 1982, 1991; McMahon, 1986; Pert, 1987; Sheikh and Sheikh, 1989; Weimer, 1976). In this regard, familiarity with the development of ideas in physics may turn out to be of invaluable significance (McMahon and Sheikh, 1984, 1989).

NOTES

1 In the TM literature pure consciousness is defined as a state in which the 'mind transcends the subtlest level of mental activity and experiences a state of complete mental quiescence in which thoughts are absent and yet consciousness is maintained'. These periods are 'characterized by the experience of perfect stillness, rest, stability, and order and by a complete absence of mental boundaries' (Farrow and Herbert, 1982: 133).
2 *Samadhi* is a state of ecstasy, in which the mind is unperturbed by outer distractions or inner turbulence. It also has been called a 'sphere of neither perception nor non-perception' where 'even the most refined of the pairs of opposites are transcended, even that between the all or nothingness, the all and the void' (Humphreys, 1987: 182).

REFERENCES

Achterberg, J. (1984) 'Imagery and medicine: psychophysiological speculations', *Journal of Mental Imagery* 8: 1–13.
—— (1985) *Imagery in Healing*, Boston, MA: Shambhala.
Achterberg, J. and Lawlis, G.F. (1979) 'A canonical analysis of blood chemistry variables related to psychological measures of cancer patients', *Multivariate Experimental Clinical Research* 4: 1–10.
Ahsen, A. (1978) 'Eidetics: neural experiential growth potential for the treatment of accident traumas, debilitating stress conditions, and chronic emotional blocking', *Journal of Mental Imagery* 2: 1–22.
Akishige, Y. (ed.) (1968) 'Psychological studies on Zen', *Bulletin of Faculty Literature of Kyrushu University* 5 and 11, Fukuoka, Japan.
—— (ed.) (1970) *Psychological Studies on Zen*, Tokyo: Zen Institute of Komazawa University.
Anand, B.K., Chinna, G.S. and Singh, B. (1961a) 'Studies on Sri Ramanand Yogi during his stay in an airtight box', *Indian Journal of Medical Research* 49: 82–89.
—— (1961b) 'Some aspects of electroencephalographic studies in yogis', *Electroencephalography and Clinical Neurophysiology* 13: 452–456.

Angell, M. (1985) 'Disease as a reflection of the psyche', *New England Journal of Medicine* 312: 1570–1572.

Arabian, J.M. (1982) 'Imagery and Pavlovian heart rate decelerative conditioning', *Psychophysiology* 19: 286–293.

Archer, J. (1673) *Everyman his Doctor*, London.

Aya, Y. (1967) 'The influence of emotions upon total serum cholesterol', *Fukuoka Igabu Zasshi Acta Medica* 58: 634–640.

Bagchi, B.K. and Wenger, M.A. (1957) 'Electrophysiological correlates of some yogi exercises', *Journal of Electroencephalography and Clinical Neurophysiology* 7: 132–149.

Bair, J.H. (1901) 'Development of voluntary control', *Psychological Review* 8: 474–510.

Banquet, J.P. (1973) 'Spectral analysis of the EEG in meditation', *Electroencephalography and Clinical Neurophysiology* 35: 143–151.

Barber, T.X. (1961) 'Physiological effects of "hypnosis"', *Psychological Bulletin* 58: 390–419.

—— (1965) 'Physiological effects of "hypnotic suggestions": a critical review of recent research (1960–1964)', *Psychological Bulletin* 63: 201–222.

—— (1970) *Suggested ('hypnotic') Behavior: the trance paradigm versus an alternative paradigm* (Medfield Foundation Report 103), Medfield, MA: Medfield Foundation.

—— (1978) 'Hypnosis, suggestions, and psychosomatic phenomena: a new look from the standpoint of recent experimental studies', *American Journal of Clinical Hypnosis* 21: 13–27.

—— (1984) 'Changing "unchangeable" bodily processes by (hypnotic) suggestions: a new look at hypnosis, cognitions, imagining, and the mind–body problem', in A.A. Sheikh (ed.) *Imagination and Healing*, Farmingdale, NY: Bayworld.

Barber, T.X., Chauncey, H.H. and Winer, H.A. (1964) 'Effect of hypnotic and non-hypnotic suggestions on parotid gland response to gustatory stimuli', *Psychosomatic Medicine* 26: 374–380.

Barber, T.X., Spanos, N.P. and Chaves, J.F. (1974) *Hypnosis, Imagination, and Human Potentialities*, Elmford, NY: Pergamon.

Barbour, W.P. (1981) 'Vividness of mental imagery and heart rate response to imagined anxiety evoking situations', unpublished honours thesis, University of Western Australia.

Bauer, R.M. and Craighead, W.E. (1979) 'Psychophysiological responses to the imagination of fearful and neutral situations: the effects of imagery instructions', *Behavior Therapy* 10: 389–403.

Bell, I.R. and Schwartz, G.E. (1975) 'Voluntary control and reactivity of human heart rate', *Psychophysiology* 12: 339–348.

Benson, H. (1975) *The Relaxation Response*, New York: Morrow.

Bevan, A.J.W. (1980) 'Endocrine changes in transcendental meditation', *Clinical and Experimental Pharmacology and Physiology* 7: 75–76.

Black, S. (1963) 'Inhibition of immediate-type hypersensitivity response by direct suggestion under hypnosis', *British Medical Journal* 6: 925–929.

Black, S., Humphrey, J.H. and Niven, J.S. (1963) 'Inhibition of Momtoux reaction by direct suggestion under hypnosis', *British Medical Journal* 6: 1649–1652.

Blizard, D.A., Cowings, P. and Miller, N.E. (1975) 'Visceral responses to opposite types of autogenic-training imagery', *Biological Psychology* 3: 49–55.

Boulougouris, J.C., Rabavilas, D.D. and Stefanis, C. (1977) 'Psychophysiological responses in obsessive-compulsive patients', *Behavior Research and Therapy* 15: 221–230.

Brown, D.P. and Fromm, E. (1987) *Hypnosis and Behavioral Medicine*, Hillsdale, NJ: Erlbaum.

Bujatti, M. and Riederer, P. (1976) 'Serotonin, noradrenaline, and dopamine metabolites in the transcendental meditation technique', *Journal of Neural Transmission* 39: 257–267.

Cannon, W.B. (1915) *Bodily Changes in Pain, Hunger, Fear, and Rage*, New York: Appleton.

Carroll, D., Baker, J. and Preston, M. (1979) 'Individual differences in visual imaging and the voluntary control of heart rate', *British Journal of Psychology* 70: 39–49.

Carroll, D., Marzillier, J.S. and Merian, S. (1982) 'Psychophysiological changes accompanying different types of arousing and relaxing imagery', *Psychophysiology* 19: 75–82.

Chaves, J.F. (1980) 'Hypnotic control of surgical bleeding', paper presented at Annual Meeting of the American Psychological Association, Montreal, September.

Colman, F. and Paivio, A. (1970) 'Pupillary dilation and mediation processes during paired-associate learning', *Canadian Journal of Psychology* 24: 261–270.

Cousins, N. (1983) *The Healing Heart*, New York: Norton.

Craig, K.D. (1968) 'Physiological arousal as a function of imagined, vicarious, and direct stress experience', *Journal of Abnormal Psychology* 73: 513–520.

Crawford, H.J. (in press) 'Cerebral brain dynamics of mental imagery: evidence and issues for hypnosis', in R.G. Kunzendorf, N.P. Spanos and B. Wallace (eds) *Hypnosis and Imagination*, Amityville, NY: Baywood.

Crowther, J.H. (1983) 'Stress management training and relaxation imagery in the treatment of essential hypertension', *Journal of Behavioral Medicine* 6: 169–187.

Das, H. and Gastaut, H. (1955) 'Variations de l'activité électrique du cerveau, du couer et des muscles suelettiques an cours de la méditation et de l'extase Yogique', *Electroencephalography and Clinical Neurophysiology* Suppl. 6: 211–219.

Davidson, J.M. (1976) 'The physiology of meditation and mystical states of consciousness, *Perspectives in Biology and Medicine* 19(3): 345–379.

Delmonte, M.M. (1985) 'Biochemical indices associated with meditation practice: a literature review', *Neuroscience and Biobehavioral Reviews* 9: 557–561.

—— (1986) 'Meditation as a clinical intervention strategy: a brief review', *International Journal of Psychosomatics* 33: 9–12.

Dossey, L. (1982) *Space, Time, and Medicine*, Boulder, CO: Shambhala.

—— (1991) *Meaning and Medicine*, New York: Bantam.

Drummond, P., White, K. and Ashton, R. (1978) 'Imagery vividness affects habituation rate', *Psychophysiology* 15: 193–195.

Dugan, M. and Sheridan, C. (1976) 'Effects of instructed imagery on temperature of hands', *Perceptual and Motor Skills* 42: 14.

Engel, B.T. (1979) 'Behavioral applications in the treatment of patients with cardiovascular disorders', in J.V. Basmajian (ed.) *Biofeedback: principles and practices for clinicians*, Baltimore, MD: Williams and Wilkins.

Farrow, J.T. and Herbert, R. (1982) 'Breath suspension during transcendental technique', *Psychosomatic Medicine* 44: 133–153.

Ford, M.R. (1982) 'Biofeedback treatment for headaches, Raynand's disease, essential hypertension, and irritable bowel syndrome: a review of the long-term follow-up literature', *Biofeedback and Self-Regulation* 7: 521–536.

Freyhan, F.A. (1976) 'Is psychosomatic obsolete? A psychiatric appraisal', *Comprehensive Psychiatry* 17: 381–386.

Furedy, J.J. and Klajner, F. (1978) 'Imaginational Pavlovian conditioning of large-magnitude cardiac decelerations with tilt as UCS', *Psychophysiology* 15: 538–548.

Gatchel, R.J. and Blanchard, E.B. (eds) (1993) *Psychophysiological Disorders*, Washington, DC: American Psychological Association.

Goldberg, B. (1985) 'The treatment of cancer through hypnosis', *Psychology: A Quarterly Journal of Human Behavior* 22: 36–39.

Goleman, D. (1988) *The Meditative Mind*, Los Angeles: Tarcher.

Gorton, B.E. (1959) 'Physiological aspects of hypnosis', in J.M. Schneck (ed.) *Hypnosis in Modern Medicine*, Springfield, IL: Charles C. Thomas.

Gottschalk, L.A. (1974) 'Self-induced visual imagery, affect arousal, and autonomic correlates', *Psychosomatics* 15: 166–169.

Gottschalk, L.A., Stone, W.N., Gleser, G.C. and Iacono, J.M. (1966) 'Anxiety levels in dreams: relation to changes in plasma free fatty acids', *Science* 153: 654–657.

Green, E.E. and Green, A.M. (1977) *Beyond Biofeedback*, New York: Delacorte.

Grossberg, J.M. and Wilson, K.M. (1968) 'Physiological changes accompanying the visualization of fearful and neutral situations', *Journal of Personality and Social Psychology* 10: 124–133.

Gruber, B.L., Hall, H.R., Hesch, S.P. and Dubois, P. (1988) 'Immune system and psychological changes in metastatic cancer patients using relaxation and guided imagery: a pilot study', *Scandinavian Journal of Behavior Therapy* 17: 24–96.

Gunville, T.M. (1991) 'Clinical applications of mental imagery: imagery, physiology and healing', unpublished manuscript, Marquette University, Milwaukee, WI.

Hall, H.R., Longo, S. and Dixon, R. (1981) 'Hypnosis and the immune system: the effect of hypnosis on T and B cell function', paper presented at 33rd Annual Meeting for the Society for Clinical and Experimental Hypnosis, Portland, OR, October.

Haney, J.N. and Euse, F.J. (1976) 'Skin conductance and heart rate responses to neutral, positive, and negative imagery: implications for covert behavior therapy procedures', *Behavior Therapy* 7: 494–503.

Hariton, E.B. and Singer, J.L. (1974) 'Women's fantasies during sexual intercourse: normative and theoretical implications', *Journal of Consulting and Clinical Psychology* 42: 313–322.

Herzfeld, G.M. and Taub, E. (1980) 'Effect of slide projections and tape-recorded suggestions on thermal biofeedback training', *Biofeedback and Self-Regulation* 5: 393–405.

Hilgard, E.R. (1965) *Hypnotic Susceptibility*, New York: Harcourt, Brace, Jovanovitch.

Hilgard, J.R. (1970) *Personality and Hypnosis*, Chicago: University of Chicago Press.

Hirai, T. (1960) 'Electroencephalographic study on the Zen meditation', *Folio Psychiatrica and Neurologica Japanica* 62: 76–105.

Hirschman, R. and Favaro, L. (1980) 'Individual differences in imagery vividness and voluntary heart rate control', *Personality and Individual Differences* 1: 129–133.

Honiotes, G.J. (1977) 'Hypnosis and breast enlargement – a pilot study', *Journal of the International Society for Professional Hypnosis* 6: 8–12.

Humphreys, C. (1987) *Concentration and Meditation*, Shaftsbury: Element Books.

Ikeda, Y. and Hirai, H. (1976) 'Voluntary control of electrodermal activity in relation to imagery and internal perception scores', *Psychophysiology* 13: 330–333.

Ikemi, Y. and Nakagawa, S. (1962) 'A psychosomatic study of contagious dermatitis', *Kyushu Journal of Medical Science* 13: 335–350.

James, W. (1890) *The Principles of Psychology*, vol. 2, New York: Henry Holt.

Jasnoski, M.L. and Kugler, J. (1987) 'Relaxation, imagery, and neuroimmodulation', *Annals of the New York Academy of Sciences* 496: 722–730.

Jemmott, J.B. and Locke, S.E. (1984) 'Psychosocial factors, immunologic mediation, and human susceptibility to infectious diseases: how much do we know?', *Psychological Bulletin* 95: 78–108.

Jevning, R., Wallace, R.K. and Beidebach, M. (1992) 'The physiology of meditation: a review', *Neuroscience and Behavioral Reviews* 16: 415–424.

Jevning, R., Wilson, A.F. and Davidson, J.M. (1978) 'Adrenocortical activity during meditation', *Hormones and Behavior* 10: 54–60.

Johnson, R.F.Q. and Barber, T.X. (1976) 'Hypnotic suggestions for blister formation: subjective and physiological effects', *American Journal of Clinical Hypnosis* 18: 172–181.

—— (1978) 'Hypnosis, suggestions, and warts: an experimental investigation implicating the importance of believed-in efficacy', *American Journal of Clinical Hypnosis* 20: 165–174.

Jones, G.E. and Johnson, H.J. (1978) 'Physiological responding during self-generated imagery of contextually complete stimuli', *Psychophysiology* 15: 439–446.
—— (1980) 'Heart rate and somatic concomitents of mental imagery', *Psychophysiology* 17: 339–347.
Jordan, C.S. and Lenington, K.T. (1979) 'Physiological correlates of eidetic imagery and induced anxiety', *Journal of Mental Imagery* 3: 31–42.
Kasamatsu, A. and Hirai, T. (1966) 'An electroencephalographic study of the Zen meditation (zazen)', *Folio Psychiatria and Neurological Japanica* 20: 315–336.
Kesterson, J. and Clinch, N.F. (1989) 'Metabolic rate, respiratory exchange ratio and apnea during meditation', *American Journal of Physiology* 256: 632–638.
King, N.J. and Montgomery, R.B. (1980) 'Biofeedback-induced control of human peripheral temperature: a critical review', *Psychological Bulletin* 88: 738–752.
Kosslyn, S. (1980) *Image and Mind*, Cambridge, MA: Harvard University Press.
Kunzendorf, R.G. (1981) 'Individual differences in imagery and autonomic control', *Journal of Mental Imagery* 5: 47–60.
Kunzendorf, R.G. (1984) 'Centrifugal effects of eidetic imaging on flash electroretinograms and autonomic responses', *Journal of Mental Imagery* 8: 67–76.
—— (1991) 'The causal efficacy of consciousness in general, imagery in particular: a materialistic perspective', in R.G. Kunzendorf (ed.) *Mental Imagery*, New York: Plenum.
Kunzendorf, R.G. and Bradbury, J.L. (1983) 'Better liars have better imaginations', *Psychological Reports* 52: 634.
Kunzendorf, R.G. and Sheikh, A.A. (1990) *The Psychophysiology of Mental Imagery: theory, research, and application*, Amityville, NY: Baywood.
Kunzendorf, R.G., Jesses, M. and Capone, D. (1995) 'Conscious images as "centrally excited sensations"', manuscript submitted for publication.
Lachman, S.J. (1972) *Psychosomatic Disorders: a behavioristic interpretation*, New York: Wiley.
Lang, P.J., Kozak, M.J., Miller, G.A., Levin, D.N. and McLean, A. (1980) 'Emotional imagery: conceptual structure and pattern of somato-visceral response', *Psychophysiology* 17: 179–192.
Laws, D.R. and Rubin, H.B. (1969) 'Instructional control of an autonomic sexual response', *Journal of Applied Behavior Analysis* 2: 93–99.
LeBouef, A. and Wilson, C. (1978) 'The importance of imagery in maintenance of feedback-assisted relaxation over extinction trials', *Perceptual and Motor Skills* 47: 824–826.
Lentz, S.L. and Zeiss, A.M. (1983–4) 'Fantasy and sexual arousal in college women: an empirical investigation', *Imagination, Cognition, and Personality* 3: 185–202.
Lichstein, K.L. (1988) *Clinical Relaxation Strategies*, New York: Wiley.
Lipkowski, Z.J. (1986a) 'Psychosomatic medicine: past and present', part I: 'Historical background', *Canadian Journal of Psychiatry* 31: 2–7.
—— (1986b) 'Psychosomatic medicine: past and present', part II: 'Current state', *Canadian Journal of Psychiatry* 31: 8–13.
Lucas, O. (1965) 'Dental extractions in the hemophiliac: control of the emotional factors by hypnosis', *American Journal of Clinical Hypnosis* 7: 301–307.
Luckhardt, A.B. and Johnston, R.L. (1924) 'Studies in gastric secretions'. I: 'The psychic secretion of gastric juice under hypnosis', *American Journal of Physiology* 70: 174–182.
Lusebrink, V.B. (1986–7) 'Visual imagery: its psychophysiological components and levels of information processing', *Imagination, Cognition, and Personality* 6: 205–218.
Lynch, J.J., Paskewitz, D.A. and Orne, M.T. (1974) 'Some factors in the feedback control of human alpha rhythm', *Psychosomatic Medicine* 36(5): 399–410.
Lynn, S.J. and Rhue, J.W. (1991) *Theories of Hypnosis: current models and perspectives*, New York: Guilford.

Margolis, C.G. (1983) 'Hypnotic imagery with cancer patients', *American Journal of Clinical Hypnosis* 25: 128–134.

Marks, I. and Huson, J. (1973) 'Physiological aspects of neutral and phobic imagery: further observations', *British Journal of Psychiatry* 122: 567–572.

Marks, I., Marset, P., Boulougouris, J. and Huson, J. (1971) 'Physiological accompaniments of neutral and phobic imagery', *Psychological Medicine* 1: 299–307.

Marzillier, J.S., Carroll, D. and Newland, J.R. (1979) 'Self-report and physiological changes accompanying repeated imaging of a phobic scene', *Behavior Research and Therapy* 17: 71–77.

Mason, A.A. and Black, S. (1958) 'Allergic skin responses abolished under treatment of asthma and hayfever by hypnosis', *Lancet* 1: 877–880.

McCanne, T.R. and Iennarella, R.S. (1980) 'Cognitive and somatic events associated with discriminative changes in heart rate', *Psychophysiology* 17: 18–28.

McClelland, D.C. (1985) 'Health psychology mandate', *American Behavioral Scientist* 28: 451–467.

McMahon, C.E. (1986) *Where Medicine Fails*, New York: Trado-Medic Books.

McMahon, C.E. and Koppes, S. (1976) 'The development of psychosomatic medicine: an analysis of growth of professional societies', *Psychosomatics* 17: 185–187.

McMahon, C.E. and Sheikh, A.A. (1984), Imagination in disease and healing processes: a historical perspective', in A.A. Sheikh (ed.) *Imagination and Healing*, Farmingdale, NY: Baywold.

—— (1989) 'Psychosomatic illness: a new look', in A.A. Sheikh and K.S. Sheikh (eds) *Eastern and Western Approaches to Healing*, New York: Wiley.

Meyer, A. (1957) *Psychobiology: a science of man*, Springfield, IL: Charles C. Thomas.

Moldawsky, R.J. (1984) 'Hypnosis as an adjunctive treatment in Huntington's disease'. *American Journal of Clinical Hypnosis* 26: 229–231.

Norris, P. (1986) 'Biofeedback, voluntary control and human potential', *Biofeedback and Self-Regulation* 11: 1–20.

—— (1989) 'Current conceptual trends in biofeedback and self-regulation', in A.A. Sheikh and K.S. Sheikh (eds) *Eastern and Western Approaches to Healing*, New York: Wiley.

Ohkuma, Y. (1985) 'Effects of evoking imagery on the control of peripheral skin temperature', *Japanese Journal of Psychology* 54: 88–94.

Olness, K., Culbert, T. and Uden, D. (1989) 'Self-regulation of salivary immunoglobulin A by children', *Pediatrics* 83: 66–71.

Orme-Johnson, D.W. (1973) 'Autonomic stability and transcendental meditation', *Psychosomatic Medicine* 35(4): 341–349.

Paivio, A. (1971) *Imagery and Verbal Processes*, New York: Holt, Rinehart & Winston.

Paivio, A. and Simpson, H.M. (1968) 'Magnitude and latency of the pupillary response during an imagery task as a function of stimulus abstractness and imagery ability', *Psychonomic Science* 12: 45–46.

Passchier, J. and Helm-Hylkema, H. (1981) 'The effect of stress imagery on arousal and its implications for biofeedback of the frontalis muscles', *Biofeedback and Self-Regulation* 6: 295–303.

Paul, G.L. (1963) 'The production of blisters by hypnotic suggestion: another look', *Psychosomatic Medicine* 25: 233–244.

Pelletier, K.R. and Garfield, C. (1976) *Consciousness East and West*, New York: Harper & Row.

Perloff, M.M. and Spiegelman, T. (1973) 'Hypnosis in the treatment of a child's allergy to dogs', *American Journal of Clinical Hypnosis* 15: 269–272.

Pert, C.B. (1987) 'Neuropeptides: the emotions and bodymind', *Advances* 3(3): 8–16.

Pickett, E. (1987–8) 'Fibroid tumors and response to guided imagery and music: two case studies', *Imagination, Cognition, and Personality* 7: 165–176.

Pope, K.S., Singer, J.L. and Rosenberg, L.C. (1984) 'Sex, fantasy and imagination: scientific research and clinical applications', in A.A. Sheikh (ed.) *Imagination and Healing*, Farmingdale, NY: Bayworld.

Pylyshyn, Z.W. (1973) 'What the mind's eye tells the mind's brain: a critique of mental imagery', *Psychological Bulletin* 80: 1–24.

Qualls, P.J. and Sheehan, P.W. (1979) 'Capacity for absorption and relaxation during electromyograph biofeedback and no-feedback conditions', *Journal of Abnormal Psychology* 88: 652–662.

Quintyn, M. and Cross, E. (1986) 'Factors affecting the ability to initiate movement in Parkinson's disease', *Physical and Occupational Therapy in Geriatrics* 4: 51–60.

Ramaswami, S. and Sheikh, A.A. (1989) 'Meditation east and west', in A.A. Sheikh and K.S. Sheikh (eds) *Eastern and Western Approaches to Healing*, New York: Wiley.

Ribot, T. (1906) *Essay on the Creative Imagination*, trans. A.H.N. Baron, Chicago: Open Court.

Richardson, A. (1969) *Mental Imagery*, New York: Springer.

—— (1978) 'Subject, task, and tester variables associated with initial eye movement responses', *Journal of Mental Imagery* 2: 85–100.

Roberts, R.J. and Weerts, T.C. (1982) 'Cardiovascular responding during anger and fear imagery', *Psychological Reports* 50: 219–230.

Ruggieri, V. and Alfieri, G. (1992) 'The eyes in imagery and perceptual processes: first remarks', *Perception and Motor Skills* 75: 287–290.

Rush, B. (1811) *Sixteen Introductory Lectures*, Philadelphia, PA: Bradford & Innskeep.

Sarbin, T.R. (1976) 'The Quixotic principle: believed-in imaginings', unpublished manuscript, Department of Psychology, University of California.

Sarbin, T.R. and Coe, W.C. (1972) *Hypnosis: a social psychological analysis of influence communication*, New York: Holt, Rinehart & Winston.

Schneider, J., Smith, C.W., Minning, C., Whitcher, S. and Hermanson, J. (1991) 'Guided imagery and immune system function in normal subjects: a summary of research findings', in R.G. Kunzendorf (ed.) *Mental Imagery*, New York: Plenum.

Schrödinger, E. (1945) *What is Life?* Cambridge: Cambridge University Press.

Schwab, J.J. (1978) *Sociocultural Roots of Mental Illness*, New York: Plenum.

Schwartz, G.E. (1971) 'Cardiac responses to self-induced thoughts', *Psychophysiology* 8: 462–467.

—— (1975) 'Biofeedback, self-regulation, and the patterning of physiological processes', *American Scientist* 63: 314–324.

Schwartz, G.E., Fair, P.L., Greenberg, P.S., Freedman, M. and Klerman, J.L. (1974) 'Facial electromyography in assessment of emotion', *Psychophysiology* 11: 237.

Schwartz, G.E., Weinberger, D.A. and Singer, J.A. (1981) 'Cardiovascular differentiation of happiness, sadness, anger, and fear following imagery and exercise', *Psychosomatic Medicine* 43: 343–364.

Shea, J.D. (1985) 'Effects of absorption and instructions on heart rate control', *Journal of Mental Imagery* 9: 87–100.

Sheehan, P.W. (1972) 'Hypnosis and the manifestations of "imagination"', in E. Fromm and R.E. Shor (eds), *Hypnosis: research development and perspectives*, Chicago: Aldine-Atherton.

Sheikh, A.A. (ed.) '(1983) *Imagery: current theory, research and application*, New York: Wiley.

—— (ed.) (1984) *Imagination and Healing*, Farmingdale, NY: Bayworld.

Sheikh, A.A. and Kunzendorf, R.G. (1984) 'Imagery, physiology, and psychosomatic illness', *International Review of Mental Imagery* 1: 94–138.

Sheikh, A.A. and Sheikh, K.S. (eds) (1989) *Eastern and Western Approaches to Healing*, New York: Wiley.

Sheikh, A.A., Kunzendorf, R.G. and Sheikh, K.S. (1989) 'Healing images: from ancient wisdom to modern science', in A.A. Sheikh and K.S. Sheikh (eds) *Eastern and Western Approaches to Healing*, New York: Wiley.

Sheikh, A.A., Richardson, P. and Moleski, L.M. (1979) 'Psychosomatics and mental imagery: a brief view', in A.A. Sheikh and J.T. Shaffer (eds), *The Potential of Fantasy and Imagination*, New York: Brandon House.

Shontz, F.C. (1975) *The Psychological Aspects of Illness and Disability*, New York: Macmillan.

Simonton, O.C., Matthews-Simonton, S. and Creighton, J. (1978) *Getting Well Again: a step-by-step, self-help guide to overcoming cancer for patients and their families*, Los Angeles: Tarcher.

Simonton, O.C., Matthews-Simonton, S. and Sparks, T.F. (1980) 'Psychological intervention in the treatment of cancer', *Psychosomatics* 21: 226–227.

Simpson, H.M. and Climan, M.H. (1971) 'Pupillary and electromyographic changes during an imagery task', *Psychophysiology* 8: 483–490.

Smith, D. and Over, R. (1987) 'Does fantasy-induced sexual arousal habituate?', *Behaviour Research and Therapy* 25: 477–485.

Smith, G.R., McKenzie, J.M., Marmer, D.J. and Steele, R.W. (1985) 'Psychologic modulation of the human immune response to varicella zoster', *Archives of Internal Medicine* 145: 2110–2112.

Smuts, J.C. (1926) *Holism and Evolution*, New York: Macmillan.

Spanos, N.P., Senstrom, R.J. and Johnston, J.C. (1988) 'Hypnosis, placebo and suggestion in the treatment of warts', *Psychosomatic Medicine* 50: 245–260.

Stock, W.E. and Geer, J.H. (1982) 'A study of fantasy-based sexual arousal in women', *Archives of Sexual Behavior* 11: 33–47.

Subrahmanyam, S. and Potkodi, D. (1980) 'Neurohumoral correlates of transcendental meditation', *Journal of Biomedicine* 1: 73–88.

Sudsuang, R., Chentanez, V. and Veluvan, K. (1991) 'Effect of Buddhist meditation on serum cortisol and total protein levels, blood pressure, pulse rate, lung volume and reaction time', *Physiology and Behavior* 50: 543–548.

Sugi, Y. and Akutsu, K. (1968) 'Studies on respiration and energy metabolism during sitting in zazen', *Research Journal of Physical Education* 12: 190.

Takahashi, H. (1984) 'Experimental study on self-control of heart rate: experiment for a biofeedback treatment of anxiety state', *Journal of Mental Health* 31: 109–125.

Thackwray-Emmerson, D. (1988) 'Stress and disease: an examination of psychophysiological effects and alternative treatment approaches', *Counseling Psychology Quarterly* 1: 413–420.

Thompson, J.K. and Adams, H.E. (1984) 'Psychophysiological characteristics of headache patients', *Pain* 18: 41–52.

Tuke, D.H. (1872) *Illustrations of the Influence of the Mind upon the Body in Health and Disease: designed to elucidate the action of the imagination*, London: J. and A. Churchill.

Vollmer, H. (1946) 'Treatment of warts by suggestion', *Psychosomatic Medicine* 8: 138–142.

Wallace, R.K. (1970) 'Physiological effects of transcendental meditation', *Science* 167: 1251–1254.

Wallace, R.K. and Benson, H. (1972) 'The physiology of meditation', *Scientific American* 262: 84–90.

Wallace, R.K., Benson, H. and Wilson, A.F. (1971) 'A wakeful hypometabolic physiologic state', *American Journal of Physiology* 221: 795–799.

Wang, Y. and Morgan, W.P. (1992) 'The effect of imagery perspectives on the psychophysiological responses to imagined exercise', *Behavioral Brain Research* 52: 167–174.

Waters, W.F. and McDonald, D.G. (1973) 'Autonomic response to auditory, visual and imagined stimuli in a systematic desensitization context', *Behaviour Research and Therapy* 11: 577–585.

Weimer, W.B. (1976) 'Manifestations of mind. Some conceptual and empirical issues', in G. Globus, G. Maxwell and J. Savodnik (eds) *Consciousness and the Brain*, New York: Plenum.

Weiner, H. (1977) *Psychobiology and Human Disease*, New York: Elsevier.

Weitzenhoffer, H.M. and Hilgard, E.R. (1962) *Stanford Hypnotic Susceptibility Scale, Form C*, Palo Alto, CA: Consulting Psychologist Press.

Wenger, M.A., Bagchi, B.K. and Anand, B.K. (1961) 'Experiments in India on voluntary control of the heart and pulse', *Circulation* 24: 1319–1325.

—— (1963) 'Voluntary heart and pulse control by yoga methods', *International Journal of Parapsychology* 5: 25–41.

West, M.A. (1979) 'Physiological effects of meditations: a longitudinal study', *British Journal of Social and Clinical Psychology* 18: 219.

—— (1987) *The Psychology of Meditation*, Oxford: Clarendon.

Whipple, B., Ogden, G. and Komisaruk, B.R. (1992) 'Physiological correlates of imagery-induced orgasm in women', *Archives of Sexual Behavior* 21: 121–123.

Whorwell, P.J. (1991) 'Use of hypnotherapy in gastrointestinal disease', *British Journal of Hospital Medicine* 45: 27–29.

Willard, R.D. (1977) 'Breast enlargement through visual imagery and hypnosis', *American Journal of Clinical Hypnosis* 19: 195–200.

Williams, J.E. (1974) 'Stimulation of breast growth by hypnosis', *Journal of Sex Research* 10: 316–326.

Willis, R.J. (1979) 'Meditation to fit the person: psychology and the meditative way', *Journal of Religion and Health* 18(2): 93–119.

Winer, R.A., Chauncey, H.H. and Barber, T.X. (1965) 'The influence of verbal or symbolic stimuli on salivary gland secretion', *Annals of the New York Academy of Sciences* 131: 874–883.

Wittkower, E.D. (ed.) (1977) *Psychosomatic Medicine: its clinical applications*, Hagerstown, MD: Harper & Row.

Woolfolk, R.L. (1975) 'Psychophysiological correlates of meditation', *Archives of General Psychiatry* 32: 1326–1333.

Yaremko, R.M. and Butler, M.C. (1975) 'Imaginal experience and attention of the galvanic skin response to shock', *Bulletin of the Psychonomic Society* 5: 317–318.

Zachariae, R., Kristensen, J.S., Hokland, P., Ellegaard, J., Metze, E. and Hokland, M. (1990) 'The effect of psychological intervention in the form of relaxation and guided imagery on cellular immune function in normal healthy subjects: an overview', *Psychotherapy and Psychosomatics* 54: 32–39.

Zikmund, V. (1972) 'Physiological correlates of visual imagery', in P. Sheehan (ed.) *The Function and Nature of Imagery*, New York: Academic Press.

Chapter 8

The placebo effect

Patrick D. Wall

SUMMARY

Day and night, the sensory apparatus of the nose, eyes, ears, skin and deep tissue steadily detects the nature of the world in which we live. This mass of unsensored data arrives continuously in the brain and spinal cord. Only a small selected fraction of the total available information affects our behaviour. A different small fraction is selected and made available for conscious perception. The manner of this selection is the subject of this chapter. A sequence of processes, alerting, orientation and attention, precedes conscious perception. It seems intuitively obvious that tissue damage and injury take precedence in attracting attention and inevitably result in conscious perceived pain. What appears intuitively obvious conflicts with the facts. The placebo effect shows that conscious perception can be dominated by expectations which may conflict with the sense data. Further-more, observations of human and animal behaviour repeatedly demonstrate that overall behaviour may relate to expectations learned from past experience rather than to the moment by moment information provided by the sense data.

INTRODUCTION

The word placebo has been used since the eighteenth century as a term for mock medicine. Its origin and meaning are usually given as a simple translation from the Latin as 'I will please'. I find that a highly improbable use of Latin by educated men of the time who would actually have said 'Placebit': 'It will please'. It seems to me much more likely that the word alludes to Psalm 116.9 'Placebo Domino in regione vivorum', which appears in the King James Bible as 'I will walk before the Lord in the land of the living'. This line beginning with 'Placebo' is the first line of the vespers for the dead. Placebo could have been the derisory word for these unpopular and expensive prayers, just as the words 'hocus pocus' come from the first line of the Communion, 'Hoc est corpus': 'This is the body [of Christ]'. This is surely the way in which Geoffrey Chaucer used the word placebo when he wrote, 'Flatterers are the devil's chatterlaines for ever singing placebo' in 1340, as did Francis Bacon in the line 'Instead of giving Free

Counsell sing him song of placebo' in 1625. This adds a more subtle meaning to the word, where the sycophant tells the listener what he expects and wants to hear, rather than the truth. That remains a placebo.

This subject is full of surprises for philosophers and neuroscientists and clinicians. Pain in contrast to suffering, is usually taken as a primary modality of sensation inevitably and automatically triggered by damage to the tissues of the body. The placebo is a powerful and widespread phenomenon which cuts the apparently inevitable link between the physical stimulus and the perceived sensory response. As we shall see, the placebo is a subtle learned effect. We are therefore faced with the traditional dualistic question of whether the placebo is a physical event or a mental process. Where precisely does the placebo intrude in the assumed separation of body and mind? Is this even a meaningful question?

This question is much more than a philosophical conundrum. It becomes a practical clinical question and a legal challenge. The question is translated into the search for the sight of action of a therapy, i.e. does it affect the body or the mind? This leads to tortuous attempts to define the placebo as a belief state separable from the purely physical effect of a drug or of surgery (White et al., 1985). In all countries, it is a legal requirement to carry out clinical trials in order to prove that the therapeutic efficiency of a new drug is superior to a placebo. A placebo here means some process by which the patient (and the therapist) are fooled into believing that they have received the new treatment, although they have in fact received some neutral substance. These trials supposedly separate 'truth' from 'belief' or 'vera' from 'placebo'. The acceptance of the method of drug trial has led to attempts to test in a similar manner other therapies such as acupuncture, homeopathy, psychoanalysis, etc. It clearly becomes progressively more difficult to fool patients into the belief that they have received the 'true' therapy. However, attempts at a clear separation persist. I will not join this attempt.

For what follows, I need go no further than Burton in 1621 in *The Anatomy of Melancholy*: 'There is no virtue in some [folk remedies] but a strong conceit and opinion alone which forceth a motion of the humours, spirits and blood which takes away the cause of the malady from the parts affected'; and 'An empiric oftentimes, or a silly chirugeon, doth more strange cures than a rational physician because the patient puts more confidence in him.'

TWO EXAMPLES OF THE PLACEBO EFFECT

I wish here to give only two contemporary examples of the effect of strong opinions from the legion of placebo effects. Surgery is rarely the subject of a placebo test, in spite of an admonition by Finneson (1969) in his book on surgery for pain: 'Surgery has the most potent placebo effect that can be exercised in medicine' (p. 30). In the 1950s it became a common practice to ligate the internal mammary arteries as a treatment for angina pectoris. Angina is a painful condition attributed to an inadequate blood supply of muscle in the heart wall. The rationale for the operation was that if the internal mammary arteries were ligated, the blood in these arteries would find alternative routes by sprouting new channels through nearby heart muscle, thereby improving the circulation in the heart. This relatively simple operation was carried out on large numbers of patients to the satisfaction of many. However, the rationale came under suspicion when pathologists were unable to detect any of the supposed new blood vessels in the heart. Therefore, two groups of surgeons and cardiologists (Cobb *et al.*, 1959; Dimond *et al.*, 1958) decided to test the rationale by carrying out sham operations to incise the skin and expose the arteries in some patients while proceeding with the full ligation in others. The patients and their physicians did not know who had the true operation and who had the sham. The majority of both groups of patients showed great improvement in the amount of reported pain, in their walking distance, in their consumption of vasodilating drugs and some in the shape of their electrocardiogram. The improvement in both groups was maintained over six months of observation. The interest here is not only the evident power of the belief that therapeutic surgery had been completed but that improvement was sustained for at least six months, in spite of the general belief that placebos have a brief and fading action.

The second example is the work of Hashish *et al.* (1988), who examined the effect of ultrasound therapy, which others had found to be the equal of steroids in reducing pain and jaw tightness (trismus) and swelling after the extraction of wisdom teeth. To determine the effective level of ultrasound, they set intensity at different levels in a manner which was unknown to the patient and the therapist. When the machine was set to produce no ultrasound, there was a marked beneficial effect, even superior to the results of the normally used intensities. Naturally disturbed by the apparently bizarre finding, the experimenters wondered if the therapeutic effect was produced by the massage of the injured area coincident with the application of the ultrasound. They therefore trained patients to massage themselves with the inactive ultrasound head with the same movements used by the professionals. This was completely ineffective. Evidently, the therapeutic phenomenon required an impressive machine and someone in a white coat to transmit the effect, even though the emission of ultrasound was not required. I introduce this particular example, chosen from many such, because the placebo therapy not only reduced the pain report but also improved the ability to open the mouth and reduced the swelling.

The reduction of pain will surprise those people who consider pain as a reliable and inevitable sensation associated with tissue damage. However, there are others who would categorize pain as a mental perception and therefore as subject to error and manipulation. These two attitudes are practical examples of the Cartesian dualistic divide, where sensation is the consequence of the working of a body mechanism while perception is a mental process. There are others who will argue that this division between body and mind is a historical artefact produced by a muddle of academic, religious, introspective argument. Whichever attitude is taken, surprise should remain that the placebo also affected the contraction of jaw muscles normally attributed to a reflex action in the flexion reflex category which loops through the medulla. Furthermore, the placebo affected the swelling, which is a classical component of the local inflammation triggered by local damage.

FOUR REASONS FOR THE DISCOMFORT PROVOKED BY THE TOPIC

Quackery

From the eighteenth century onwards, the word placebo became attached to quackery. As a rational medicine developed, placebo could be used as a word to hammer Burton's 'empirics and silly chirugeons'. Beyond this, even the rational physicians were not above the use of a placebo as a form of deception, either for diagnostic purposes or to get rid of unwanted or unprofitable patients. This, in turn, provoked the ethical and practical discussion of whether the doctor–patient relationship would survive the discovery by patients that doctors used deception on occasions. This debate on the role of truth-telling and paternalism in the clinic continues (Rawlinson, 1985) with discussion of such phrases as 'the benevolent lie'. As awe and trust by the patient for the paternal doctor fade, so does the frequency of informed consent and of the placebo response. In 1807 Thomas Jefferson wrote:

> One of the most successful physicians I have ever known has assured me that he used more bread pills, drops of coloured water and powders of hickory ashes than of all other medicines put together . . . I consider this a pious fraud.

A tiresome and expensive artefact

A considerable fraction of the huge cost of clinical trials for a new drug resides in the legal requirement for a placebo trial. Not only is the expensive delay assigned to the fault of a meddling bureaucracy, but the existence of a fraction of patients who show placebo responses is considered to be of no intellectual interest but simply an intrusion in the search for true mechanisms.

One attractive short cut is to compare the new therapy with an established one without a placebo stage in a cross-over trial. This does not address the possibility that both therapies are placebos. In two surveys of tests for the effectiveness of manipulation, osteopathy and chiropractic for pain, the great majority were shown to be inadequate, while the acceptable trials produced contradictory answers (Koes et al., 1991, 1992).

A question of logic

The very mention of a placebo trial is likely to be taken as a hostile questioning of the logic on which a therapy is based. To request an investigation of the placebo component which is an inevitable part of any therapy is to invite anger. Anger confuses the question of whether something should work with the question of whether it does work. Too bad.

The reality of the senses

Everyone assesses their own sanity by cross-checking their sensation with objective reality. On the rare occasions where there is a mismatch, special names are applied – hallucination, illusion, delusion, madness, drunkeness, etc. For anyone, there is a simple intuitive sense apparent on reading Descartes (1644):

> If for example fire comes near the foot, the minute particles of this fire, which you know move at great velocity have the powers to set in motion the spot of skin of the foot which they touch, and by this means pulling on the delicate thread which is attached to the spot of the skin, they open up at the same instant the pore against which the delicate thread ends [in the brain] just as by pulling on one end of a rope one makes to strike at the same instant a bell which hangs at the other end.

It seems so reasonable that we should possess sensory mechanisms which represent the state of the world as reliably as the tolling of the bell represents action at the end of its rope. It seems equally reasonable that we should possess a separate entity, the mind, which can decide whether to ignore the bell or write a poem about it. Even a philosopher like Bertrand Russell who questioned Cartesian dualism still required a reliable sensory apparatus that generated sensation as the closest representation of events the machinery would permit. Sensation for him was generated by a continuous uncensored flow of information. If this flow was faulty or variable, then even a great cognitive brain would necessarily be faulty. If the sensory apparatus was censored or corruptible, then sense could become nonsense and reality an individual construct of a particular mind. We have many reasons and facts which lead us to reject that conclusion. We trust our senses, the five senses of Aristotle. Pain appears to us as the sensation provoked by injury. A broken leg provokes an appropriate intensity and location of pain. Placebos in no way affect the leg and its fracture but modify the sensation of pain and its perception. No wonder the topic provokes a sense of discomfort.

DIVERSIONS GENERATED TO AVOID A CONSIDERATION OF THE NATURE OF PLACEBO RESPONSES

When doctors who are not involved in a therapy under trial learn that it turns out to be a placebo, they howl with laughter. When you are the subject in a trial and discover that you have reacted to a placebo, as I have, you feel a fool. When you are the proponent or inventor of a therapy, whether based on contemporary rationale or old-fashioned faith, you are resentful of the need for placebo testing. If the test reveals a substantial placebo component in the response, myths are created to eliminate consideration of the placebo effect. These add to the four general reasons for discomfort with the effect.

Myth 1: the placebo diffentiates between organic and mental disease

This is the most dangerous and cruel attitude which has been used by physicians and surgeons when they detect placebo responses. An example is shown in the reaction of the profession to the true or sham operation on the internal mammary artery described above (Cobb *et al.*, 1959; Dimond *et al.*, 1958). Amsterdam *et al.* (1969) describe patients with angina in whom there appears to be an adequate circulation in the coronary arteries. It is then immediately assumed, without evidence, that these are the patients who would respond to a placebo while those with true cardiac ischaemia could not. This idea had already been suggested by psychiatrists using the phrase 'somatic hallucination' (Farrer, 1964). Clearly, this approaches the diagnosis of hysteria (Merskey, 1989), although in hysteria the somatization fails to initiate any known organic disease so that the alert diagnostician can differentiate hysteria from the condition it mimics. Here we have the proposal that some patients mimic an organic disease so precisely that a diagnostic test, the placebo, is needed to separate the two classes. The proposal is very attractive to those who seek an absolute separation of organic from functional disease and who believe that every true pain is precisely causally related to an observable organic lesion. The proposal is dangerous nonsense if one considers the hundreds of papers, of which 986 are reviewed in Turner *et al.* (1980), where placebo responses are described in patients suffering pain appropriate to a diagnosed overt organic lesion, such as postoperative pain or cancer.

I will simply relate two illustrative anecdotes. A patient with classical causalgia following a near miss on his sciatic nerve by a bullet had responded to a saline injection interspersed in a regular series of morphine injections. A very senior orthopaedic surgeon concluded that there was therefore nothing wrong with the man, by which he meant there could be no causative lesion in this surgeon's territory of interest, i.e. peripheral nerves and bones, and therefore this was a mental condition as proven by the placebo response. The patient's pain and the vascular signs disappeared with a sympathectomy of the leg, a procedure of which the patient had no knowledge or expectation. This patient's pain was caused by a peripheral nerve lesion and cured by a peripheral lesion.

The second anecdote is related by Professor Collins, who became head of neurosurgery at Yale. In a forward hospital in Korea, while operating on a series of casualty admissions, he began to suffer severe abdominal pain which was obviously acute appendicitis. Faced with extreme emergency casualties, he ordered the theatre sister to give him an injection of morphine. His pain subsided and he completed the surgery, after which he himself became a patient and his inflamed appendix was removed. Returning to duty after his recovery, he was leafing through the operating room report book when he came across the sister's entry: 'Major Collins ordered a morphine injection so that he could continue operating but, since he appeared distressed, I thought it best to give him an intramuscular injection of saline.'

Myth 2: the placebo is the equivalent of no therapy

This is clearly not true. The placebo has a positive effect. If cancer patients receive narcotics at regular intervals, the secret substitution of a single saline injection in the series of morphine injections results in the relief of pain and other signs and symptoms in the majority of patients. Furthermore, the time course of relief imitates that produced by the administration of the narcotic. The saline injection is not the same as missing an injection, since the placebo produced a decrease in pain while missing an injection would be followed by an increase in pain.

Myth 3: a fixed fraction of patients respond to placebos

This myth is widely stated in papers and textbooks, with the figure of 33 per cent being commonly quoted. The idea is to label a fraction of the population as mentally peculiar. Where these sources quote the origin of the myth, they refer to Beecher (1955), who gives the figure of 35.2 per cent. However, this figure is an average of Beecher's own eleven studies, each of which varied widely from the average. Double-blind studies show the fraction of placebo responders varying from close to 0 per cent (Tyler, 1946) to near 100 per cent (Liberman, 1964), depending on the circumstances of the trial. Clinical pains are associated with a larger number of placebo responders than experimental pains (Beecher, 1959). The subtlety of the conditions has commercial as well as theoretical interest. Capsules containing coloured beads are more effective than coloured tablets, which are superior to white tablets with corners, which are better than round white tablets (Buchaleq and Coffield, 1982). Beyond this, intramuscular saline injections are superior to any tablet but inferior to intravenous injections. Tablets taken from a bottle labelled with a well-known brand name are superior to the same tablets taken from a bottle with a typed label. My favourite is a doctor who always handled placebo tablets with forceps, assuring the patient that they were too powerful to be touched by hand. More seriously, I will discuss the conversion of experimental subjects to placebo responders (Voudouris et al., 1989, 1990). There is no fixed fraction of the population that responds to placebos.

Myth 4: placebo responders have a special mentality

This proposal is an extension of the fixed-fraction myth. It proposes that there are groups in the population with distorted mental processes which lead them to confuse true therapies with placebos. For those who cannot imagine that a normal person would ever make such a mistake, the idea is attractive. It was first proposed by Beecher (1968) and promptly dropped. With the rise of personality psychology, there were any number of pejorative mental tendencies which could be detected in the population by the analysis of the answers to questionnaires. Some of these seemed attractive labels to hang on those who responded to placebos to differentiate them from the normal subject who would never make such a silly mistake. These labels include suggestible, hypnotizable, neurotic, extrovert, introvert, acquiescent, willing to please and unsophisticated. For anyone who rates high on masochism in a personality questionnaire, I suggest they wade their way through the thirty-six papers on the topic in Turner *et al.* (1980) and the many more in White *et al.* (1985). Most papers report no correlations with personality type and the rest are contradictory.

Myth 5: pain is a multidimensional experience and the placebo affects only a part

Beecher (1959) made an intuitive introspective common sense division of one's personal reaction to pain as having two separable dimensions: one deals with intensity and the other with reaction. This is reminiscent of Cartesian sensation followed by perception. Melzack and Casey (1968) even assigned different parts of the brain to create these two dimensions, which gave a new respectability to this ancient idea. Melzack and Torgerson (1971) then analysed the way in which people used words about pain and derived three dimensions: sensory, affective and evaluative. From this, the widely used McGill Pain Questionnaire evolved. Up till now, four dimensions have been isolated (Holroyd *et al.*, 1992). Gracely *et al.* (1978) and Gracely *et al.* (1979) examined the placebo response to discover if all dimensions of pain were equally involved. They used volunteer experimental normal subjects who received gradually rising electrical shocks to the teeth. The subjects were asked to rate separately the intensity of the pain and the unpleasantness of the pain, i.e. Cartesian sensation and perception, or Beecher's intensity and reaction, or Melzack's sensation and affect. The subjects were then given a saline injection with the assurance that they were receiving a powerful analgesic. The intensity of the pain was completely unaffected, while at low shock levels the unpleasantness was markedly reduced but at higher intensities it was unaffected. This important experiment would seem to bring us back to the most classical position: sensation as a body mechanism is unaffected by a placebo at any stimulus level. Minor unpleasantness as a mental perception is affected by the mental suggestion implicit in the presence of a placebo. When the stimulus intensity rises, the appropriate unpleasantness perception regains its proper place, in spite of implied suggestion from the placebo. These clear experiments would seem to remove the mystery from the placebo and to return the entire subject to classical dualism. Gracely *et al.* (1978) went on to show that diazepam, a tranquillizer, could produce exactly the same effect.

Up to this point one could say that the experiments support a particular version of Cartesian dualism in which there is a reliable sensory apparatus unaffected by these manipulations and that sensation is observed by a mental apparatus which assigns unpleasantness to the pure sensation and which is subject to suggestion and to tranquillizers. However, Gracely *et al.* (1979) went on to investigate the effect of fentanyl, a narcotic, on the same type of pain and the result is summarized in the title of their paper: 'Fentanyl reduces the intensity but not the unpleasantness of painful tooth sensations'. This abolishes the idea that a reliable sensory apparatus feeds a dependent mental apparatus which assigns unpleasantness. The three experiments taken together suggest that there are two separate dimensions, intensity and unpleasantness, which can be manipulated independently. We should now ask if the placebo result, i.e. intensity is unaffected but low level unpleasantness is affected, can be taken as a general statement about analgesic placebos. The first prediction would be that placebos would work on minor pain but not on severe pain, but that is precisely the opposite of Beecher's observations (1955) and those of Lasagna *et al.* (1954). The second prediction is that patients responding to a placebo would report the pain intensity unchanged while the unpleasantness was relieved, but patients with migraine or postoperative pain or cancer report relief of both aspects. Even in experimental situations, both threshold and intensity are affected by placebos (Voudouris *et al.*, 1989, 1990). My conclusion is that the identification of distinct categories of pain experience is a valid and useful aspect of pain study but that the placebo effect can change these dimensions separately or together, depending on the circumstances of suggestion, expectation and instruction.

Myth 6: the placebo effect may be dissected away to reveal the pure therapeutic action

For this myth to be true, the therapeutic effect of an active compound would have to be free of its own additional placebo component. Strong evidence shows that two responses are not separable in practical tests. In an extensive series of tests on postoperative pain, Lasagna *et al.* (1954) identified placebo reactors and nonreactors. They then gave a fixed dose of morphine to the two groups and found an adequate analgesic response in 95 per cent of the placebo reactors and only 55 per cent of the nonreactors. A much more subtle problem was revealed by Beecher (1968) on examination of the matrix of results from double-blind cross-over studies of morphine versus saline. If the first administration contained morphine, the patient learned that this trial involved powerful medicine and tended to give a strong response to the second administration, which was saline. If the first test dose was saline, the response to the second, which contained morphine, was weak. It is obvious that this problem will also affect the results of trials where the relative effects of two active compounds are being compared. There will be a carry-over effect of the first trial on the results of the second.

It is apparent that the patient or subject is searching for subtle hints of what to expect and that these expectations affect responses. This raises the question of the comparable nature of the active test and the placebo test. It does not take a connoisseur to distinguish intravenous morphine from saline, because the morphine produces such obvious immediate side effects. This problem has led to the use of placebos that produce some obvious effect, such as vasodilatation, which are assumed to have no direct therapeutic effect but give the subject an impression of receiving powerful medicine. The introduction of active placebos produces a series of problems: the placebo and active compound rarely precisely mimic each other; the specific inactivity of the placebo is questionable; the patient may find the placebo's effects distasteful. These problems apply even more to other forms of therapy. What is a comparable manoeuvre against which to test acupuncture? The nature of acupuncture is well known to 90 per cent of the world's population.

Because, as we shall see, it is the expectation of the subject which is crucial, the obverse is the question of secrecy. It is assumed in therapeutic trials that the subject is not aware of the expectation of the proponent. Can that be achieved in practice? Sometimes the secrecy is shattered in obtaining consent: 'We would like you to help us in a trial of a new, safer form of aspirin.' Almost always, the person who administers the therapy, who may not know which pill is blank and which is 'true', will be aware of the general nature of what is being tested. This person's expectations can be covertly infectious. Patients talk to each other and reach a consensus; the strong effects of this covert expectation are shown by Evans (1974). He examined the relation between the relative effect of a range of analgesics versus placebos in twenty-two published double-blind trials. If the placebo effect was independent of the therapeutic effect, the placebo fraction of responders would have been the same in all trials while the drugs ranged in a series of therapeutic potency. The results all show that the stronger the drug, the stronger the placebo response. Evans divided the pain reduction produced by the placebo by the reduction produced by the drug. The answer is a fixed 55–60 per cent over the entire range from weak to strong analgesics. So much for the blindness of these double-blind trials. So much for the clear separation of placebo and therapeutic effects.

These six myths do not permit us to dispose of the placebo. It is evidently a common and powerful phenomenon which needs explanation.

CLASSES OF EXPLANATION

Affective

Gracely *et al.* (1978) propose that the placebo effect works on the unpleasantness of pain while leaving the intensity dimension unaffected. I gave reasons above for believing that their experiments represent a special case which does not apply universally, especially in clinical cases. Evans (1977) proposes that the placebo operates by decreasing anxiety. However, the results show that there is a weak and variable interaction with various types of anxiety and it is clear that anxiety reduction is a component of the placebo effect rather than the cause of it.

Cognitive

By far the commonest proposal is that the placebo effect depends on the expectation of the subject. There is nothing subtle about this. Placebo reactors can be identified before the trial by simply asking the subject what they expect to be the outcome of the therapy. Those who doubt do not respond to the placebo, while those with high expectations do (reviewed by Bootzin, 1985). Lasagna *et al.* (1954) investigated many aspects of postoperative patients who responded to placebos and to analgesic drugs and conclude: 'a positive placebo response indicated a psychological set predisposing to anticipation of pain relief.' They add: 'It is important to appreciate that this same anticipation of pain relief also predisposes to increase the effect of morphine and other pharmacologically active drugs.' In a trial of two drugs versus placebos on 100 patients, Nash and Zimring (1969) tested specifically for the role of expectation. The two drugs had no effect which would differentiate them from the placebo, but there was a strong correlation between the measured expectation and the placebo effect. Expectation is given a number of related names, such as belief, faith, confidence, enthusiasm, response bias, meaning, credibility, transference, anticipation, in thirty of the papers in the bibliography of Turner *et al.* (1980).

Expectation is a learned state and therefore young children do not respond to placebos as adults do, because they have had neither the time nor the experience to learn. Similarly, in adults, the learning of expected effects will depend on culture, background, experience and personality. A desire to believe, please and obey the doctor will increase the effect while hostility decreases it. Obviously, part of the expectation of the patient will depend on the expectation, enthusiasm and charisma of the therapist and there are many reports on this doctor–patient interaction. Expectation in a laboratory experiment may be more limited than in a clinical setting, which may explain why rates and intensities of placebo effects tend to be less in the laboratory than in the clinic (Beecher, 1959).

Conditioning

There are many reports of drug anticipatory responses in animals (Herrnstein, 1965; Siegel, 1985). These come in two forms. In the first, the animal has been given one or more trials on an active drug and is then given a saline injection; it proceeds to mimic the behavioural or physiological response which was observed after the administration of the active drug. In the second type, the animal mimics the actions which it mobilizes to neutralize the effect of the active compound. For example, if animals have experienced a series of injections of insulin that lower the blood sugar, a saline injection in the same setting as the insulin injection results in a rise of blood sugar, which would be one of the animal's reactions to counteract the insulin-induced decrease (Siegel, 1975). In cultures not raised on *Winnie the Pooh*, *Wind in the Willows* and *Watership Down*, it is customary to deny animals the luxury of cognitive processing and to ascribe such phenomena to classical Pavlovian conditioning.

This led to the proposal that the human placebo response had the characteristics of a conditioned response (Wickramasekera, 1980; Reiss, 1980). The idea is that active powerful drugs produce a powerful objective physiological response in the same manner that food produces salivation, the unconditioned stimuli and responses. However, giving the drug is inevitably associated with a pattern of other stimuli, such as a hypodermic injection. It is proposed that these are the equivalent of unconditioned stimuli coupled with the conditioned stimulus. It is then proposed that if these incidentally coupled stimuli are given alone, they will provoke the same response as the original drug; just as with the dog, coupling a bell with food eventually leads to the ability of the bell by itself to provoke salivation. The similarity goes beyond the proposed production of a conditioned response. If a placebo is given repeatedly in some, but not all, trials, the effect declines. This is a characteristic of Pavlovian responses, where simple repeated ringing of the bells leads to a steady decline of the salivation unless the conditioning is reinforced by the occasional coupling of the bell with food.

All such comparisons between widely differing processes lead to argument about similarities and differences, identities and analogies (Wall and Safran, 1986). However, the idea led to a series of clever experiments by Voudouris et al. (1989, 1990). The first stage was a repeat of a type of trial which had been reported many times before. Volunteer subjects were given rising electric shocks and the current was established, in full view of the subject, at which the shock became painful and the level at which it became intolerable. Then a bland cream was rubbed on the area, the subjects were assured that it was a powerful anaesthetic, and the shock trial was run a second time. A small fraction of the subjects demonstrated a placebo response by reporting pain and intolerable pain at a higher shock level than they had on the first trial. This established the placebo response rate in these circumstances. They then started again with a new group of subjects and determined their threshold and tolerance shock levels. The cream was applied and – now came the clever and novel part of the experiment – the strength of the electric shocks was secretly reduced, unknown to the subject or observer. When the trial was run now, the subject observed that much higher numbers on the shock machine were achieved before pain was felt and before the pain reached the tolerance limit. These subjects believed that they had tested on themselves the truth of the remarkable anaesthetic properties of the cream. Next, after one such apparent demonstration of the efficacy of the cream, a trial was run in the original conditions, i.e. the strength of current was returned to its original level. The cream was put on and the shock level raised. On this trial, large numbers of the subjects became placebo reactors. The only difference in these newly produced placebo responders was that they had 'experienced' in some fashion the apparent anaesthetic properties of the cream. Clearly, this result can have important practical implications. Whether the change in the subjects was cognitive or conditioned must remain an issue for debate and further experiment. Brewer (1974) concludes that 'there is no convincing evidence for operant or classical conditioning in adult humans' which is free of cognitive awareness of the situation. It may be that the passionately maintained differences between cognitive and conditioned responses will collapse.

Response-appropriate sensation

I wish to introduce a novel proposal, which is that certain classes of sensation are locked into the response that is appropriate to the situation, in contrast to the classical view that sensation is always locked into a stimulus which provokes it. I refer *only* to certain types of body sensation and not to those sensations related to the outer world, such as sight and sound, where psychophysics shows a precise lawful relation between stimulus and sensation. However, the psychophysics of pain differs wildly from that of other senses (Sternbach and Tursky, 1964). This special class includes pain, hunger, thirst, vertigo, fatigue, sleepiness, feeling too hot and too cold. In this class of sensations, each member is associated with disease where the sensation is not coupled with the appropriate stimulus. For pain, this is a major clinical problem, to be discussed below. This proposal for a separate class of sensations has been approached in a series of steps (Wall, 1974, 1979).

In diseases where overt pathology is an integral part of the diagnosis, such as osteoarthritis, the amount of pain is poorly related to the amount of pathology. In other diseases, such as angina pectoris, an appropriate evocative pathology, such as occluded coronary arteries, is obvious in some cases but not all. In other painful conditions, no appropriate peripheral pathology has been identified. These include trigeminal neuralgia, migraine, atypical facial neuralgia, temporo-mandibular joint syndrome, post-encephalitic myalgia syndrome and fibro-myalgia. The most extreme example of an uncoupling of pain from injury occurs in emergency analgesia following abrupt injury. Beecher (1959) reported that 70 per cent of soldiers admitted to a forward hospital with severe battle injuries did not complain of pain. In the less dramatic setting of a city hospital, 40 per cent of patients admitted after the common accidents of civilian life reported no pain at the time of the accident (Melzack *et al.*, 1982); another 40 per cent reported high levels of pain. There was no obvious relation between the location or severity or nature of the injury and the amount of pain reported at the time of the injury. Three characteristics of this analgesia are crucial to its understanding. First, the patient is usually fully aware of the injury and its consequences but describes the initial sensation in neutral words, such as 'blows' or 'thumps'. Second, in hospital the analgesia is precisely located only to the original injury and does not apply to subsequent stimuli such as the introduction of an intravenous line. Third, by next day all are reporting the expected pain. Similar behaviour is observed in animals after injury (Wall, 1979).

While the body sensations under discussion appear poorly related to a provocative stimulus, each is inevitably linked with attention and with a predictable response: for hunger, eating; for thirst, drinking, etc. For pain, three phases of response are observed: to attempt to avoid further injury, to seek aid and safety, and to recover from injury (Wall, 1979). The third phase includes immobilization of the painful part, avoidance of contact to the painful area, withdrawal and sleep. All three response patterns are observed in animals as well as in humans.

If, then, pain and the other sensations discussed are variably linked to the provocative stimulus but reliably locked into the response, would it not be reasonable to propose a brain mechanism by which the brain analyses some internal body states in terms of the biologically relevant behaviour, and that certain sensations signal the outcome of that analysis rather than the input on which the analysis was based? Just such a brain mechanism has been explored by the ethologists who followed Hess, Tinbergen and Lorenz. In ethological schemata, the brain continuously monitors the flow of information from the internal and external sensory apparatus. Next, a biological priority is assigned to a fraction of the input and the appropriate motor pattern is released. Let us propose that humans too incorporate such an apparatus in their brains and that the initial stages do not necessarily intrude on consciousness. Let us propose further that conscious pain appears only after the priority assignment stage and that pain is sensed consciously at the same time as the release of the motor pattern. The ethological motor patterns of vertebrates are *not* fixed action patterns or reflex discharges; they require reference to the sensory system in order to shape the correct response. The combination of an empty stomach and the sight of a nearby bill releases the herring gull pecking motor pattern. However, the herring gull chick still needs to use its sensory apparatus to locate the red spot on the mother's bill in order to peck at it. In other words, there are two sequential uses of the sensory input. The first is to assign priority and the second is to guide the motor behaviour. It is proposed here that pain appears as a conscious phenomenon only in the second epoch of sensory analysis after the period during which priority is established but consciousness is not alerted.

For pain and the placebo response, I propose that before the placebo, the unconscious priority decision mechanism had assigned priority to the motor pattern and sensation of pain: after the placebo, which is a stimulus with its learned powerful association with pain relief, the unconscious priority decision mechanism reverts to selecting a non-pain state. This new situation assigns a lower priority to pain and allows the release of the next most biologically appropriate pattern. This two-stage analysis process could also provide a rational basis for the other apparently paradoxical absence of pain, emergency analgesia. Pain is the obvious reaction to overt injury but other actions and sensations may take precedence. For the soldier in action, impending death has the well-known property of 'concentrating the mind' and much more elaborate life-preserving actions and reactions take precedence over the reaction to localized injury. This begs the obvious question of why one sensation should take precedence over another. Why could they not both be felt simultaneously, or at least alternate rapidly? The probable answer reinforces the linking of this type of sensation to motor pattern. It is not biologically permissible to release two motor patterns simultaneously. It would be disastrous to attempt to advance and retreat at the same time. Animals in ambiguous situations exhibit what Tinbergen called displacement activity. A herring gull in a threat posture suddenly switches on a nest building motor pattern and rips up tufts of grass. Obviously, sensation should not be considered to result from an all-or-nothing switch. Priorities would vary in their strength and duration, which would be mirrored in the strength and persistence of attention and sensation.

For an hypothesis to be useful it has to be more than an analogy (Wall and Safran, 1986); it has to be both testable and deniable. For the placebo response, this requires probing inside the brain, but that itself requires a definition of what would be the object of the search, which leads me to the final section.

WHAT PROCESSES WOULD ONE EXPECT TO DISCOVER IN THE BRAIN?

Any philosophical statement inevitably predicts the existence of some neural process. Therefore, observations of neural processes, neurophysiology, could be used to validate philosophical proposals.

Dualism

Descartes made such a proposal which has dominated philosophical and neurophysiological thinking. In modern times, it predicts identifiable components of the brain which will reliably detect, transmit and create specific fractions of sensation that are representations of specific fractions of the real world. The components of this sensory body mechanism would be line-labelled, modality dedicated and hard wired. They would feed information to an entirely separate and different process, the mind.

Over the past century, neurophysiology has developed powerful and precise techniques capable of describing the first stage of the Cartesian prediction about sensory mechanisms. I find nothing in these observations which validates Descartes' prediction for body sensation (Wall and Jones, 1992). It is true that the individual nerve fibres which run from the tissues to the central nervous system can be described in terms which satisfy Descartes' prediction. However, as soon as the information which these nerve fibres carry enters the central nervous system, a quite different process takes over. The information transmitted is no longer locked simply and only into the stimulus. It is shaped and formed by processes normally assigned to the second separate mental stage. In other words, there is no evidence for a 'pure' sensory stage. The information passes through a gate zone where the data which is transmitted to the rest of the brain depends on the contingencies of other events in the periphery and on the brain state which orders and permits and shapes the arriving messages. The sensory consequences are not the passive slave of the stimulus but an active selective process of the brain itself.

I will illustrate this active process which begins at the entry point to the brain by referring to the work of Dubner *et al.* (1981), Bushnell *et al.* (1984) and Duncan *et al.* (1987).

They recorded in monkeys from first-order central cells which receive information from nerve fibres from the skin. By all classical criteria, these cells fulfil perfectly the requirements of Cartesian sensory transmission cells – their discharge rigidly and reliably reflects a particular stimulus applied to a unique area of skin. The cells signal in a lawful fashion the location, intensity and nature of the stimulus with such reliability that the signal was the same in both awake and anaesthetized monkeys. These workers then trained the animals to use a stimulus in a discrimination task in which the correct response was rewarded. The form of the trial was that the animal was first given a warning signal that the trial was about to begin, next the stimulus was applied, and then the animal was rewarded with a drink of orange juice if it reached out and pushed a button if, and only if, the stimulus was of a particular intensity. When the training began, of course, the cell responded only to the skin stimulus and not to the warning signal or any of the other events. However, when the animal had successfully solved the problem and was fully trained, most of the cells produced a brief burst of activity after the warning signal. This novel period of cell discharge mimicked the discharge of the cell which always occurred after the stimulus to be discriminated was presented. This means that the trained brain had created a virtual input which ran over the same pathway as the input provoked by the real stimulus. A precise model of the expected input precedes the input actually provoked by the expected stimulus. The literature contains several examples of this creation of inputs without stimuli in classical and operant conditioning.

The phantom limb

The phantom limb has been a challenging paradox for philosophers and neurologists. Descartes was aware that he had set a trap for himself in the very rigidity of his proposed sensory mechanism. He writes in *Meditations on a First Philosophy* (1641):

> It is manifest that notwithstanding the sovereign goodness of God, the nature of man, in so far as it is a composite of mind and body, must sometimes be at fault and deceptive. For should some cause, not in the foot but in another part of the nerves that extend from the foot to the brain, or even in the brain itself, give rise to the motion ordinarily excited when the foot is injuriously affected, pain will be felt just as though it were in the foot and thus naturally the sense will be deceived: for since the same motion in the brain cannot but give rise in the mind always to the same sensation and since this sensation is much more frequently due to a cause that is injurious to the foot than by one acting in another quarter, it is reasonable that it should convey to the mind pain as in the foot.

Descartes has set himself a double trap. He realizes that in his original scheme, if the foot is amputated, a hole should appear in the body map, since no signals can originate from the missing foot. He therefore proposes a typically brilliant way out in which the nerves generate a false signal which fools the mind into thinking that the foot is still there. Even this clever idea does not stand inspection. If nerves to the arm are blocked with a local anaesthetic, the arm does not seem to be missing, but is immediately replaced by a strong and precise sensation of a phantom arm (Bromage and Melzack, 1974). We have all experienced this phenomenon at the dentists after a local anaesthetic block has made a lip numb. In spite of the fact that the lip is completely numb, we feel the presence of a swollen attention grabbing lip which we keep touching. That is a phantom lip. The relevance of this to Descartes' false signal explanation is that the local anaesthetic produces no false signals in the nerve. It simply blocks all the normal traffic in the nerve. Therefore, some process central to the block must have detected an absence of the normal input and has created, by an active process, an attention getting imitation arm. This brain is not the passive Cartesian brain totally dependent on its sensory input but an active reactive and creative brain. It has created a virtual reality to be checked against the actual reality.

The placebo effect

I consider the placebo effect to be equal but opposite to the phantom in defining the operation of the brain. In one a state is created, in the other a state is abolished. In the placebo response, there is no known mechanism and no evidence that the activity of the afferent peripheral nerves is changed in any way. Yet the state of the brain is radically changed to a new state. It must be emphasized again that this change is not limited to conscious perception. A patient whose severe cancer pain disappears in response to a placebo not only states verbally that the pain has gone but also shows appropriate changes of blood pressure, heart rate, respiration, gut motility, pupil size, etc. This complete pattern of body and mind alteration differs from some cases of hypnotic suggestion where the verbal report may conflict with the autonomic body system changes.

It would seem to be evident that a selection process is in operation to determine the content of conscious sensory perception. One factor in this selection is the information in the input message from the sensory nerves. However, it is equally apparent that the content of this message is not necessarily dominant. If other input messages or past experiences combine to propose that some other form of behaviour and perception is more appropriate to the biological needs of the organism, the other solution takes precedence.

REFERENCES

Amsterdam, E.A., Wolfson, S. and Garlin, R. (1969) 'New aspects of the placebo response in angina pectoris', *American Journal of Cardiology* 24: 305–306.

Beecher, H.K. (1955) 'The powerful placebo', *JAMA* (Journal of the American Medical Association) 159: 1602–1606.

—— (1959) *Measurement of Subjective Responses*, New York: Oxford University Press.

—— (1968) 'Placebo effects: a quantitative study of suggestability', in H.K. Beecher and L. Lasagna (eds) *Non-specific Factors in Drug Therapy*, Springfield, IL: Thomas Publishers.

Bootzin, R.R. (1985) 'The role of expectancy in behaviour change', in L.P. White, B. Tursky and G.E. Schwartz (eds) *Placebo: theory research and mechanisms*, New York: Guildford.

Brewer, W.F. (1974) 'There is no convincing evidence for operant or classical conditioning in adult humans', in W.B. Weimer and D.S. Palermo (eds) *Cognition and the Symbolic Process*, New York: Wiley.

Bromage, P.R. and Melzack, R. (1974) 'Phantom limbs and the body schema', *Canadian Anaesthetics Society Journal* 21: 267–274.

Buchaleq, L.W. and Coffield, K.E. (1982) 'An investigation of drug expectancy as a function of colour, size and preparation', *Journal of Clinical Pharmacology* 2: 245–248.

Burton, R. (1621) *The Anatomy of Melancholy*, Oxford: Cripps.

Bushnell, M.C., Duncan, G.H., Dubner, R. and He, L.F. (1984) 'Activity of trigemino-thalamic neurons in monkey trained in a thermal discrimination task', *Journal of Neurophysiology* 52: 170–187.

Cobb, L.A., Thomas, G.I., Dillard, D.H., Merendino, K.A. and Bruce, R.A. (1959) 'An evaluation of internal mammary artery ligation by a double blind technique', *New England Journal of Medicine* 20: 1115–1118.

Descartes, R. (1641) *Meditation on a First Philosophy*, Paris.

—— (1644) *L'Homme*, Paris.

Dimond, E.G. Kittle, C.F. and Crockett, J.E. (1958) 'Evaluation of internal mammary ligation and sham procedure in angina pectoris', *Circulation* 18: 712–713.

Dubner, R., Hoffman, D.S. and Hayes, R.L. (1981) 'Task related responses and their functional role', *Journal of Neurophysiology* 46: 444–464.

Duncan, G.H., Bushnell, M.C., Bates, R. and Dubner, R. (1987) 'Task related responses of monkey medullary dorsal horn neurones', *Journal of Neurophysiology* 57: 289–310.

Evans, F.J. (1974) 'The placebo response in pain reduction', in J.J. Bonica (ed.) *Pain*, New York: Raven.

—— (1977) 'The placebo control of pain', in J.P. Brady, J. Mendels, W.R. Reiger and M.T. Orme (eds) *Psychiatry: areas of promise and advancement*, New York: Plenum.

Farrer, G.R. (1964) 'Psychoanalytic theory of placebo', *Diseases of the Nervous System* 35: 655–662.

Finneson, B.E. (1969) *Diagnosis and Management of Pain Syndromes*, Philadelphia, PA: Saunders.

Gracely, R.H. (1989) 'Psychophysical assessment of human pain', in C.P. Chapman and J.D. Leoser (eds) *Issues in Pain Measurement*, New York: Raven.

Gracely, R.H., McGrath, P. and Dubner, R. (1978) 'Validity and sensitivity of ratio scales, manipulation of effect by diazepam', *Pain* 5: 19–29.

—— (1979) 'Fentanyl reduces the intensity but not the unpleasantness of painful tooth sensations', *Science* 203: 1261–1263.

Gracely, R.H., Woskee, P.J., Deeter, W.R. and Dubner, R. (1982) 'Nalozone and placebo alter postsurgical pain by independent mechanisms', *Society of Neurosciences Abstracts* 8: 264.

Hashish, I., Finman, C. and Harvey, W. (1988) 'Reduction of postoperative pain and swelling by ultrasound: a placebo effect', *Pain* 83: 303–311.

Herrnstein, R.J. (1965) 'Placebo effect on the rat', *Science* 138: 677–678.

Holroyd, K.A., Holm, J.E. and Keefe, F.J., Turner, J.A., Bradley, L.A., Murphy, W.D., Johnson, P., Anderson, K., Hinkle, A.L. and O'Malley, W.D. (1992) 'A multi–center evaluation of the McGill Pain Questionnaire: results from more than 1700 chronic pain patients', *Pain* 48: 301–312.

Koes, B.W., Bouter, L.M. and Beckerman, H., van der Heijden, G. and Knipschild, P.G. (1991) 'Exercises and back pain, blinded review', *British Medical Journal* 302: 1572–1576.

Koes, B.W., Bouter, L.M. and Beckerman, H. (1992) 'Randomised clinical trials of manipulative therapy and physiotherapy', *British Medical Journal* 304: 601–606.

Lasagna, L., Mosteller, F., von Felsinger, J.M. and Beecher, H.K. (1954) 'A study of the placebo response', *American Journal of Medicine* 16: 770–779.

Liberman, R. (1964) 'An experimental study of the placebo response under three different situations of pain', *Journal of Psychiatric Research* 2: 233–246.

Melzack, E. and Casey, K.L. (1968) 'Sensory, motivational and central control determinants of pain', in D. Kenshalo (ed.) *The Skin Senses*, Springfield, IL: Thomas Publishers.

Melzack, R. and Torgerson, W.S. (1971) 'On the language of pain', *Anesthesiology* 34: 50–59.

Melzack, R., Wall, P.D. and Ty, T.C. (1982) 'Acute pain in an emergency clinic, latency of onset and descriptive patterns', *Pain* 14: 33–43.

Merskey, J. (1989) 'Pain and psychological medicine', in P.D. Wall and R. Melzack (eds) *Textbook of Pain*, Edinburgh: Churchill Livingstone.

Nash, M.M. and Zimring, H.E. (1969) 'Prediction of reaction to placebo', *Journal of Abnormal Psychology* 74: 569–573.

Rawlinson, M.C. (1985) 'Philosophical reflections on the use of placebos in medical practice', in L.P. White, B. Tursky and G.E. Schwarz (eds) *Placebo: theory research and mechanisms*, New York: Guilford.

Reiss, S. (1980) 'Pavlovian conditioning and human fear: an expectancy model', *Behavioral Theory* 11: 380–396.

Siegel, S. (1975) 'Conditioning insulin effects', *Journal of Comparative Physiological Psychology* 89: 189–199.

—— (1985) 'Drug anticipatory responses in animals', in L.P. White, B. Tursky and G.E. Schwarz (eds) *Placebo: theory, research and mechanisms*, New York: Guilford.

Sternbach, R.A. and Tursky, B. (1964) 'On the psychophysical power functions in electric shock', *Psychosomatic Sciences* 1: 217–218.

Turner, J.L., Gallimore, R. and Fox-Henning, C. (1980) 'An annotated bibliography of placebo research', *Journal Suppl Abstracts Service American Psychological Association* 10: 22.

Tyler, D.B. (1946) 'The influence of a placebo and medication on motion sickness', *American Journal of Physiology* 146: 458–466.

Voudouris, N.J., Peck, C.L. and Coleman, G. (1989) 'Conditioned response models of placebo phenomena', *Pain* 38: 109–116.

—— (1990) 'The role of conditioning and verbal expectancy in the placebo response', *Pain* 43: 121–128.

Wall, P.D. (1974) '"My foot hurts me", an analysis of a sentence', in R. Bellairs and E.G. Gray (eds) *Essays on the Nervous System*, Oxford: Clarendon.

—— (1979) 'On the relation of injury to pain', *Pain* 6: 253–264.

Wall, P.D. and Jones, M. (1992) *Defeating pain*, New York: Plenum.

Wall, P.D. and Safran, J.W. (1986) 'Artefactual intelligence', in S. Rose and L. Appignanesi (eds) *Science and Beyond*, Oxford: Blackwell Scientific Publications.

White, L., Tursky, B. and Schwarz, G.E. (eds) (1985) *Placebo: theory, research and mechanisms*, New York: Guilford.

Wickramasekera, I. (1980) 'A conditioned response model of the placebo effect', *Biofeedback Self-regulation* 5: 5–18.

Chapter 9

What and where are conscious experiences?

Max Velmans

HARD QUESTIONS AND EASY QUESTIONS

The problems surrounding consciousness may be divided into the 'hard questions' and the 'easy questions' (Chalmers, 1995). Hard questions have to do with fundamental theoretical problems such as 'What *is* consciousness?', 'How could purely physical activities give rise to subjective conscious states?', or, conversely, 'How could a subjective conscious state have a causal influence on the activities of neurons?' 'Easy questions' are those which appear open to existing methods of empirical research; for example, the contingent relationship of given states of consciousness to given states or functions of the brain. What makes a hard question hard is that, given our current understanding of consciousness and how it relates to the brain, it is not clear what *kind* of answer would satisfy us.

There is little doubt that with some of the easy questions advances have been made. For example, over the last thirty years cognitive psychology has given us a glimpse into the sheer complexity of human information processing and this has allowed a far more detailed study of how given conscious states relate to preconscious and nonconscious processing than was ever envisaged by Freud (cf. Baars and McGovern in Chapter 4 above; Gardiner in Chapter 3 above; Kihlstrom in Chapter 2 above; Velmans, 1991a, and Chapter 1 above). Neuropsychology has yielded insights into some of the neural conditions for consciousness (cf. Libet in Chapter 5 above), the many dissociations of consciousness, and the accompanying modular organization of the brain (cf. Young in Chapter 6 above). Clinical investigations have provided considerable evidence that altered states of consciousness (produced by imagery, hypnosis, placebos, etc.) can affect states of the body/brain as well as vice versa (cf. Sheikh *et al.* in Chapter 7 above; Wall in Chapter 8 above).

As with any productive science, the research findings have often been surprising and suggest the need for theoretical development. For example, the effects of imagery, hypnosis and placebos on a wide range of bodily functions and basic sensations such as pain suggest that, to some extent, the latter may be subject to cognitive influences (imagination, suggestion, expectation). If so, the distinction between voluntary and autonomic nervous system activities may not be as rigid as it is generally thought to be. The fact that neuropsychology has revealed so many dissociations of consciousness prompts us to ask by what means consciousness comes to be integrated in everyday experience (the 'binding problem'). The evidence that much of psychological processing is preconscious and nonconscious challenges us to find what if anything is special about conscious processing.

Such data gathering and theoretical development are part of the normal business of science. In the study of consciousness, however, the easy questions are never far from the hard questions. Decisions about what consciousness is, for example, will influence decisions about what to look for when searching for its neural causes or correlates. Decisions about whether consciousness *could* have some causal influence on the activity of neurons will influence how one thinks of the function of consciousness within some global model of mental functioning, and about how best to interpret the clinical evidence for the effects of psychological states on bodily processes.

Hard questions may also be asked about methodology. Some theorists treat consciousness as an inferred construct, to be investigated, like inferred nonconscious processes, from a third-person perspective (see Baars and McGovern in Chapter 4 above). Other theorists treat conscious states as psychological data in their own right and stress the need to supplement traditional third-person accounts of brain functioning with first-person accounts of what is experienced (see Libet in Chapter 5 above; Velmans, 1991a, 1991b). A similar debate has taken place over the best way to decide whether a process is conscious – with some theorists arguing in favour of behavioural criteria and others stressing the centrality of subjective experience (see Kihlstrom, in Chapter 2 above, for a review).

Consequently, we cannot evade the hard questions for long, and it is to this that we now turn our attention.

WHAT IS CONSCIOUS ABOUT A CONSCIOUS PROCESS?

In cognitive psychology there are many experiments that have contrasted processes which are or are not accompanied by consciousness in order to isolate functional differences between them (in perception, learning, memory, etc.). There is broad consensus that, in time, such studies may reveal those aspects of brain processing that relate most intimately to consciousness. But there is less consensus about whether such studies will reveal the nature and function of consciousness *as such*. According to Baars and McGovern (Chapter 4 above), the study of conscious processing *is* a direct study of consciousness as such. By contrast, Libet (Chapter 5 above), Gardiner (Chapter 3 above) and Velmans (1991a, 1991b) are careful to distinguish *third-person* studies of brain processing from *first-person* investigations of conscious experience. Deep philosophical differences lie buried in these fundamental distinctions.

A study of brain processing *could* only be a study of consciousness as such, if consciousness *is* just a form of brain processing (a form of philosophical reductionism). Elsewhere (Velmans, 1991a, 1991b, in press) I have argued against premature closure on this issue. It is widely recognized (even by its proponents) that philosophical reductionism gives no adequate understanding of the phenomenology of conscious experience. It is less well understood that reductionism also obscures how consciousness as such *relates* to the processes which cause or correlate with it in the brain.

Reading this text, for example, involves 'conscious processing' in the sense outlined by Baars and McGovern (Chapter 4 above). But what, we might ask, is conscious *about* the processing? As one reads one is conscious of the print on the page, of feelings of understanding and so on, but one is *not* conscious of the processing itself. Operations such as grapheme analysis, pattern recognition, grapheme to phoneme conversion, syntactic analysis, semantic analysis, inferences from prior knowledge, and the effects of prior verbal context, operate *nonconsciously* (and can only be inferred). Nor do we have any scientific or introspective grounds for believing that the experiences we have somehow *enter into* such nonconscious operations. That is to say, reading is 'conscious' only in the sense that it *results* in conscious experiences. In short, the processes involved in reading are not *themselves* conscious in any sense. And that leaves the question of whether consciousness *is* a brain process an open one (see Velmans, 1991a, 1991b, 1993b, for a detailed discussion).

WHAT IS CONSCIOUSNESS?

At first glance this looks like an easy question, as consciousness is something that we all have. However, no question has been the subject of greater confusion. In Chapter 1 above I have argued that definitions need not be final for research to get under way. It is enough that definitions are sufficiently similar for different investigators to be able to agree that they are investigating the same thing. As science begins to unravel the causes of consciousness, the functions of consciousness, how consciousness relates to nonconscious processing and so on, our understanding of what consciousness *is* will deepen – for the reason that such relationships form part of the *meaning* of the term (its connotative meaning, or sense). Such mutual focusing of attention followed by exploration of the nature of what is attended to (and how it relates to other things) is fundamental to how phenomena come to be understood in a socially shared way. In this respect, coming to understand the nature of consciousness is no different to coming to understand the nature of anything else.

Of course, in order to learn *what* something is, it is useful in the initial instance to know *where* it is, so that one can point to it – enabling the attention of different investigators to be focused upon it. But where does one point, when one is pointing at consciousness?

WHERE IS CONSCIOUSNESS?

Where dualists and reductionists think consciousness to be

According to Descartes the material world is composed of *res extensa*, a substance that has both location and extension in space. Consciousness is formed out of *res cogitans*, a substance which thinks, but which has no location or extension in space. If this is right, then one cannot point at consciousness, as it has no location. At best, one might be able to point at the place where consciousness interfaces with the material world. According to Descartes this place is the pineal gland, located in the centre of the brain.

Modern reductionist philosophers (e.g. Dennett, 1991; Searle, 1993) argue that consciousness is nothing more than a state or function of the brain. It might be difficult to point with any precision at such states or functions, as they are likely to be distributed properties of large neuronal populations (cf. Dennett and Kinsbourne, 1992). Nevertheless, if one *had* to point one would point at the brain.

In short, classical dualists and reductionists disagree vehemently about *what* consciousness is, but they agree (roughly) about *where* it is. In so far as consciousness can be located at all, that location is somewhere in the brain.

A common sense view of consciousness

In earlier writings (Velmans, 1990, 1993a) I have argued that this currently popular view has no basis either in science or in everyday experience. In order to decide where consciousness is (or whether it has any location) one has to attend to its *actual* phenomenology. It is true that there are some experiences which seem to be poorly localized in space, or at best localized somewhere in the head or brain, just as dualists and reductionists claim. Examples include thoughts and vague feelings such as the verbal thoughts, feelings of understanding and so on which accompany reading (as described above). However, most experiences have a very different phenomenology – for example, experiences of the body or of the external world.

Let me illustrate this with a very simple example. Suppose you stick a pin in your finger and experience a sharp pain. Within philosophy of mind, pain is generally regarded as a paradigm case of a conscious, mental event. Now, where is the pain? Hampered by their theoretical presuppositions, dualists and reductionists take this to be a rather difficult question. However, if *forced* to point they would point (vaguely) in the direction of the brain (see comments by Nagel, Harnad, Searle, Marcel, and Dennett, following Velmans, 1993a). I take this to be a very simple question. The pain one experiences is in the finger. If one had to point at it one should point at where the pin went in. Any reader in doubt on this issue might like to try it.

Let me be clear that this sharp difference of opinion is about the *experience* of pain and *not* about the antecedent physical causes (the deformation and damage to the skin produced by the pin), or about the neural causes and correlates of pain.

The proximal neural causes and correlates of pain are undoubtedly located in the brain. However, in science, the causes or correlates of a given event are not ontologically identical to that event. For example, the movement of a wire through a magnetic field causes an electrical current to flow through the wire. But that does not mean that the electrical current is ontologically identical to the movement of the wire through the magnetic field. Nor, if one reverses this experiment, is it right to say that the current one passes through a wire is ontologically identical to the surrounding magnetic field produced as a result.

The current is in the wire and the magnetic field is distributed in the space around the wire. They cannot be the same thing for the reason that they are in different places. Similarly, innervation of appropriate pain circuitry in the brain may cause an experience of pain in the finger. These cannot be the same thing, because they are in different places.

No, I am not being facetious. This simple example demonstrates a general principle which leads one away from both dualism and reductionism towards a 'reflexive' model of how consciousness relates to the brain and the physical world (cf. Velmans, 1990). In many respects, there is no difference between these theoretical positions. For example, dualism, reductionism and the reflexive model agree that there may be physical and neurophysiological *causes* and *correlates* of a given experience within the brain – and that we can leave it to science to discover what these are (the so-called 'easy questions'). But they disagree about the nature and location of the *effects* (the resulting experiences). Dualists claim that experiences have no location or extension in space (although they interface with the brain). Reductionists claim that all experiences are in the brain. The reflexive model claims that experiences are *where we experience them to be*. If the pain seems to be in the finger, then that is where the pain is. There is no *other* or *second* experience of pain in the brain, or 'nowhere' to point at. This, I submit, is common sense.

A REFLEXIVE MODEL OF HOW CONSCIOUSNESS RELATES TO THE BRAIN AND THE PHYSICAL WORLD

But is this consistent with science? In the reflexive model the sequence of events in perception (in highly simplified form) is as follows. An input stimulus activates peripheral and central nervous system activity to produce a representation of that stimulus in the brain of a subject (S). S's brain encodes the properties of the stimulus, which for exteroceptive stimuli and many interoceptive stimuli will include its location and extension in three-dimensional space. A mental model of the stimulus is formed which may be influenced by previous experiences stored in memory, by expectations and so on. From the third-person perspective of an external observer (E), the mental model in S's brain appears to take a neural or other physical form. Indeed, from the perspective of E, this is all that can be observed of S's representation of the input stimulus, as E cannot observe S's experience of the stimulus.

If S had no experience of the stimulus, E's description of S's perceptual processing in terms of peripheral and central nervous system activity might now be complete. Indeed in functional terms there might be nothing to distinguish S's perceptual processing from that of a nonconscious robot designed to emulate such processing.

But if appropriate conditions are met (if the stimulus is suprathreshold, if it is attended to, etc.), S does have an experience. The *form* that the experience takes is determined by the way the input stimulus is modelled by the brain, but it is the *result* or conclusion of the modelling process that is manifest in S's experience. One aspect of such modelling is judging where things are. Consequently, damage to S's finger is represented both in S's resulting mental model and in S's consequent experience (accurately) as an event taking place in the finger. Damage to S's finger is not manifest in S's experience as a pain in the brain.[1]

In sum, damage to S's finger ends up as a pain in the finger. That is why the entire process is 'reflexive'. If S pricks a finger with a pin, there is only *one* experience of pain that results – the pain that S experiences in the finger. E has no access to S's experience, and so has no evidence that S is mistaken about where the pain is. On the contrary, E can easily confirm S's report by sticking a pin into his or her own finger. In this way, the observation that sticking a pin in a finger produces pain in the finger is intersubjective and repeatable (thereby fulfilling the basic conditions for scientific investigation of this phenomenon – see Velmans, 1993a). Given this, why do many philosophers and scientists currently *insist* that the pain *must* be in the brain?

WHY SHOULD ANYONE THINK THAT PAIN IS IN THE BRAIN?

One reason has to do with the dominance of the third-person perspective in science – which can be caricatured as: 'If you can't see it from the outside it doesn't exist!' This was the driving force behind the now discredited behaviourist approach to psychology. And it persists in a more sophisticated form in current, reductionist philosophies of mind. If one views the brain from the outside one can only observe brain states, not conscious experiences. Consequently, the reductionists argue, in so far as conscious experiences exist they must *be* brain states and must therefore be *in* the brain. In essence, this approach attempts to reduce what is observed from a subject's first-person perspective to what can be observed from an external observer's third-person perspective. Reductionist philosophers accept that this seems to conflict with common sense (conscious experiences seem very different to brain states), but they maintain that one day science will *discover* these to be one and the same.

Needless to say, no such discovery has yet been made. Given this, reductionist philosophers have had to content themselves with trying to show what kind of discovery *could* show experiences and brain states to be one and the same. I will not review these arguments in detail, as my aim is to present an approach that is consistent with science *and* common sense. Commonly, however, reductionists argue that if science manages to discover the neural *causes* of consciousness and can consequently *explain* the occurrence of consciousness in neural terms, then consciousness will have been shown to be nothing more than a state of the brain (see, for example, Place, 1956; Churchland, 1988).

The counterargument to this is that causes are not ontologically identical to their effects (see the discussion of electricity and magnetism above). Penfield and Rassmussen (1950), for example, *caused* their patients to have somatosensory experiences by direct electrical stimulation of the somatosensory cortex via microelectrodes. However, this *resulted* in sensations of numbness and tingling in different regions of the *body*, not in the brain. In any case, nearly *all* theories of the consciousness–brain relationship accept that antecedent neural causes of given conscious experiences can in principle be found, while retaining very different views about the nature of the effects (the conscious experiences that result). This is true, for example, for interactionist dualism (which assumes a two-way causal interaction of consciousness with the brain), epiphenomenalism (which assumes that brain states cause conscious experiences but not vice versa) and emergent interactionism (which assumes that consciousness emerges from brain activity and then supervenes over the activity from which it emerges). The reflexive model also urges scientific investigation of the neural and psychological causes of given experiences. But a pin in the finger still produces a pain in the finger, not a pain in the brain.

One might of course ask how, if the neural causes and correlates of pain are in the brain, does the resulting experience of pain get to be in the finger? This is a scientific question rather than a philosophical one, roughly analogous to well-known puzzles in science like how is action at a distance possible (in gravity), how can remote events remain connected (Bell's theorem in quantum mechanics) and so on. In such instances, we simply have to accept, given the evidence, *that* such things take place and get on with examining the detailed conditions under which they take place. The main difference in the case of pain localization is that a *psychological* process rather than a *physical* process is involved. Elsewhere (Velmans, 1990) I have called this process 'perceptual projection'.[2]

EVIDENCE FOR PERCEPTUAL PROJECTION

The experience of pain in the finger is initiated by stimulation of the afferent pain fibres which terminate there. But perceptual projection of pain to the finger cannot be explained by this purely physical connection – for, if the entire arm is severed from the body, pain may be still be experienced in the now, nonexistent hand of a 'phantom limb'!

Livingston, for example, reports that:

In 1926, a physician, who had long been a close friend of mine, lost his left arm as a result of gas bacillus infection. . . . The arm was removed by a guillotine type of amputation close to the shoulder and for some weeks the wound bubbled gas. It was slow in healing and the stump remained cold, clammy, and sensitive. . . . In spite of my close acquaintance with this man, I was not given a clear impression of his sufferings until a few years after the amputation, because he was reluctant to confide to anyone the sensory experiences he was undergoing. He had the impression, that is so commonly shared by layman and physician alike, that because the arm was gone, any sensations ascribed to it must be imaginary. Most of his complaints were ascribed to his absent hand. It seemed to be in a tight posture with the fingers pressed closely over the thumb and the wrist sharply flexed. By no effort of will could he move any part of the hand. . . . The sense of tenseness in the hand was unbearable at times, especially when the stump was exposed to cold or had been bumped. Not infrequently he had a sensation as if a sharp scalpel was being driven repeatedly, deep into . . . the site of his original puncture wound. Sometimes he had a boring sensation in the bones of the index finger. The sensation seemed to start at the tip of the finger and ascend the extremity to the shoulder, at which time the stump would begin a sudden series of clonic contractions. He was frequently nauseated when the pain was at its height. As the pain gradually faded, the sense of tenseness in the hand eased somewhat, but never in a sufficient degree to permit it to be moved. In the intervals between the sharper attacks of pain, he experienced a persistent burning in the hand. The sensation was not unbearable and at times he could be diverted so as to forget it for short intervals. When it became annoying, a hot towel thrown over his shoulder or a drink of whisky gave him partial relief.

(cited in Melzack, 1973: 51–53)

Phantom limbs also demonstrate that perceptual projection is not confined to experiences of pain. Melzack, in his review of phantom limb experiences, reports that:

Most amputees report feeling a phantom limb almost immediately after amputation of an arm or a leg. . . . The phantom limb is usually described as having a tingling feeling and a definite shape that resembles the real limb before amputation. It is reported to move through space in much the same way as the normal limb would move when the person walks, sits down, or stretches out on a bed. At first, the phantom limb feels perfectly normal in size and shape – so much that the amputee may reach out for objects with the phantom hand, or try to get out of bed by stepping onto the floor with the phantom leg. As time passes, however, the phantom limb begins to change shape. The arm or leg becomes less distinct and may fade away altogether, so that the phantom hand or foot seems to be hanging in mid-air. Sometimes the limb is slowly 'telescoped' into the stump until only the hand or foot remain at the stump tip.

(Melzack, 1973: 50)

In addition to such tingling and kinaesthetic sensations, amputees report a variety of other sensations, including pins and needles, itching, sweating, warmth or coldness and heaviness in their phantom limbs (Melzack, 1973; Craig, 1978).

Such evidence supports the view that the experienced body, including its experienced location and extension in space, is, in part, a construction formed by mental modelling within the brain. I have previously (Velmans, 1990) reviewed evidence that similar constructive processes involving perceptual projection take place in normal exteroception; that is, in audition and vision. I will not repeat that review here. Suffice it to say that in audition, the proximal stimulus is vibration at the eardrum, but sounds are generally experienced to be localized in the space beyond the body surface, not at the surface of the eardrum or in the brain. The factors which govern spatial localization in audition have been extensively investigated (cf. Blauert, 1983). In vision, the factors which govern the perceived size, shape, location and movement of objects in space have been investigated in many different ways. Of particular relevance to the study of perceptual projection are the varied demonstrations of how information arranged on a two-dimensional surface may under appropriate circumstances be interpreted by the brain to have arisen from a three-dimensional scene, resulting in the two-dimensional information being experienced as objects and events in three-dimensional space. Recent examples include holograms and virtual realities. Another recent demonstration is provided by stereoscopic pictures (Figure 9.1), a development of the random-dot stereograms initially developed by Julesz (1971) to investigate depth perception. Some of these appear, at first glance, to be multicoloured, random patterns on a two-dimensional surface. However, if one focuses one's gaze *behind* the surface the random patterns gradually form into shapes arranged in three-dimensional space. What is particularly striking about such pictures is that the transition from a two-dimensional pattern to three-dimensional shapes occurs sufficiently slowly to experience perceptual projection *in action*.

Elsewhere (Velmans, 1990, 1993a) I suggest that such demonstrations of perceptual projection exemplify the operation of normal exteroceptive and interoceptive processing. Of course, not all experiences are given a clear location or extension in space. For example, experienced thoughts and other 'inner' experiences, such as visual images, vague feelings and so on, represent the ongoing results of problem solving, planning and other cognitive and conative activities taking place within the brain itself. Consequently, in so far as these 'inner' experiences have any location, they are (loosely) experienced to be within the head or brain. As before, mental modelling places such events more or less where they actually are. By contrast, events which originate in the body or beyond the body surface, once modelled by the brain, are reflexively projected in the form of experienced events within the body or beyond the body surface.

Such inner, body and external experiences together form the contents of consciousness, which are none other than the contents of our everyday phenomenal world. We normally *call* some aspects of this phenomenal world the 'physical world' (the experienced body and its experienced surround). But the appearance of such 'physical' entities and events remains, in part, a construct of the brain. The appearance *represents* the entities and events which are detected by the sense organs in a biologically useful way, but it is not *identical* to those

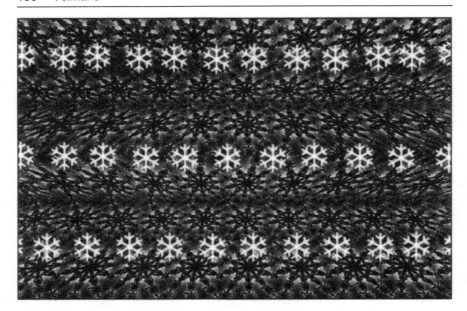

Figure 9.1 A stereoscopic picture of 'snowflakes'. To experience the picture in depth, bring the picture up to your nose and look *through* it, so that the picture is completely blurred. Now, leaving your eyes relaxed and looking through the picture, gradually move the picture away to a distance of a foot or more, and a three-dimensional scene should form. Notice that once an experienced three-dimensional scene is formed it is possible to inspect different parts of it without losing the experience of depth. This is an example of 'perceptual projection' in action, demonstrating the brain's ability to create an experience of depth, in spite of the fact that the cues are arranged on a two-dimensional surface

Source: Reproduced with permission from 3D Magic, taken from the 3D Magic Portfolio, published by Dragon's World, London

entities and events (the 'things themselves'). Physics, for example, would represent the same entities and events in a very different way (in terms of relativity, quantum mechanics and so on).

To those accustomed to thinking in a dualist or reductionist way the claim that the phenomenal world includes what we normally think of as the 'physical world' may seem odd. But note that this is entirely consistent with what *we actually experience*. With our eyes open, we experience a phenomenal world spread out before us in space, not a world in the brain (or without any location). Nor is this way of looking at things new. The view that the phenomenal world is a representation constructed by the mind is central to the philosophy of Immanuel Kant (1969 [1781]), along with the separation of the phenomenal world from some grounding reality (the 'thing itself'). The extension of consciousness to include the external world as experienced occurs also in the work of Ernst Mach (1897 [1885]), William James (1950 [1890]), Alfred North Whitehead (1932) and Bertrand Russell (1948), as well as in the scientific theorizing of Charles Sherrington (1942), Wolfgang Kohler (1966) and Karl Pribram (1979). It is also a basic assumption of phenomenology (cf. Spinelli, 1989). Needless to say, different theorists have argued for this position in different ways, and their opinions about the consequences also differ.

CONSEQUENCES OF THE REFLEXIVE MODEL

The reflexive model gives an account of how consciousness relates to the brain and the physical world which is neither dualist nor reductionist. Experiences arise from a reflexive interaction of initiating stimuli with perceptual processing. This interaction results in an experienced, phenomenal world which includes what we normally think of as the 'physical world'. That is, what we normally think of as the physical world is *part of* what we consciously experience; it is not *apart from* it. If so, there can be no unbridgeable divide separating the contents or 'qualia' of consciousness from experienced physical phenomena.

This has many interesting consequences for the dualist vs. reductionist debate within philosophy of mind, the issue of realism vs. idealism, and the relation of psychology to physics. These have been discussed in Velmans, 1990 and 1993a. Initial attempts have also been made to challenge aspects of the model (see Gillett, 1992; Rentoul, 1992; Wetherick, 1992 – and the replies by Velmans, 1992a, 1992b; see also the discussion with Marcel, Nagel, Gray, Searle, Libet, Humphrey, Wall, Lockwood, Shevrin, and Dennett, following Velmans, 1993a). I do not have space to recount these discussions here. In what follows I deal only with some of the main implications of the reflexive model for psychological science.

CONSEQUENCES FOR PSYCHOLOGICAL THEORY AND RESEARCH

1 The most obvious advantage of the reflexive model is its ecological validity. We experience the phenomenal world to be outside our heads. We do not experience this world to be inside our brains. Having a model which reflects what we actually experience, encourages exploration of *how* it comes to be that way. For example, it encourages the study of perceived spatial localization and extension, and in particular the mechanisms underlying perceptual projection. It also encourages the study of how perceptual processes in the brain combine to produce an integrated, three-dimensional, phenomenal world.
2 The model potentially enables a more unified understanding of a wide range of phenomena experienced to have both spatial location and extension, including phenomena as diverse as lucid dreams, hallucinations, eidetic imagery, the creation of virtual realities, the construction of a body image and the normal

perception of events in a three-dimensional space. Accepting perceptual projection as a normal process (when it operates on representations of events out in the world) also makes it easier to understand what happens in pathological or artificial situations. For example, hallucinations can be understood to result from mental models which are erroneously subject to perceptual projection (following a breakdown of the usually reliable modelling of 'inner' versus 'external' events). And three-dimensional virtual realities can be understood to arise from artificial stimulation of the same projective processes which create normal, phenomenal worlds.

IS A SCIENCE OF CONSCIOUSNESS POSSIBLE?

It should be clear from the various chapters in this book that a science of consciousness is possible, as it is *actual* and flourishing. But it has often been claimed that the study of consciousness can never be a proper science, as consciousness and its contents have characteristics that are quite unlike the natural world. These assumptions about consciousness still persist.

Consider, for example, the situation depicted in Figure 9.2, in which a subject (S) is asked to focus on a stimulus (say a cat) while an experimenter (E) tries to observe what is going on in the subject's brain. E has access to S's brain states but has no access to what S experiences. Other experimenters can also access S's brain states. Consequently, what E has access to is thought of as 'public' and 'objective'. S's experiences, by contrast, are considered to be 'private' and 'subjective'. If so, how could S's experiences provide a database for science?

Note that this radical difference in status of the data accessible to E and S is enshrined in the very words we use to describe what they perceive. That is, E makes 'observations', whereas S merely has 'subjective experiences'. The presumed 'objectivity' of E's observations and the 'subjectivity' of S's experiences also motivates reductionism in current philosophy of mind (for example, attempts to demonstrate that S's experiences are nothing more than the brain states observed by E).

But the reflexive model gives a very different story. According to the model, both E and S inhabit phenomenal worlds which are *each*, in a sense, private to themselves. E and S are no different in this respect from you and me. I cannot access your experienced world and you cannot access mine. In the situation depicted in Figure 9.2, E's private phenomenal world includes the events E observes in S's brain, while S's private phenomenal world includes the cat.

It is true that other experimenters (E_1 to E_n) could also focus their attention on the events in S's brain and observe what E observes. In this way, their observations may become 'public' in the sense of being communally shared. However, each observation remains private to a given experimenter. When the observations made by different experimenters are sufficiently similar, they become 'intersubjective'; if they can be made on more than one occasion they also become 'repeatable' (cf. Velmans, 1993a). But it is equally true that other subjects (S_1 to S_n)

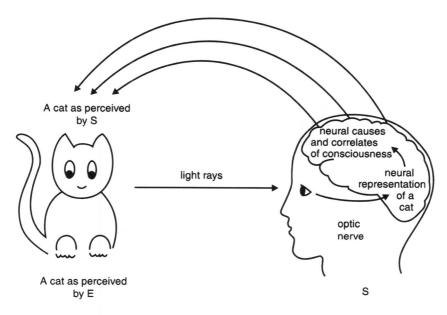

Figure 9.2 A reflexive model of the causal sequence in visual perception. Light rays from a cat (as perceived by an experimenter, E) impinge on the eye of a subject, S. Impulses travelling up the optic nerve produce neural representations of the cat within S's central nervous system. Information within this neural representation is formed into an 'experiential model' of the cat; that is, into the cat as perceived by S. To S, the cat as perceived is out in the world, not in his head or brain. In this, the cat that S experiences is similar to the cat that E experiences, although it is viewed from the perspective of S rather than the perspective of E. In short, an event in the world is *experienced* to be in the world, which makes the causal sequence reflexive

Source: Adapted from Velmans, 1990

could focus their attention on the cat and observe what S observes. In this sense, what S observes can also be made 'public', 'intersubjective' and 'repeatable'.

Note that this does not apply only to observed cats but also to less tangible experiences such as images and pains. For example, S_1 to S_n might all report that a pin in the finger produces a pain in the finger, or that a dose of aspirin reduces the pain. The fact that staring at a red spot produces a green after-image is similarly 'public', 'intersubjective' and 'repeatable'. In short, there is nothing *intrinsic* about the epistemic status of E's observations which distinguishes them from those of S.

The same principle can be illustrated in another way by asking E and S to turn their heads, so that E switches attention to the cat, while S switches attention to what is going on in E's brain. In this situation, E becomes the 'subject' and S becomes the 'experimenter'. Following current conventions, S would now be entitled to think of his or her observations (of E's brain) as 'public and objective' and to regard E's observations of the cat as 'private and subjective'. But this outcome is absurd – as nothing has changed in the character of the observations of E and S other than the focus of their attention.

In sum, the effect of this analysis is to remove *the pretence* that observations have nothing to do with the 'conscious experiences' of observers, and that E's observations are 'objective' while S's experiences are 'subjective'. Either E or S can make observations that are objective in the sense of being dispassionate, truthful and so on. But *neither* E nor S can make observations that are objective in the sense of having nothing to do with what they experience. Both E and S observe or experience phenomenal worlds, which arise from a reflexive inter- action of attended-to entities and events with perceptual processes. *What* E or S observe depends entirely on their focus of attention.

There is a good deal more to be said about the implications of the reflexive model for the relation of 'public' to 'private' events, and for 'subjectivity', 'intersubjectivity' and 'objectivity' (cf. Velmans, 1993a). It should also be stressed that I have given a very simplified analysis of the basic procedures involved in the study of conscious experiences. The contents of consciousness vary greatly in their stability, repeatability, reportability, measurability and so on. Consequently, the methods appropriate to investigating such phenomena also vary.

But it should be clear that the reflexive model gives quite a different view about whether the study of the phenomena that we experience can ever be a science. If the above analysis is correct, the 'phenomena' observed by experi- menters are as much a part of the world that they experience as are the 'subjective experiences' of subjects. If so, the *whole* of science may be thought of as an attempt to make sense of the phenomena that we observe or experience.

NOTES

1   Note that this description allows that the *information* (about the finger) encoded in S's mental model in the form of a brain state may be identical to the information (about the finger) manifest in S's experience. But it does not follow that S's experience is nothing more than S's brain state. The same information may be formatted in very different ways without one format being ontologically identical to another. For example, the information about a TV programme encoded in the form of magnetic variations on videotape may be identical to that displayed in an accompanying picture on a screen, but the picture is not ontologically identical to the magnetic variations on the tape. The issue of how a given experience might relate to its correlated mental model is more fully discussed in Velmans, 1991b, section R9.3; 1993b, sections R5, R6.
2   Psychological processes may, in part, *be* physical processes. But I have distinguished psychological from physical processes to emphasize that nothing *physical* is 'projected' from the brain to the finger to produce the experienced pain. I do not, for example, wish to resurrect Empedocles' theory that there is a 'fine interior fire' in the eye, whose light emanates from the eye to 'light up' the world. Rather, 'perceptual projection' is a 'conscious psychological process' in the sense outlined above. That

is, it involves brain processes which *result* in a conscious experience. The experience is 'projected' in the sense that, from the perspective of the subject, it is located in the phenomenal space beyond the brain (in the finger), rather than in the region of its neural causes or correlates.

REFERENCES

Blauert, J. (1983) *Spatial Hearing: the psychophysics of human sound localization*, Cambridge, MA: MIT Press.

Chalmers, D. (1995) 'Facing up to the problem of consciousness', *Journal of Consciousness Studies* 2(3): 200–219.

Churchland, P.S. (1988) 'Reductionism and the neurobiological basis of consciousness', in A.J. Marcel and E. Bisiach (eds) *Consciousness in Contemporary Science*, Oxford: Clarendon.

Craig, K.D. (1978) 'Social modelling influences on pain', in R.A. Sternbach (ed.) *The Psychology of Pain*, New York: Raven Press.

Dennett, D.C. (1991) *Consciousness Explained*, London: Allen Lane.

Dennett, D.C. and Kinsbourne, M. (1992) 'Time and the observer: the where and when of consciousness in the brain', *Behavioral and Brain Sciences* 15: 183–200.

Gillett, G. (1992) 'Consciousness, intentionality and internalism', *Philosophical Psychology* 5(2): 173–180.

James, W. (1950 [1890]) *The Principles of Psychology*, New York: Dover.

Julesz, B. (1971) *Foundations of Cyclopean Perception*, Chicago: University of Chicago Press.

Kant, I. (1969 [1781]) *Critique of Pure Reason*, trans. J.M.D. Meiklejohn, London: Dent.

Kohler, W. (1966) 'A task for philosophers', in P.K. Feyerabend and G. Maxwell (eds) *Mind, Matter and Method: essays in philosophy of science in honour of Herbert Feigl*, Minneapolis: University of Minnesota Press.

Mach, E. (1897 [1885]) *Contributions to the Analysis of Sensations*, trans. C.M. Williams, Chicago: Open Court Publishing.

Melzack, R.(1973) *The Puzzle of Pain*, Harmondsworth: Penguin.

Penfield, W. and Rassmussen,T.B. (1950) *The Cerebral Cortex of Man*, Princeton, NJ: Princeton University Press.

Place, U. (1956) 'Is consciousness a brain process?', *British Journal of Psychology* 47: 44–50.

Pribram, K.H. (1979) 'Behaviorism, phenomenology and holism in psychology: a scientific analysis', *Journal of Social and Biological Structures* 2: 65–72.

Rentoul, R. (1992) 'Consciousness, brain and the physical world: a reply to Velmans', *Philosophical Psychology* 5(2): 163–166.

Russell, B. (1948) *Human Knowledge: its scope and its limits*, London: Allen & Unwin.

Searle, J. (1993) 'The problem of consciousness', in *Experimental and Theoretical Studies of Consciousness*, Ciba Foundation Symposium no. 174, Chichester: Wiley.

Sherrington, C.S. (1942) *Man on his Nature*, Cambridge: Cambridge University Press.

Spinelli, E. (1989) *The Interpreted World: an introduction to phenomenological psychology*, London: Sage.

Velmans, M. (1990) 'Consciousness, brain, and the physical world', *Philosophical Psychology* 3(1): 77–99.

—— (1991a) 'Is human information processing conscious?', *Behavioral and Brain Sciences* 14(4): 651–669.

—— (1991b) 'Consciousness from a first-person perspective', *Behavioral and Brain Sciences* 14(4): 702–726.

—— (1992a) 'The world as-perceived, the world as-described by physics, and the thing-itself: a reply to Rentoul and Wetherick', *Philosophical Psychology* 5(2): 167–172.

—— (1992b) 'Reply to Gillett', *Philosophical Psychology* 5(2): 181–182.

—— (1993a) 'A reflexive science of consciousness', in *Experimental and Theoretical Studies of Consciousness*', Ciba Foundation Symposium no. 174, Chichester: Wiley.

—— (1993b) 'Consciousness, causality, and complementarity', *Behavioral and Brain Sciences* 16(2): 404–416.

—— (in press) 'The limits of neurophysiological models of consciousness', *Behavioral and Brain Sciences*.

Wetherick, N. (1992) 'Velmans on "Consciousness, brain and the physical world"', *Philosophical Psychology* 5(2): 159–162.

Whitehead, A.N. (1932) *Science and the Modern World*, Cambridge: Cambridge University Press.

Name index

Subject index